PREFACE TO THIRD EDITION.

IN submitting to the general public the third edition of *Tales and Ballads of Wearside*, I beg to thank them for the especial favour shown in their kind appreciation of the two former issues. The sole reason for the republication of this book is that (although the volume is out of print, and the type long since broken up) an almost daily demand for copies continues to be made on the publisher and myself; and apart from the United Kingdom, I have received letters from many places in the British Colonies and the United States. This demand I attribute not so much to the ability of the writer as to the purely local nature of the stories and ballads, and the true delineation of old Sunderland character, which cannot fail to remind the real native—wherever he may be—of the place of his birth, and at the same time call up sweet home visions, and pleasant recollections of the favoured haunts of his childhood.

I have contributed two additional stories and two local ballads to the present edition of this book. The original of " The Keelman Preacher " will be easily recognised by all old Sunderland residents, and " Their First Six Months' Bill " is a local tale, fully descriptive of the old system of wood shipbuilding, which bears a marked and decidedly striking contrast to the gigantic undertakings in marine architecture carried out in the present day at the vast shipbuilding establishments of Messrs. Laing, Doxford, Thompson, Short, and others.

"The Keelman's Message" is a true typification of the River Skipper sixty years ago; while the "Legend of Lowther Hall" should possess a rich interest for all those who first saw light in Sunderland Parish proper.

Lowther Hall (or Castle, as some assert) was supposed to have stood on Sunderland Moor, looking towards the sea, and was in the possession of a family of that name. It is said that many many years ago the German Ocean had encroached so much on the land, that during one more than usually fierce north-east gale in the month of October, the waves, lashing themselves into a foaming fury, beat so heavily, and with such angry force against the banks, that the earth crumbled away, and the hall—or castle, whichever it might have been—"toppled its head" lower than its foundations, and was buried beneath the waters. I can remember, when a very little boy, standing at my mother's knee, and listening, with all the keen interest which is so characteristic of childhood, to the story of the destruction of Lowther Hall. And I can also remember her telling me that in the time of her grandfather—who was a fisherman—the stones of the building could be seen, when the water was in a state of placidness, deep down on the sandy bottom, outside the beacon rocks. I can find no historical trace of a family residing at or near Sunderland, and bearing the name of Lowther; but strange to say, a road leading from the moor to the sea-beach, before the formation of the South Docks, was invariably called by the natives "Lowther's bank."

In launching the third edition of *Tales and Ballads* on the ocean of public favour, I have an eager hope that it will be driven in its course towards the haven of success, by pleasant and propitious gales.

THE AUTHOR.

SUNDERLAND,
        September 1882.

Tales & Ballads of Wearside

John Green

TALES AND BALLADS

OF

WEARSIDE.

By JOHN GREEN.

FOURTH EDITION.

LONDON:

WALTER SCOTT, 24 WARWICK LANE,

PATERNOSTER ROW.

1885.

PRINTED BY WALTER SCOTT,
FELLING,
NEWCASTLE-UPON-TYNE.

TO

JOHN WRIGHT WAYMAN, Esq., J.P.,

Red House, Hendon,

A GENTLEMAN DESCENDED FROM THE HARDY RACE OF
WATERMEN, WHOSE PRIMITIVE HABITS AND PECULIAR
CHARACTERISTICS ARE HEREIN DELINEATED,

THIS VOLUME,

A FRAGILE LINK

CONNECTING THE PAST OF SUNDERLAND WITH

ITS PRESENT,

IS RESPECTFULLY INSCRIBED

BY

THE AUTHOR.

PREFACE TO FOURTH EDITION.

IN the early part of the year 1880, humbly, hopefully, yet still with no small amount of trepidation, I submitted to the reading public some ninety pages of modest duodecimo. This unassuming *brochure*, gentle reader, was my first edition of *Tales and Ballads of Wearside*. The doubts entertained by me for the success of this little book were soon dispelled; indeed, so great was the demand, that a third edition—now also out of print—appeared early in 1882. I need hardly say how much I was pleased with the favourable notices in the local press, and the reproduction, in review, of some of the shorter stories; and I may be pardoned if I give in the Preface to this edition, now grown and developed into a full-sized crown 8vo volume, a few of those same notices.

"His stories of the comical sayings and doings of the keelmen, pilots, and sailors of the Wear, related in the robust dialect of the locality, are exceedingly amusing. The author of *Tales and Ballads of Wearside* is a true humorist, and a pleasing and versatile writer."— *Weekly Chronicle*, 1880.

"The narratives are pithy and brief, and are told in that homely conversational style which none but an adept at anecdotal narration can hope to succeed in. Of the numerous tales, where all are so good, there is a difficulty in making a selection, but for brevity's sake we give the following as samples of the humour pervading the volume."— *Sunderland Daily Post*, 1880.

"It consists of short tales admirably told, and well worth the telling, and a few ballads which possess a quaint and peculiar interest. We may open the book at any page, and be sure of coming across something good ; but the full flavour of Mr. Green's humour appears in his nautical sketches, such as "Running the Blockade off the Elbe," "Chartered by the Seck," and others rich in the vernacular. The ballads comprise "Legend of the Lambton Worme," "Ralph the Boatman," and "Click him an' catch him," and they display respectively powers of dramatic expression, pathos, and broad humour. We are tempted to produce "Chartered by the Seck."—*Sunderland Weekly Echo and Times*, 1880.

"Mr. Green knows well the people of whom he writes, their characteristics, idiosyncrasies, and dialect ; and in the work he gives living pictures of many types. By sea-going people, and those connected with them, this volume will be perused with lively interest. One of these stories we quote under the title of "The Pilot Poet."— *South Durham and Cleveland Mercury*, 1880.

"There is little need on our part to state that those *Tales and Ballads* are likely to be popular. A graphic and genial writer, the author has given a few short sketches which will not fail to give the reader an hour's enjoyment."—*Hexham Herald*, 1880.

The story of "Balmston ; or, No Greater Love," is not limited to locality, and is therefore calculated to possess a more general interest. In it I have endeavoured to record with accuracy and precision some of the stirring events of the memorable " Forty-Five."

THE AUTHOR.

August 1885.

CONTENTS.

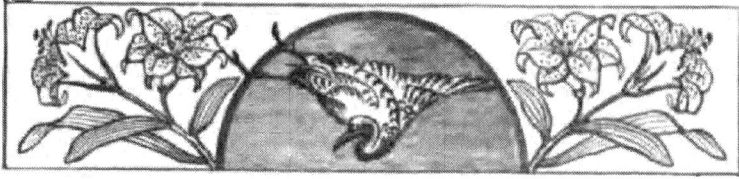

Balmston ; or, No Greater Love.

A STORY OF THE "FORTY-FIVE."

CHAPTER I.

"And let concealment, like a worm i' the bud,
Feed on her damask cheek."
— *Twelfth Night.*

ON a cold, windy, and stormy night in the drear November of Seventeen Hundred and Forty-four, two apparently seafaring men were seated in the smallest room of a small public-house, in a small, narrow thoroughfare, or cross passage, between Warren Street and Silver Street, in the old town known as Sunderland-by-the-Sea. Those two individuals of the genus *navis* were quietly—and evidently in a manner perfectly satisfactory to themselves— imbibing a sort of liquid which at this particular

2

period was held in special favour by the seagoing
people of the north-east coast of Britain. The
beverage in question was denominated "purl," but
whether this appellation was fitly chosen or not
is another matter. It was compounded of the
following ingredients—viz., warm ale, with a small
quantity of rum or gin, at the option of the drinker,
while to the liquids were added sugar and nutmeg,
and sometimes cinnamon. The older man, to judge
by his appearance, would be verging close on the
half-century. He had a rough, weather-beaten look,
and despite the dim, uncertain light in the room,
not a few iron-grey hairs were plainly conspicuous
amid the sombre hirsute growth on his storm-
pelted visage. His upper-surface attire consisted of
a sort of pea-jacket, or reefer, profusely and rather
absurdly adorned with large horn buttons; his brown,
shaggy fearnought trousers were half-hidden by a
pair of unusually long sea-boots; while on the un-
polished deal table, close to his elbow, lay a sou'-
wester, on which the rain-drops were still glistening.
His companion—who was evidently the junior by
some fifteen or sixteen years—was attired in a
somewhat similar fashion; his complexion appeared
too fresh, and too fair, for a man whose characteristic
garb denoted a thorough salt-water life. His features
were clear-cut and faultless, and his hair was of
auburn tint, evidently possessing a natural tendency
to curl.

The elder, whose name was Bill Jones, was the first to set the conversational ball rolling. Sending a thick spiral column of blue smoke from the comprehensive aperture between his lips, he said, in a decided voice—

"It's a dirty night at sea, Capytine Chedville."

"Bah!—yes!" assented the other, with a slightly foreign accent, so slight as to be almost imperceptible; and then, shrugging his shoulders, he added, in an undertone—"*Il fait bien mauvais temps.*"

"I'll tell ye what it is, Capytine Chedville," resumed Jones, taking his pipe from his mouth and waving the stem in a dignified manner, like the *baton* of a musical conductor, "it aint a bit o' use thinkin' o' puttin' to sea in this ere weather. The wind's east—aye, east an' by south, I'll venture to say—an' more'n that, d'ye see, it's blowin' two-thirds of a gale; an' I say this, if we was outside this blessed minnit, it's my humble 'pinion the *Mary Ann* would be ashore this side o' Blackhall rocks in less nor two hours."

"No, no!" interrupted the other, with a deprecatory head-shake. "The wind is east and by north, and were it even to the southward of east, the little *Mary Ann* knows her work."

"Aye, aye," muttered Jones, falling back in his chair, and almost concealing himself in a smoke cloud. "That's just the way; an old salt like me, that's lived on the water for nigh onto six-and-thirty years, is to have his velocity questioned by a Johnny Raw, that's never been on a leeshore all his life, mayhap. I'll tell ye what it is, Capytine Chedville"—and here Jones brought his fist down on the table with such terrific force that the glasses actually danced again—"if the wind's not to the south'ard of east, I aint fit to be a keelman, much less skipper of a sea-going craft."

"You know how vastly important my business is?" said Chedville, quietly.

"Why, yes," replied Jones, "partlin's I do, and partlin's I don't, and if I was to be hung to-morrow for my complication (I believe that's the word the land-lubbers use), why I should be hung nearly in the dark. But this 'ere, Capytine Chedville," he added, pulling from his pocket a leathern bag apparently well filled with gold—"this 'ere kind o' whispers to me, d'ye see, that there's more risk in this 'ere business than in a strong no'th-easter."

"Bah!" exclaimed the other, impatiently. "Why talk of risk? you have been face to face with danger since you were a boy."

"Why, that's almighty truth, now," said Jones, in softened accents, "and I don't think I should be the least bit afeared to founder; it's a sort of honourable death, d'ye see, an' what's more, it's nat'ral. Now, here's one of your land-lubbers: well and good; he walks all his lifetime, 'ceptin' his first twelve months, atop o' the earth, an' when his proper time comes he goes under it. Now, here's a sailor : look at *him;* he's been a-sailin' and a-sailin' all his lifetime atop o' salt water, and when his proper time comes he goes under it ; and where's the difference? Why, there aint any, least-ways not as far as I can see ; but to be hung up like an anchor to a cathead, a boat to a davit, or a big skate to a schooner's main-boom, or maybe to have your head clipt off by the neck joint, why that's quite another matter, d'ye see. And if such a cat——what d'ye call 'em ?—was to happen, these 'ere shiners would be no good, as I aint got no heirs, nor 'ministrators, nor 'sassinators, nor nothin' o' that sort."

"'Twould make no great matter if you had, *mon ami,*" said Chedville, smilingly, "for in that case, if I understand your laws rightly, the Crown would be legally, if not justly, entitled to your effects. But, *peste,* we are straying away from the subject. It is now eight o'clock, by twelve it will be high water, and if there is the slightest possible chance, the *Mary Ann* must to sea."

"Why, if she must, why, then, in course she must," was the logical remark of Jones, as he indulged in a long, deep draught of the "purl;" "but, hark'ee, Capytine Chedville," he continued, after recovering his breath, "I know my terms exactly, and I have the build and rig o' that 'ere

agreement from stem to starn—aye, from the bottom
of the keel to the royal-mast head, as a man might
say—an' this 'ere is something like the true bearin's
on't. In the first place, I takes you as my mate
in the *Mary Ann*, to sail under the colours of one
Peter Thornton (which there aint no such person,
leastways, not as I knows on); and, in the second
place, I permits you to fetch and carry dispatches
(which, in course, I knows nothin' about whatsom-
ever), 'atween this 'ere and the coast of France;
but there aint nothin' specified about puttin' to sea
in an easterly gale, blowing away every rag of
canvas, and sending the *Mary Ann* slap-bang to
Davy Jones' locker. No, no, Capytine Chedville,
there aint nothin' o' that in the agreement—least-
ways, if there is, I would just like you to point it out."

"No, there is not," returned the other; "but you
are to afford me every facility to reach France or
England, just as I may wish, and it is most
desirable that I should be in the good old town of
Abbeville in a few days from this."

"Well, as I said afore, and as I say agin, there's
a nasty lump of a sea, and the wind's south of
east; I'll maintain that agin the Pope, or any other
larned man in the universe; but, spite of all, I'll
put to sea to-night, an' mind this, Capytine Chedville, if the *Mary Ann's* hammerin' her bottom out
under Huntlyfoot to-morrow mornin', don't go for
to say that Bill Jones was the lubber as did it."

"*Au diable !*" exclaimed Chedville. "Huncliff-foot, forsooth! If the wind holds we shall have passed through Yarmouth Roads before to-morrow midnight; and now, Jones, with your permission, I will go and make preparations for the voyage. You may expect me on board by half-past ten o'clock; have your crew ready, and let us be off."

"Aye, aye," said Jones, "leave all that 'ere to me; we'll take top high-water for it, as there's a heavy send on the bar."

The two men now left the public-house, Jones taking his way towards the river; while Chedville, or Thornton, departed in the direction leading through Burleigh Street, then the most fashionable and aristocratic locality in the parish of Sunderland. About the middle of a narrow crossing running east and west. and affording a communication between Burleigh and Vine Streets, the younger sea-man halted before a house of singularly unpretending appearance, and knocked gently at the door. It was speedily opened by an elderly female, who met Chedville with a welcome smile.

"Now, mother Willis," he said, as he entered the house, "we are going to sea to-night, so please get my things ready at once."

"What, to-night, Mr. Thornton ?" the old woman asked, in undisguised astonishment; "why, it's blowin' a perfect hurricane."

"Not quite, good mother," Chedville answered;

"but it is a nasty night, nevertheless. But you see, when we are once outside, we have a fine wind."

"Why, only to think now," commented Mrs. Willis, "Mary went out about half-an-hour since, and as she was going, she said to me, 'Mother,' says she, 'Mr. Thornton will never go to sea to-night.' And I says, 'I'm sure he won't, Mary dear, for it's blowin' great guns from the north-east; it's a'most as wild a night,' says I, 'as when your poor dear father was lost off the Tees.'"

This allusion to the departed Willis evidently awakened unpleasant, or rather, sad and sorrowful memories, causing the widow to wipe the extreme corner of her right eye with one of the ultimate angles of her brown holland apron.

"Well, gale or no gale, we're going, mother," said Chedville. "I have to be aboard by half-past ten, and as I have a letter to write, I will go to my room and finish that before supper."

The good woman immediately produced a candle-stick from a cupboard in the kitchen, and after lighting the candle she handed it to Chedville, who at once ascended a narrow, old-fashioned staircase leading to his apartment. After closing and care-fully locking the door, he seated himself before a small table, and producing from a secret pocket a thin parcel of papers, all folded lengthwise, and bearing special endorsements, he began to read them attentively, one by one, a sarcastic or contemptuous smile flitting occasionally over his handsome face.

" *C'est incroyable,*" he said at last, " how cool these good Jacobites seem to be! they think a rising should be delayed until finer weather. Bah! a man's patriotism must be lukewarm at best when cold weather turns it to ice, and it can only be thawed into active life by a summer sun. Well, well; it's not quite so bad either, for some of them say ' the Prince' must be his own judge in the matter, and others, while wishing me to unfold their own opinions to his highness, desire me also to inform him, that whatever decision he may ultimately arrive at, they pledge themselves to stand or fall by his side. *Fort bien !* on the whole, I think my time has not been ill-spent; but alas! I am too painfully conscious of the want of enthusiasm on this side of the Tweed, and in my opinion Prince Charles Edward, in riding out this revolutionary gale, must consider the Scotch people his best bower anchor."

Chedville now proceeded to make certain memoranda in cipher, which, with the packet, was consigned to a secret pouch; he next drew forth a pair of small, elaborately-finished pistols, and having tried the locks, and carefully examined the primings, he replaced them with a grimly satisfied smile.

Meanwhile, in the room below a totally different scene was being enacted. Following Chedville's departure from the kitchen, a young woman entered it. She was apparently about eighteen, plainly although neatly and cleanly attired, her figure well rounded and graceful, slightly below the average height of womankind, deep blue eyes fringed with dark lashes, while her hair of auburn hue hung in undulating folds down her back, flowing "like an alpine torrent, which the sun dyes with his morning light." This girl was the only child of the widow Willis.

"Mary, my dear," began the mother, as soon as the daughter had seated herself, "what do you think? Mr. Thornton is really going to sea to-night."

"Good heaven!" the girl exclaimed, turning pale. "What, in such weather as this? Oh, mother, he should not go to-night."

"You forget, my dear, he cannot help himself. He is only mate of the ship, and if she goes he must go too; but, bless you! he seems to think nothing about it. But hush, dear; I hear him coming downstairs."

The loud tread of Chedville's heavy boots could now be heard distinctly; and shortly afterwards he entered the kitchen, bearing in his hand the candle-stick.

"Ah, Mary," he exclaimed, as he caught sight of the girl, "has your mother told you that we go to sea to-night?"

"Yes, Mr. Thornton," she replied; "and oh, dear me, what a fearful night to go to sea in!"

"Not at all," said Chedville, laughingly; "there's a fine wind, and when we are once outside we will scud along merrily. And now, Mother Willis, supper, if you please. Here, Mary, take this key, and in the little cupboard in my room you will be able to find a prime bottle of cognac, which never acknowledged the sovereignty of King George by the payment of a sous duty."

Mary took the key from Chedville's hand with a smile, and tripped lightly upstairs; meanwhile Mrs. Willis set herself earnestly to work with the evening meal, and the frying-pan was soon hissing and spluttering a somewhat inharmonious accompaniment to the song of the tea kettle. Mary returned with the bottle, and Chedville, whose temporary residence in the house had evidently made him thoroughly acquainted with its peculiar wants and characteristic shortcomings, proceeded, with the aid of a common two-pronged fork, to give liberty to the imprisoned *eau de vie*.

"Now, Mary, three glasses, quick," he shouted, good humoredly, "and come along here, Mother Willis; you must drink success to the *Mary Ann;*" and filling two small glasses for the ladies, and pouring out half-a-tumbler for himself, he said, "Here's a quick passage to the sweet little craft. Health, long life, and happiness to you both, and the same to—— *le fils de mon pere*," he added, in an undertone, as he drank off the contents of his glass. "Now, then," he continued, "let's have supper. I am precious hungry, I can tell you."

Mrs. Willis promptly responded by placing the viands on the table, the modest banquet consisting of steaks, onions, and potatoes—the latter being cut into thin slices, and fried crisp and brown in the fat.

Chedville positively insisted that Widow Willis and her daughter should sit down beside him before he commenced to ply his knife and fork, and then he began with an earnest alacrity which fully compensated for the previous delay.

After supper was over he drew forth a curious old watch, and looking at the dial he said, " It just wants a quarter of ten. You must have another small drop of brandy each, and then I'm off aboard." Mary Willis began to make an excuse, but Chedville would take no denial.

"Now look you, Mary," said he, filling her glass, " while you are sipping this little drop I'll sing you a good sea-song."

This promise apparently vanquished all Mary's *scruples*, for she put her rosy lips to the *dram*, and took a wee, wee sip, as Chedville, in a deep, manly voice (quite rich enough to build a baritone reputation on, even in those days), broke into the following nautical rhyme :—

> " A double reef in the topsails, boys,
>   For the gale is coming fast ;

The billows rise, and the wind, my boys,
   Like a sapling bends each mast.
The huge green wave laps the deck, my boys,
   And now, o'er the topmast heads,
The wild white spray dashes fast, my boys,
   Like the flakes stern winter sheds.
     O ! a double reef in the topsails, boys,
      For the gale is coming fast ;
     The billows rise, and the wind, my boys,
      Like a sapling bends each mast !

" The land we left last night, my boys,
   Far abaft lies dim and low ;
But still 'tis green in our hearts, my boys,
   As merrily on we go.
Pull with a will on each brace, my boys,
   She now holds galley way,
And if the wind stands true, my boys,
   We'll Cherbourg sight to-day.
     O ! a double reef in the topsails, boys,
      For the gale is coming fast ;
     The billows rise, and the wind, my boys,
      Like a sapling bends each mast ! "

As the song proceeded, Chedville more than once cast a half-inquiring, half-uneasy glance at the face of Mary Willis, and he failed not to observe an expression on her fine features, indicative of something beyond the mere pleasurableness which his vocal efforts were calculated to create ; and as the last note of the chorus died away, he said to himself—

"*Pardieu !* I verily believe this little girl is in love

with me.   What beauty! what animation!   But have
a care, Monsieur Pierre Chedville; marriage with
her is an impossibility, and to betray youth, beauty,
and innocence is not in your line, *mon ami.*"

Rising from his seat, he shook Mrs. Willis by the
hand; and imprinting a kiss on the fair forehead of
the young girl, he picked up a roughly-stitched canvas bag, and throwing it over his shoulder, exclaimed,
in hearty tones—

"Good-bye for a while.   We shall soon meet again,
if all goes well."

In another moment he was gone, and when the
sound of his footsteps had faded quite away into
silence, and the little narrow street had regained all
its usual lone quiet, Mary Willis flung her arms
round her mother's neck, and burst into tears.   For
some time no word was spoken ; the mother permitted the daughter to weep on, merely patting her
head in loving tenderness ; at length she said,
soothingly, her hand still resting on the rich auburn
hair—

"My poor child, don't, oh, don't give way to grief
like this."

"God be with him, mother," exclaimed the poor
girl, "and may His all-powerful arm guard and
protect him through every danger!   Oh! if he but
knew how fondly, how dearly, how truly I love
him!"

"But he doesn't know it, Mary dear," said Mrs.

Willis, winding her arms tenderly round her daughter, "and my poor lass must remember, that he has said nothing to waken up love in her heart, though he may have done much to gain her respect and esteem."

" Ah, mother," Mary answered, in sad, weary tones, "do not remind me of that. We do not always bestow our love on the man who is most anxious and wishful to hold our hearts' best affections. No, no! true womanly devotion rises into life, makes its own choice, goes forth where it wills, and to whom it wills, uncontrolled, uncontrollable. His manly look, his frankness and kindly feeling, his true nobleness of nature, have all done more, far more to win my love than the most sincere protestations of another could have ever accomplished. And, mother dear, it was needless, nay, it was unkind to remind me that he had said nothing to awaken in my breast the faintest glimmer of hope that he would ever regard me as a sweetheart ; for who, amongst those to whom he is known, could have found that out sooner than I ?—I, who watched his every look, hung with delight on his every word, lived happy in his kindly smile, which meant everything—everything but the love I would gladly die to possess."

CHAPTER II.

"The breeze, like the old one, will kick us
  About on the boisterous main;
And one day, if death doesn't trick us,
  Perhaps we may come back again."

—*Old Song.*

BILL JONES, Pierre Chedville, and four able-bodied seamen, comprising the entire crew of the brigantine *Mary Ann*, stood at their various stations on the deck of the little vessel, as she worked her way over Sunderland bar, with a very indifferent sea prospect.

"She'll never carry that mainsail to-night," Jones observed to Chedville, as he came from the helm, having been relieved by one of the hands.

"I'm afraid not," was the reply; "we shall have to give her the storm trysail instead."

Although the wind was well in from the eastward, and blowing fresh, the little craft kept gradually edging away from the land, being considerably assisted by the set of the tide. After beating off for some time, the vessel was at length allowed to go free, and then, like a high-mettled steed, with the bridle bit hard gripped between its teeth, the *Mary Ann* darted swiftly away. Her speed through the water might be fairly computed by the loud hissing of the angry foam, as it was hurled back from her bows, and mingled, with apparently instinctive reluctance, with the deep blue underneath. Occasionally a sheet of water would cast itself with a heavy thud on the forecastle deck, causing the little vessel to tremble and vibrate through every timber. Primitively constructed, the brigantine possessed a manifest advantage over the vessels of our own time ; excepting the bulwarks from the hawse to the after timber heads, she was open right fore and aft, the main rail being supported by widely-spaced stanchions. There was an obvious utility in this style of build, for the water shipped, being unchecked by a close bulwark, speedily found its way from the deck. The *Mary Ann* had now been going free for some five or six hours, when Jones came again on deck. Though still dark, a faint, transient glimmer in the east heralded the near approach of day.

"Where d'ye think we are now, Thornton?" asked the skipper, as he walked aft to Chedville, who held the tiller.

"Why, to the south of Whitby, I should say," was the reply, given somewhat doubtfully. "But hark! what was that? As I live I hear shore breakers."

3

"And by the heavens above us!" exclaimed Jones, excitedly, "I see land right ahead, and may I be keel-hauled if it isn't Flamborough; we're right in by Hunmanby, like a rat in a trap."

"She'll never go off," said one of the men.

"We'll try her, anyhow," Jones answered, sharply, "an' that'll show willin'. Set the mainsail," he shouted. "Now then, bear a hand, my lads; we have no time to spare."

The order was promptly executed, and the large sheet of canvas bellied out almost to bursting by the force of the wind.

"Now then, Thornton," came the cheery voice of Jones, "hard a-starboard, hard over, my lad."

The brigantine now began to walk off, but she was so far in the bight that the chance of her ultimately weathering the headland seemed next to impossible; in fact, if the quick eye of Jones had not taken in their perilous position at a single glance, she would have struck on the rocks in a few minutes, at a spot where the hazard of life would have been great indeed.

By the time the *Mary Ann* had worked off the length of the headland, broken water could be seen on both lee and weather sides, and for a few moments she was so close to the dangerous point that a biscuit might have been easily shied ashore; still the little craft did her duty nobly and well. Once, however, there came a decided lull, and this was indeed the most serious moment of their great peril, for the *Mary Ann*, like some huge sea-monster bereft of life, lay tossing helplessly among the breakers ; but again, down came the wild storm breeze with a violence so terrific that the vessel heeled over before its force, until covering board waterway and three strakes of her lee deck amidships were buried in the bubbling foam. Still, clear and distinct through the tempest, high even above that euroclydon roar, the voice of Jones could be heard—

" Starboard, hard a-starboard, hard over, for your life."

Chedville instantly obeyed the command, and the prow of the little craft came proudly up to the wind, as though, like a fatally wounded tiger, she had formed the desperate resolve of making a grand dying charge on her relentless enemy. Another moment and the dread point was weathered; a louder gust, a more terrific roar of the baffled, mad wind, and jib and topmast staysail were split, torn, and flying away in patches to leeward. On how little hung the fate of the gallant vessel! Had this accident to her canvas befallen two short minutes earlier, she would have become a total wreck, and her entire crew would have been inevitably dashed in pieces on the cruel rocks of that wild and rugged shore.

" I don't see nothin' for it," Jones exclaimed, after

gazing for a moment ruefully at the remnants of
the two sails flying landward like a flock of ill-
omened sea birds; "I don't see nothing for it but
to run into the bay, and come to an anchor."

"I quite agree with you," said Chedville. "Dis-
abled as we are, we have no other alternative."

When well sheltered under the lee of the headland, the anchor was dropped from the bows, and
the good ship *Mary Ann* was soon riding safely,
Flambro' Head bearing E.N.E., and Bridlington W.
and by N.

"Now, my lads," said Jones addressing the crew,
"you've been just as near kingdom come to-day as
ever you were since you were born of your mothers,
and if this ere ship hadn't ha' been the sweetest,
wisest, prettiest, little darling of a craft that ever
danced a jig on salt water, to the music of a stiff
nor'easter, she'd never ha' worked out o' that d——d
hole, I can tell you. And now, boys," he continued,
"as soon as you get your breakfast, you'll turn to
and bend 'tother jib and 'tother staysail; that was
the winter staysail, and a good-un, nearly bran new,
but it's gone half-a-mile inland by this time, and
it aint a bit use to fret about it."

By nine A.M. the wind had not only considerably
abated its force, but had, still more fortunately,
shifted a point or two further north, and the *Mary
Ann*, having repaired damages, weighed and proceeded on her voyage. Nothing of importance

occurred during the remainder of the passage. She passed through the Downs, took a departure from Beachy, and on the fourth day after leaving Sunderland she entered the port of St. Valery, and was there moored in safety.

Chedville—after holding a private conference with Jones in the cabin of the little vessel—was put ashore on the north bank of the river Somme, just as the day was gradually deepening into twilight, and the shadows of the quaint old houses were lengthened out to their utmost stretch by the slowly sinking sun. After walking about a mile from the town, in an easterly direction, he came to a large house or chateau, which, by its outward appearance, plainly indicated the residence of some fortunate individual occupying a by no means humble position in the country of Louis the Fifteenth. By this time night had succeeded the intermediate faint obscurity, and Chedville, opening a small iron gate, hastened his steps up the white sand walk intersecting a broad level lawn, and mounting the stone steps in front of the mansion, plied the large knocker with a sort of impatient vigour.

The clanking fall of a heavy chain was heard, the large door suddenly opened, and an old man appeared on the threshold, holding in his hand a small silver lamp of exquisite workmanship. Raising the light fairly on a level with his white head, he gazed, with hand-shaded eye, at the visitor for an instant, and then exclaimed, joyfully, " *Quelle surprise ! Monsieur le Comte.*"

"Just myself, Jacques," replied the other, in the same language, as he entered the house. "Just myself, and, look you, safe and sound."

"Ah, my dear master," said the old man, with a head shake, expressive equally of sorrow and deprecation, as he closed the door behind Chedville, "why will you persist in taking those long, hazardous journeys ? "

"Why ? " the other repeated, laughingly, letting his hand fall gently and tenderly on the shoulder of the ancient *serviteur.* "Do you not already know why I undertake them, silly man ? Those errands, fraught with peril and danger as they may be, will probably be the means, or rather let me say, to some extent the means, of restoring the true representative of the Stuart line to his own hereditary rights and privileges—but there, there, I know what you are going to say, my old fidelity ; I can almost see the words on your lips ; you are going to ask what possible concern I can have with Prince Charles Edward and the Stuart succession ? Bah! not much, that I will grant you ; I have *La Belle France*, and I am satisfied. But apart from all this there is in those same expeditions a charm, a bewitching delight, begotten and engendered by the very danger and peril you speak of ; and in the excitement I feel a pleasure which—although you,

Monsieur Jacques, may not understand—seems necessary to my very existence. But enough of this ; have dinner in half-an-hour, and order the carriage to be ready immediately afterwards ; I go to Abbeville this evening."

" This evening, Monsieur Pierre ? "

" This evening, my friend ; *J'ai des affaires in-dispensables."* As Chedville spoke, he entered a well-lighted apartment, most elaborately furnished. A cheerful wood fire blazed on the hearth-stone, the walls were hung with pictures of rare value, some of them limned by artists well known to fame, while every article of furniture was high wrought, highly finished, and bore unmistakable marks of antiquity. In one part of the room hung a full-length portrait of a very beautiful lady, apparently between twenty-five and thirty. The background showed a richly-wooded landscape, with an old castle or chateau in the distance, and sundry figure groupings representing a *fête champêtre.* The lady was attired in one of those attractive · and rather picturesque costumes worn by court dames in the time of *Louis Quatorze.*

Stepping on to a couch, Chedville imprinted a loving kiss on the fair face looking so life-like from the canvas ; and in a deep, tremulous voice, he said—" *Ma mère, voici ton fils. Nous n'avons rien de secret l'un pour l'autre."*

CHAPTER III.

"There are hills beyond Pentland, and lands beyond Forth ;
If you've lords in the south, we hae chiefs in the north."
—*Jacobite Song.*

IN a room in a large, old-fashioned mansion, in a quiet quarter of the quaint
old town of Abbeville, about thirty
gentlemen were assembled. The room
in question was fairly furnished, and brilliantly
illuminated. At one end, immediately below a large
stained-glass window, was erected a platform or
daïs, on which was placed a large chair of antique
shape, covered with rich crimson velvet. In the
centre, and running almost the entire length of the
apartment, tables of highly polished wood were
closely ranged, strewn carelessly with despatches,
plainly written, and in cypher, and other apparently
important MS. matter. Chairs having the distinctive
features of antiqueness flanked the tables on either
side. The place of honour—viz., the crimson chair
on the daïs, was occupied by a young fair-haired
man, seemingly not more than twenty years of

age. His dress, in keeping with the attire of most of the gentlemen present, was that of a French courtier of the period.

A gentleman, apparelled in a suit of black, and seated immediately below the daïs, evidently held the post of secretary or amanuensis. There were also present two ecclesiastics, whose sacerdotal habiliments were abundantly scented with the fragrance of the City of Seven Hills. But chiefly conspicuous in this heterogeneous assembly was a tall, raw-boned man of more than threescore, arrayed in full Highland costume; and although the tartans were faded and worn, he presented a picturesque appearance, affording a striking contrast to those around him. His beard and deep hanging moustache were grizzled—in fact the latter might be said to be almost purely white; he had been obviously a remarkably handsome man in his prime, and—*maugre senility*—evident traces of manly beauty still lingered lovingly on his face, as though loath to leave the poor forlorn exile in age and adversity.

The occupant of the place of honour was Prince Charles Edward, the "Young Chevalier," celebrated in story and in song; and at the time of the reader's introduction to this Jacobite gathering, the young Pretender was addressing those about him in a warm and fervent manner.

"Gentlemen," said he, "you will, I am sure, readily believe me when I tell you that I have

weighed this matter well and carefully; I have
viewed it from every side and in all aspects before
coming to a conclusion ; and, in my humble opinion,
a rising in the South of England—apart from its
positive futility—would be exceedingly unwise and
impolitic. ·I grant you that better and greater facil-
ities offer themselves for a landing in England than
elsewhere, and were I invading Britain with a
large and powerful army, I should most assuredly
adopt the plan advocated so strenuously by some
of our most trusty friends—viz., debarkation on
the coasts of Kent or Devon ; but, gentlemen, I
beg to remind you that any aid, beyond good
wishes, and a truly earnest prayer for our ultimate
success, may not be expected from His Majesty of
France, and for our brave little band to attempt a
landing on English soil would be a forlorn hope
indeed. Now, I am sure you will agree with me
in this—that it is my strict duty (apart from a
policy which should be self-apparent) to set up the
standard of my father in a part of the country
where I may be able to count, not only on the
most valuable assistance, but on the readiest and
most expeditious aid ; and only in the extreme
North of Scotland can we rely for prompt succour
and support. We have, as you well know, the
pledged word of the heads of many powerful clans,
and I need hardly tell you that clansmen march
with their chiefs either to victory or to death, with-

out question or debate ; though their numbers are a thousand, there is but one heart, but one mind. Now, on the other hand, in England, and also in the Scottish Lowlands, a totally different state of things exist. Every man, with but few exceptions, has a free will, an independent judgment, and is only guided or constrained by his own personal feeling ; and admitting, merely for the sake of argument, that the popular thought in Britain on this matter is so nicely and so evenly balanced that the smallest feather weight would turn the scale either way, still, with the certain knowledge that at least three-fourths of the Highlanders are with us, it would be unwise to attempt a landing, excepting to the north of the Tay on the east, or to the north of the Firth of Clyde on the west. What say you, McLean, to a landing in England ?"

"England, forsooth!" said the old Highlander to whom the question was addressed by the Prince. "I would just as soon shove my legs into a pair o' lowland breeks. I tell ye this, and I ken it to be true, that no sooner will the Royal standard be unfurled in the Hielans than mair than five thousand guid braidswords will leap frae their scabbards, and be flashin' in the bright sunshine ; and that, I conceive, wad be something to start the campaign. Five thousand Hielan' men, each with a guid claymore in his fist, wadna' be laughed at or lightly turned aside, as the Laird o' Ross there can tell ye."

"You must not appeal to me, McLean," said Ross, with quiet dignity. "I am no authority on this matter."

"Ye say true, laird," returned the old man, evidently much nettled, "ye say very true; but your ancestors, laird, could gie good caution, I wot, for their valour."

"My ancestors!" repeated Ross, warmly. "Sir, I would have you know that my forbears never yielded so much as an inch of ground even before a host of Highland robbers."

"Robbers!" exclaimed the old man, starting to his feet, and grasping the hilt of his broadsword with convulsive energy. "Robbers! did I hear ye apply that term to the clan McLean?"

"No!" replied Ross. "You did not. I never mentioned your clan, and there is indeed but little cause for your virtuous indignation, for I presume you will not deny that some of the Red-shanks, wearing your ain tartan, have gone back to the hills mair than once in your ain time, with twenty or maybe thirty head of cattle before them, that were never bought wi' siller."

To what length this extreme provocation (the more exasperating and provoking because of its exceeding truthfulness) would have carried the old Highlander, we are not prepared to say, but peace having been restored through the intervention of friends, and finally at the command of the Prince, the chief and the laird resumed their respective seats, scowling at each other in bitter defiance. This too-apparently expressed want of unanimity and concord was an ill augury of the ultimate success of the cause of the Jacobites.

"Might I ask your Royal Highness," said one gentleman, rising to his feet, "the particular line of march after mustering forces in the Highlands?"

"In that case," answered the Prince, "we shall be entirely governed by circumstances. I shall undoubtedly, as a matter of policy, labour to reach and occupy Edinburgh as soon as possible; for the Scottish capital once in the hands of my royal father, will invest the campaign with an essential dignity of power, gladden the hearts of our friends in the south, reassure the timid and wavering, and incline those who are halting between two opinions to declare at once for the House of Stuart."

"We have, your Royal Highness," pursued the previous speaker, "but little reliable information as to the intentions of many persons of distinction and influence in the south, the representatives of old loyal families who have done good service for King James in the past."

"I am happy to say," returned Prince Charles, "that we have some earnest friends working for us in the south of England, through whom we from time to time receive the most hopeful promises of adherence and support on the part of the heads of

the old Jacobite houses; and furthermore, even now
we are awaiting the return of one of our most
valued and trusted allies, who will be able to show
us most clearly the state of feeling in the counties
of Durham and Northumberland."

As the Prince was speaking this last sentence, an
attendant announced " Le Comte D'Aubray," and
our friend Chedville, in the dress of a courtier, with
a jewelled order flashing bright and sparkling rays
from his breast, entered the apartment, saluting the
Prince and his friends by a courteous though somewhat stately recognition.

"We bid you welcome, monsieur le Comte," said
Charles, "and trust you are the bearer of pleasant
and hopeful tidings."

"I have done my best to promote the interests
of the cause of *votre altesse;* and if my errand has
not been so successful as might have been desired,
the unsatisfactory result is due more to the luke-
warmness—and in some instances cold apathy—of
your friends, than to the inertitude or indolence of
your humble ambassador."

"Before proceeding with other business," said
Ross, "I move that we have the report of our
excellent friend le Comte D'Aubray."

"Undoubtedly," answered Charles Edward. "I
am sure your wish will have the general concurrence."

"Your Royal Highness," began Chedville, "I shall
be most happy to impart to this company the in-

formation I possess. I have succeeded—I may be
permitted to say with some difficulty, and occasionally some little danger—in gaining personal, and in
certain instances lengthy interviews, with the whole
of the gentlemen whose names were inscribed on my
letter of instructions when leaving France ; and
nearly all of them, while professing their true and
staunch adherence to the royal cause, protest
strongly, as you will see by these papers, against a
rising in any part of Britain, until the onward march
of the coming year shall have given an assurance
of finer and more genial weather. There are some
few who, although holding the same opinions, nevertheless express their willingness to leave the matter
entirely in the discretion of your Royal Highness ;
and whatever decision you may be pleased to arrive
at, in the exercise of your own wisdom, they pledge
themselves to stand or fall in your cause."

Chedville's remarks were listened to with deep
and earnest attention, and the latter part of his
speech evoked a subdued applause.

The secretary now read from the documents
handed to him the names of the various northern
Jacobites interviewed by D'Aubray, after which the
Laird of Ross rose, and addressing the Prince, said—

" I crave pardon, your Royal Highness, but by
some unintentional oversight the name of a most
loyal and influential gentleman has been omitted
in the copy of instructions given to the Comte ; I

allude, your Highness, to Kenard Maxwell, a gentleman of sterling integrity and worth, and well known, I believe, to the major part of this assembly."

"Does the gentleman of whom you speak command much influence?" asked the Prince.

"Not in England, your Royal Highness," replied Ross; "but the bare knowledge of the fact that he had embraced our cause would gain for us many powerful friends in the Lothians. Kenard Maxwell is a Scotchman of property, good family, and long descent. He removed to England on his marriage with a lady of considerable wealth. His estate, as I am given to understand, lies on the north bank of the river Wear, some five miles from the seaport town of Sunderland ; and his residence, to the best of my recollection, is known in the locality as Balmston House."

" Our trusty friend, the Comte D'Aubray," said the Prince, "contemplates another journey to England, and will doubtless have an opportunity of waiting on this gentleman ; meanwhile, our secretary will see that proper credentials are furnished him for that purpose."

One of the priests, in a speech remarkable for its wily craft, argued in favour of the right and left promulgation of the religious sentiments, convictions, and faith of the Prince, contending, in language calmly yet most artfully worded, that this would most assuredly draw to his side the great mass of the catholic gentry in England and Scotland, many of whom were still standing on neutral ground.

The disquisition of the reverend gentleman was somewhat brusquely interrupted by Chedville, who said, that so far from agreeing with him, he could assure the Prince, on the strength of his own personal knowledge and individual observation, that such a course would prove inevitably disastrous and calamitous to the cause they had so much at heart.

"I must confess," continued the Comte, "that I am both surprised and grieved to hear a proposal of this nature made—a proposal to force on the people of Britain the same dominative creed which has already been so unpropitious to your royal house; for if there is truth in history, James the Second was unquestionably hurled from his seat solely for that he pricked the people a little too severely with the papal spur. The religious convictions or opinions of your Royal Highness, whatever they may be, are not matters for public parade in the present day: between God and your own conscience let them lie. If it should prove necessary to introduce the religious element in any mode or guise whatever, be it your duty, as it is your best policy, to promise freedom of worship to all sects and all denominations of Christian people."

Those sentiments were endorsed by the Laird of Ross, and re-echoed by the majority of the gentlemen present, and the priest resumed his seat,

4

evidently disappointed and chagrined. After several important matters had been considered, the Jacobite council broke up, the Prince observing that with the assurance of aid from so many friends in England and in Scotland, and the voluntarily proffered services of so many subjects of His Majesty of France, the result of the coming campaign could not be otherwise than favourable to the royal cause. "Our next meeting," he added, "will be at Paris a week hence, when we trust to have the pleasure of your company, and the benefit of your valuable counsel. May we rely on you, Monsieur le Comte?"

"I am afraid not, your Royal Highness," replied Chedville, to whom the question was addressed. "If all goes well, I expect to sail for England in a few days, and will do my best to screw 'to the sticking place' the courage of your north-country friends. I shall also make it a special business to see this same Kenard Maxwell, of whom I trust to give you a good account on my return to France."

The gentlemen, after paying court to the young Chevalier, retired one by one, and the Prince and Chedville were left together.

"Now, D'Aubray, *mon ami*," said Charles Edward, "I know well thou art a man of superior intelligence and admirable penetration—nay, nay," he added, seeing Chedville express something of gestural deprecation, "do not think I flatter. Alas, alas!

I cannot go further and say, with our equally unfortunate cousin of Denmark—

"For what advancement may I hope from thee?"

when 'tis from thee, dear friend, and men with souls as true and noble as thine own, I hope for future prosperity. I know thou art candid, and that thou, after weighing well thy thoughts, dost always speak the true sentiments of thy mind ; therefore, tell me what thou judgest of this, our high emprise."

"That," replied Chedville, "even with all the wisdom your Royal Highness is pleased to credit me with, I cannot answer at the moment. If I were to hazard an opinion founded on present experience and observation, it would be favourable to your cause; but pardon me, your Highness, for the premonition, if I am compelled to warn you that the opposition of your foes will be greater, stronger, and far more determined than many of your friends would have you believe."

"Ha!" exclaimed Charles, "there I shall not be beguiled. But there is another matter which gives me much cause for grief and uneasiness. Can'st not make a guess, D'Aubray?"

"I can," Chedville answered promptly. "Your Royal Highness alludes to the almost constant quarrels, bickerings, and petty broils amongst so many of your friends. This is not only common, but natural, and by no means exceptional under the existing circumstances, and it certainly calls for no

special wonderment. Consider for a single moment
they are men who, in addition to the loss of large
estates, have had their tempers further soured by
that adversity which is almost invariably the *vade
mecum* of the poor exile ; but when the time for
decisive action arrives, this same sourness of disposition, which at present finds its only vent in
morose, splenetic, and petulant speech, will tend
to—nay, fully succeed in making them daring and
desperate men."

"Thanks, *bon ami*," said Charles ; "and soon I
hope to see the dawn of that day which will enable
me, if not fully to requite, at least to repay in
some small degree your excellent and truly valuable
services in my cause otherwise than with my poor
thanks. And now," the Prince continued, in a more
cheerful tone, "what say you, D'Aubray, shall we
go and put a few coins, like our dear father's triple
kingdom, on the hazard ? "

"Your Royal Highness must pardon me," Chedville answered, seriously ; " I never enter a gaming-
house. A gambling dispute, resulting in *une affaire
d'honnéur*, robbed me of both parents at an early
age. *Pauvre mére*."

"*Pardon, mon cher ami*," said Charles Edward,
hastily, and with considerable feeling, "it pains me
to think I have unwittingly recalled to your mind
a deep sorrow. For myself, D'Aubray, I find in
those same games of fickle chance something so near

akin to my own desperate fortunes, that the excitement and suspense arising from the very uncertainty of the ultimate results, gives to me an unfailing degree of pleasure which no other source can really supply. And now *adieu, monsieur,*" continued the Prince, grasping Chedville's hand with a cordial clasp, "and believe me, I shall ever consider the Comte D'Aubray one of my best and dearest friends."

"Your Royal Highness may at all events look upon me as one of the most personally disinterested associates in your present enterprise."

CHAPTER IV.

"Mark the condition and the event, then tell me
If this might be a brother?"

—Tempest.

BALMSTON was a large old-fashioned
country house, wanting only a very few
architectural embellishments outwardly
to transform it into a mansion of some
pretensions. This rural residence stood on the north
bank of the river Wear, about five miles westward
from the port of Sunderland. The site of the house
evinced capital taste on the part of the builder,
standing, as it did, backward from the stream on a
gently rising ground. Immediately below it, and
margining the limpid water, was a thick close wood,
covering to some extent the sloping bank, and extending to the south-east for nearly a mile. Balmston
House looked fairly enchanting, and showed a truly
picturesque beauty, when viewed from the river or its
south shore, in the glad summer time—just at that
particular period of the year when the trees had
donned their greenest and brightest attire, when the

wild flowers bloomed in the rich full noontide of their
natural loveliness, and the tall meadow-grass swayed
backwards and forwards, or, rather, rose and fell with a
languid, undulatory motion, as though intoxicated with
the amorous breath of the soft-sighing June breeze.
The house, and a very considerable portion of the
land round about, was the property of Mr. Kenard
Maxwell, of whom mention has already been made.

Balmston was an estate which had only come into
Maxwell's temporary possession by marriage. The
property, being strictly entailed, would at his death
pass into the hands of his only child, a daughter, at
this time about eighteen years of age. Kenard was a
Scotchman by birth, descended from an ancient
family, known and respected in the Lothians. He
was the eldest of two sons, and heir to the paternal
acres. Maxwell's first meeting with the lady who
subsequently became his wife was in Edinburgh, and
with him it was most assuredly a case of love at first
sight. Ruth Eden was the daughter of a decidedly
" well - to - do " English gentleman of the north-
country.

Kenard's love for the lady was a pure and honest
affection : no single thought of her father's wealth
tended to increase or intensify the ardour of
his attachment. With his brother, James Maxwell, it was quite a different affair. He saw the
lady—fully appreciated and admired her beauty,
Not much in this—no man made up of flesh.

blood, and youth could help it ; but, after all, the
" tocher" was

> " The jewel had charms for him."

As a younger son the income of James was by no
means large, and to hold a position in society he
depended to some extent on the liberality of his more
fortunate brother, who, by the way, was invariably
kindly generous, open-hearted, and loving.   James
Maxwell, like Sir Pertinax M'Sycophant, had come—
some time previous to the advent of this semi-divine
specimen of femininism—to the conclusion " that a
matrimonial adventure, prudently conducted, wad be
the readiest gate he could gang for the bettering of
his condition ;" and as a golden opportunity now
presented itself, his attention to Miss Eden was constant, obsequious, and servile; while poor Kenard,
whose love was pure and inviolate, spoke for a time
only from his eyes, in visible but inaudible language.

Ruth Eden, though young, was a shrewd observer,
and was soon able to accurately weigh up James
Maxwell's devotion.   Deducting the useless tare to
" a pennyweight," she was quite able to discern the
difference between unalloyed gold and brass, and
consequently the advances of the younger son were
acknowledged by the lady with a coolness so
decidedly icy, that James could not fail to see that
she preferred " his room to his company."   Kenard
and Miss Eden, on the other hand, soon began to

understand each other, for, as we have already shown, love, like murder, though it should have no tongue, yet will it speak. After some little time, the all-important question was put by Maxwell; and the lady (after experiencing a slight tremulous quivering in the heart's region, by no means painful or even unpleasant) uttered deliciously low, and in a manner becoming the occasion, the wished-for monosyllable, which came sweeter to the ear of the lover than the most angelic music, and made him unspeakably happy. Maddened by the thought that his brother had triumphed where he had himself so ignominiously failed, James Maxwell went to work with the wicked design of thwarting, by any means, fair or foul, the full consummation of Kenard's fond desire. Chance soon lent him the opportunity. Taking advantage of the temporary absence of the elder, he managed, by that crafty insidiousness which certainly appeared to be the chief characteristic of his evil nature, to circulate in the society in which Miss Eden was daily moving a report that Kenard was about to wed another. James was questioned one day on the subject, in Ruth's presence, by a young lady, who, to do her justice, was quite ignorant of the existence of anything like a tender attachment between Miss Eden and the elder Maxwell. James denied the truth of the report, but in a manner so thoroughly embarrassed and confused, that it could not fail to convince those present that it was no lying rumour.

During the evening Ruth felt it to be her duty
to take James Maxwell to task for the vague,
halting, and singularly perplexed method employed
by him in contradicting the idle story.

"My dear Miss Eden," he replied, "I have to
confess to you that I was so much taken by
surprise, that I scarcely knew what I was saying;"
and then, he added, in a lower tone, as if speaking
to himself, "How, in the name of fortune, has this
unhappy affair got wind?" Ruth heard—as he
evidently intended she should—the latter sentence,
and turned sharply round on him, her cheeks richly
suffused, and her eyes sparkling with indignation.

"Sir," she exclaimed, "do you mean to say
that you really believe there is a single word of
truth in the report so wantonly circulated by these
fashionable scandalmongers?"

"Alas! Miss Eden," he answered, demurely, "I
would not attempt to deceive you, nor would I for
the world's wealth give you a moment's pain; but
when you question me so directly, then, as an
honest man, I am bound to answer you truth-
fully, having no other choice. I am sorry to say—
and I know you will pardon me, for this is
unquestionably a matter of duty and right—I am
sorry to say that my brother Kenard has acted
most unfairly towards you; but I am also bound
in honour to tell you, that up to this time I never
knew, nay, never for one moment thought that

duplicity or double-dealing formed any part of his character. My brother—dear Miss Eden, if this communication pains you, I crave forgiveness—my brother is about to wed another lady, and he is even now at the house of her father arranging the necessary marriage settlements."

Ruth turned pale as death, but her faith in Kenard's honour, her trust in his love, had not yet departed.

"James Maxwell," she said, "I cannot, nay, will not, believe this."

"Pardon me, I pray you," he continued, interrupting her; "why should I, or rather let me say, how could I deceive you in a matter which must of necessity come to your own knowledge in a short time? I have myself seen some of the correspondence between this young lady and my brother Kenard, and I have now in my possession a letter written by him to her father. You know his hand well; read this, and you will be fully convinced that I have spoken the sad truth."

Ruth took the proffered letter, almost unconsciously, and, after a pause, she suffered her eyes, now growing dim and moist, to fall on the paper. The letter was addressed to a certain Alexander McDonald, and its contents ran thus :—

"My dear sir—I will be with you early in the *next* week, for the purpose of arranging the pre-

liminaries necessary before the marriage can take
place. I beg to assure you I am in a position to
make such settlements as cannot fail to give you
the highest satisfaction. I pray you to excuse me,
in that I do not write at greater length, but I have,
as you must be aware, much work in hand in con-
nection with this happy business, which, I need
hardly say, is of the weightiest importance to yours,

"KENARD MAXWELL."

Miss Eden stood motionless, the missive in her
hand, like a sculptural triumph, hewn from a faultless block of marble.

Was this real? she asked herself deep down
in her own heart; was she awake, or under the
torturing influence of some painful dream? No, she
could not be deceived; it was no dream, no halluci-
nation; the hand was known to her, alas, too, too
well, it was Kenard's and Kenard was faithless—
false to the vows he had so repeatedly made with
such apparent truth. She felt for a moment as if
all the blood in her veins had become congealed
and turned to ice; and then it rushed, a warm,
powerful, impetuous flood-tide, back to the heart,
and filled its vessels nigh to bursting. Despite the
great mental and physical anguish under which
Ruth laboured; despite the sad, lone feeling engendered by the shattering to pieces of her life's
idol; despite all this, she turned her pale yet brave

face towards James Maxwell, and holding him with her eye, she said, in a voice apparently uninfluenced by the slightest emotion, "It is enough. I need not ask you how you came by this letter. I can easily conceive the manner; and while feeling myself deeply wronged, and remembering too keenly the fact that your brother has broken his pledged word to me, and set at nought his trothplight, still I fail to find an excuse for your despicable baseness in playing the triple *rôle* of traitor, thief, and spy."

Dropping the letter on the ground, Miss Eden walked calmly away, leaving James Maxwell in a decidedly unenviable state of mind. He thought to have made a scene, and in soothing the affliction of the lady he anticipated a bright and fortunate result.

Mr. Eden and his daughter left Edinburgh the next day; and James Maxwell, although able to congratulate himself on the full and complete success of the plot against his brother's happiness, had still to make the sad, humiliating self-confession that his chances of gaining either the respect or love of the wronged lady had in nowise been improved.

→✳✣✳←

CHAPTER V.

"But well y wote y hadde not done
Hur to displease, but in great mone
She hath me left, and ys agone ;
For sorwe my hert doth blede."
—*John Lydgate.*

A FEW days after the departure of Ruth Eden and her father, Kenard returned to the Scottish capital, and learnt, to his utter astonishment, how abruptly their visit had terminated. The love-stricken young man immediately penned a letter to the lady, expressing his great sorrow at her enforced removal from Edinburgh before his return ; and to his still greater surprise and bewilderment he received a frigid reply to his note, in which Miss Eden very briefly stated that her movements could be of very little moment or consequence to Kenard Maxwell. Feeling fully assured that during his short absence he had been cruelly slandered, he wrote a second time, protesting, in love's warmest phraseology, his deep devotedness

to the lady, and beseeching her to give him a reason
for the brief and cold missive he had received. This
epistle, which contained the outpourings of a full,
true, and faithful heart, would have unquestionably
restored matters to their former footing, had it not
been cleverly intercepted and confiscated by James
Maxwell.

Kenard—who loved Ruth Eden as well as man
ever loved woman since the world began—felt this
blow keenly ; but still, though the iron had entered
his soul, though the hidden fox was gawning at his
heart, he was, like the Spartan boy of old, by a
strong effort of human will, enabled to bury his great
pain and sorrow in his own breast, and present
himself, calm and unruffled, before the world of his
own society.

About six months after the unexpected and
abrupt departure of Ruth Eden and her father
from Edinburgh, business of some importance carried Kenard Maxwell into South Northumberland.
Journeying on horseback near the close of a fine
autumn day, in the immediate vicinity of Glenwelt
(rather an uncanny district at this particular period),
our traveller was aroused from a fit of musing by
the sharp report of fire-arms, and looking up he
saw straight before him, and at no great distance,
a carriage, round which three or four men
were standing. Kenard came at once to the
conclusion that the vehicle had been attacked by

footpads, and hastily snatching his pistols from their holsters, he galloped to the rescue.

Before he reached the spot, those "minions," not only "of the moon," but afternoon too, as it seemed, had succeeded in dragging from the carriage an elderly gentleman, apparently rendered insensible by the ruffians, who began to rifle him in a deliberate and systematic manner. One of the old man's hands still grasped the weapon he had so recently discharged evidently without effect.

The tramp of his horse's hoofs became louder as Kenard left the moorland for the hard road, and the resonant beat was now conveyed to the ears of the robbers. Seeing but one man approaching, they apparently resolved to stand their ground and await the assault. Maxwell, nothing daunted, rode so furiously upon them that they were constrained for their own safety to step hastily aside; and— holding the bridle firmly between his teeth—he discharged both weapons in passing, and with good effect, for two of the ruffians fell to the ground. Replacing his pistols, he wheeled his charger, and grasping firmly his heavy riding whip, he proceeded to attack the other two, but they, seeing half their number already *hors de combat*, and the coachman and footman rapidly recovering from the terror which for a time had paralysed them both, took to their heels, seeking shelter in a thick wood at no great distance. Kenard dismounted, and having lifted the old gentleman carefully from the ground, he consigned him to the charge of his attendants, and then approaching the vehicle, he found it occupied by a lady, who had evidently swooned. To permit a free current of air, Maxwell threw open the door of the carriage, and while performing this act, he found, to his utter amazement, that the occupant was none other than Ruth Eden.

Maxwell raised the lady gently from her recumbent position, and when, on opening her eyes, she beheld the face of the man she had so fondly and truly loved looking down into her own, the features wearing an expression of extreme tenderness, not unmixed with sorrow, she was for the moment utterly oblivious of their now altered positions, and entirely forgetful of the deep, sombrous cloud between them. Ruth threw herself on Maxwell's breast, exclaiming, " Kenard, thank heaven ! " When she was fairly recovered, and had again become thoroughly conscious, she blushed deeply, and withdrawing in a manner decidedly cold and dignified from Kenard's embrace, Ruth proceeded to aid her father. Mr. Eden (for the old gentleman was none other) had partially regained his senses, but loudly complained of much pain and suffering from the wound inflicted on him by the ruffians. After drinking a little wine he was assisted into the carriage, and in reply to a question from Maxwell the lady stated that they were then on their way to Carlisle, where her father had business of some importance to arrange. Kenard at once proffered his services as an escort to the nearest town, an offer which Miss Eden accepted with gelid, yet still courteous thanks.

One of the footpads was found to be dead, and the other, who was dangerously wounded, was conveyed to Greenhead, and there handed over to the safe keeping of the constable. This representative of the law, after a short inspection, recognised him as "a Bewcastler," whose past history, though generally known, was not over appreciated in that particular locality.

Kenard proposed a halt, in order that the wound inflicted on Mr. Eden might be properly attended to; and the old gentleman finding that the little inn at Greenhead afforded passable accommodation for "man and beast," fell in at once with Maxwell's proposal, and resolved to stay till next morning.

The village surgeon was called in. He was a man about fifty, stoutly built, with the word "Brandy" written on his face in plain and legible characters. His miscellaneous and diversified vestments were a study: he was garbed in the coat of a clergyman, the waistcoat of an itinerant tinker, the breeches of a horse-couper, and the boots of a jockey. This worthy, after clipping away a portion of the hair, discovered a severe but not dangerous cut on the head of the old gentleman, and having carefully dressed the same, he looked for a moment seriously wise, and rigidly sober, then prescribed " rest, and great care."

After some conversation with Maxwell, Mr. Eden, acting on the advice of the rural Galenist, retired to his apartment, and Kenard and the young lady were left *tête-a-tête* in the best parlour of the house, which, although not elegantly furnished, was nevertheless a comfortable room.

The conversation for some time, as might be expected, was carried on in a decidedly reserved, frigorific, and precise manner. Both lady and gentleman in look and in speech evinced a desire to approach a certain subject, but were apparently held back by a kind of indefinable awe. At length Ruth—in allusion to the day's adventure—said, " I am sure my dear father will fully estimate and appreciate your gallant services on our behalf; but for your timely aid, he would have been unquestionably the loser of a large sum of money, and those wicked men might even have taken his life."

" The knowledge of being able to aid or assist Miss Eden is in itself a guerdon sufficient; and," continued Kenard, warming as he spoke, " though I may have good reason to complain of that lady's past treatment of my poor self, I would still think it happiness to lay down my life in her service."

" I thank you most sincerely, Mr. Maxwell," said

Ruth, with stately grace, and looking vastly surprised, "but you must really pardon me if I am compelled to ask you when and where cause for complaint was given you by Ruth Eden?"

"Madam!" exclaimed Kenard, rising hastily to his feet, an ironically bitter smile playing the while on his handsome face, "I cannot for one moment entertain the thought that you would, at such a time as this, knowingly or wantonly wound the feelings of the man who has already suffered—aye, undeservedly suffered—so much wrong at your hands."

It was now the lady's turn to be indignant, and with a somewhat flushed face, but with a proud, haughty glance darting from her eye, she looked straight at Maxwell for a single moment; then rising from her seat, and grasping the back of her chair with almost convulsive force, she said, in slow, distinct, and apparently unemotional tones—

"Mr. Maxwell, when I heard—and you can doubtless imagine with what feelings I did hear it—when I heard that you had transferred the love and the affection which I foolishly deemed had been already given absolutely to me, to another lady, I did not even reproach you; I endeavoured to think the best. Nay, hear me out," she added, hastily, seeing Kenard about to speak. "I thought, or at all events I schooled myself to think and believe, that you had found one more beautiful, more charming in mind, form, and manner, than her to whom you had rashly, and peradventure foolishly, pledged your first love ; and I said, 'It is better he should discover his error in time ; it is better he should now draw back, and retrace the false step he has taken—better this than that the dread knowledge of an unhappy mistake should come upon him in after years, when fate had cast both our lives to flow on together in one stream—when there were bonds between us which death alone could snap asunder.' But now, sir, when you—you upbraid me with having done you wrong, I can only say, I find in Mr. Kenard Maxwell that which to this moment I never expected to discover—deceit, dissimulation, and what I can least of all pardon and forgive—unblushing effrontery."

"Madam, you do me grievous wrong. When, where, and how have I done these things you now so freely lay to my charge ? "

" Are you not married to a certain Miss McDonald ? "

" Heavens ! No, madam."

" Are you not about to wed this lady ? "

" No, madam."

" Did you not attend at her father's house with the design of arranging and drawing up the necessary marriage settlements ? "

" For myself ? "

"Yes."

"No, madam."

"I saw your own letter to Mr. McDonald, in which you plainly stated that you would be with him within a week for that purpose."

"Might I ask Miss Eden in whose hands she saw this same letter."

"In the hands of your own brother, James Maxwell."

"Good Heaven!" exclaimed Kenard, the truth flashing upon him at once, "what a villain! Sit you down, Ruth," he added, taking her hand almost roughly; "we have been groping like children in the dark, but, thank heaven, we are coming into the glorious sunshine at last."

Miss Eden obeyed the stern mandate of Maxwell mechanically, looking like one in a dream.

"I may tell you at the outset," he continued, in deeply impressive tones, "that I never loved till I saw you, and since that time I have never loved or professed an attachment for another, and come weal come woe, let good or ill betide, Ruth Eden will be the first and last love of Kenard Maxwell. My brother, I am now aware, loved, or pretended to love you also, and his purpose in showing you that letter was doubtless to induce you to withdraw your affection from me, and transfer the same to himself. I have a cousin, Miss Eden— one William Maxwell—to whom my poor father was guardian. At his decease I was compelled, by virtue of my altered position, to accept the same trust, although my ward was my junior by little more than six years. William Maxwell became devotedly attached to a certain Miss McDonald, a young lady of great beauty and sterling worth, whose acquaintance he made during a short visit to Perthshire; and six months before attaining his majority he earnestly entreated my permission to marry her. Mindful of his happiness, I made such inquiries as, holding the position of guardian, I deemed essential; and so pleased was I with the result of my investigations, that I joyously gave my consent to their union, and the day for the wedding was fixed. Now, Miss Eden, you will readily understand that in consequence of my cousin being still under twenty-one years of age, his affairs were entirely in my hands as his warden, and all pecuniary arrangements were of necessity to be made by me. In furtherance of this object, I wrote Mr. McDonald, appointing a time to meet him, so that all preliminary matters might be settled. I had already promised my cousin that I would be present at the marriage. Judge then of my great surprise when, on my arrival at the house of the lady's father, I found the principal parties in a state of alarm and even dismay, in consequence of the non-delivery of my letter. I soon put this matter right by an assurance that a letter had

been despatched by me, which must have been
diverted by some unfortunate circumstance from
its proper course. I stayed to witness the ceremony
by which two truly loving people were made happy,
and then returned to Edinburgh to find—what ?
that you and your father had left it in the most
abrupt and mysterious manner, without a line,
without a word for me. I wrote you immediately
on my arrival, and received in return for my communication a note so cold, so cruel, and apparently
so heartless, that its perusal drove me to the verge
of madness.   On reflection, I came to the conclusion
that slander had been busy during my short absence,
and I penned another letter, telling you of my un-
dying love, and daring the proof that I had at
any time or in anywise rendered myself unworthy
to hold the esteem and the affection of Miss Eden.
That letter—the humble, earnest protest of a wounded,
nay, of an almost broken heart—you did not deign
to answer."

"Pardon me, Kenard," exclaimed Ruth, tearfully.
"Pardon me ; I never received it, so help me, heaven !"

"You did not ?   Then my unnatural brother must
have succeeded in intercepting that also."

" O! Kenard," said the poor girl, now weeping
bitterly, "think you it was no trial to me ? Can
you see no difference?   Am I now aught like the
same laughing, happy girl you first met in Edinburgh ? Do you see the same fresh bloom on my

cheek, the same glad smile on my face? Ah! no, no! Believe me, dear Kenard, I have suffered, suffered greatly."

She was now clasped in his arms, her head lay pillowed on his manly breast; the dark cloud which for a time had hovered pall-like over them was swept away, and their former sky once again canopied them, in all its pristine pellucidness.

"Ruth, love," said Kenard, imprinting a kiss on her ready lips, "I must plead guilty to the utterance of a·falsehood even now."

"Indeed, Kenard," Ruth returned, looking up into his face with a sweet smile; "what was it?"

"One of your questions," he replied, "ran thus: Are you not about to wed? If you remember, love, I answered, No. You will forgive me, I am sure; the falsehood was not wittingly told, for heaven knows I dreamt not my happiness was so near."

Maxwell accompanied Miss Eden and her father to Carlisle, and on their arrival he wrote to his brother, informing him that his treachery had been discovered, and that his evil devices had utterly failed in their desired effect. James, as may be expected, was afraid to meet Kenard; he started for London almost on the receipt of the letter, and soon, through the influence of friends high in power, he succeeded in obtaining a good emolumental appointment under the existing goverment, and abjuring the creed of his family, and the political principles so early imbibed, he attached himself and his fortunes to the house of Hanover. The brothers never met again in this life. Three months after their reconciliation at the little inn at Greenhead, Kenard Maxwell and Ruth Eden were married. They resided in Scotland for some time, but on the death of the lady's father they removed to Balmston. After five years of undisturbed felicity, a sad misfortune befel Kenard; the sunshine of true happiness, which had gilded his life-path day by day, was gone, and his way was darkened by the dusky cloud of a sad bereavement. A malignant fever broke out on the Balmston estate, and Mrs. Maxwell, ever foremost in good works, paid daily visits to the stricken tenantry, supplying them with suitable food and medicine, and administering to them kind words of comfort and whisperings of hope. But alas! just when the fever began to show unmistakable signs of abatement, and all were in high expectation that the pestilential malady would by God's mercy pass away, the lady of Balmston was herself stricken, and died after a few days of extreme suffering.

It would be almost impossible to portray the deep grief and poignant distress of poor Kenard. Great fears for his reason were at one time entertained. Regardless of rest or food, he sat beside the clay-cold mortal remains of the woman he had so fondly, so devotedly loved; and even after they were removed, and shrouded in God's acre, he still occupied the death chamber, and refused to be comforted. After some time, a kind female friend, who possessed a knowledge of the human heart, and understood the true source whence human sympathies flow, carried into the room to him his daughter, a little laughing fairy, scarce four years old. The lady placed the child on Kenard's knee, and left the apartment without uttering a single word. The effect was magical! The secret spring was touched, the fount of tears hitherto dried up began to stream; and kissing the little smiling face again and again, he exclaimed, in a voice half choked by sobs—

"Yes! yes! my child, for thy sake I will live on."

CHAPTER VI.

"On Christmas eve the bells were rung ;
On Christmas eve the mass was sung ;
That only night in all the year
Saw the stoled priest the chalice rear.
The damsel donned her kirtle sheen ;
The hall was dressed with holly green ;
Forth to the woods did merry men go,
To gather in the mistletoe."

—Marmion.

THE morning of the 24th day of December, in the year of grace 1744, broke bright and clear; and a moderately thick covering of snow lay on the ground, and the frost was intensely keen and biting.

In the large hall of Balmston House, on this same morning, a more than middle-aged man, habited in an almost entirely worn-out plaid jacket, a pair of trousers of an almost unconceivable pattern, and having on his head the peculiar flat cap or bonnet worn by the Scotch, was, with two male assistants, busily engaged in decorating the walls of this particular apartment with holly, when he was suddenly interrupted in his work of adornment by a sweet, musical voice calling out—

"Donald, Donald Spey !"

"Deil's in the glaikit lassie," muttered the old man; "she'll no gie me a moment's peace this blessèd day." And then, in a louder tone, he cried, "I'm here, Miss Flora, here in the ha'."

A light, lively, elastic footfall was heard for a moment, and Flora Maxwell entered, a tall, lovely brunette, with hair as dark as the raven's wing, and quick, piercing eyes of the same sombre hue.

Her attitude as she took her stand in the hall was easy and graceful. Her faultless figure was such an one as the painter or the sculptor would love to delineate ; only that enforced admiration of the original would have most assuredly prevented the artist devoting the time and labour requisite for the completion of the copy.

"Well, Donald," she said, "have you got plenty holly ? "

"I dinna ken," replied Donald, laconically; "gin there's plenty for yoursel, my leddy, I wot there's mair than eneugh for me."

"And the mistletoe, Donald ? "

"Hoot awa wi' ye, Miss Flora," cried the old man, impatiently. "Did ye no say ye wad gang alang wi' me an' help pu' the mistletoe your ainsel ? "

"To be sure I did, crusty old Donald Spey; but I really had forgotten it for the moment, and I thank you for reminding me. Won't it be nice, Donald, to be able to say to my lady friends this evening, 'Look there now! With my own hands I gathered all this mistletoe, in order that the happy Christmastide may bring you plenty of kisses'? But oh! dear Donald—Donald Spey, what are you doing? Did ever any one behold holly put up in this queer fashion? I'm sure you once had a taste for this kind of work."

"Oh, aye!" returned Donald, coming slowly down from his elevated position, and regarding his more recent decorative performances somewhat ruefully; "it's a mistake, my leddy, it's a mistake althegither; the diel's in me this mornin', Miss Flora. I gat sicken a fright yestreen, that I kenna for certain whether I'm stannin' o' the soles o' my feet or the top o' my crown."

"A fright, Donald!" asked Miss Maxwell. "And pray what sort of a fright did you get?"

"I saw the Brownie."

"The what?"

"The Brownie."

"The Brownie?"

"Aye, my leddy, the Brownie o' the Maxwells."

Flora burst into a loud fit of laughter, much to the annoyance of the old man.

"Aye, aye, Miss Flora," he muttered, in high

dudgeon, "ye may laugh, but it's aye true for a' that."

"But, Donald, where did you see this preternatural individual?"

"Just in the garden, my leddy; but he was no in the kilt as he appeared when your grandfeyther Archie Maxwell gaed awa'."

"Ah," said Flora, maliciously, "no doubt, Donald, he's a Brownie of taste, and conforms cheerfully to the manners, customs, and even costumes of the times. It would be no surprise, as far as I am personally concerned, to see this ghostly visitant in breeches and a bob-wig."

"Vera weel, my leddy," returned Donald, completely nettled at the playful badinage of Miss Maxwell, "ye dinna believe in't, but ye'll see him yer ainsel before ye come till your deeth bed; aye, an' it's just matterless where ye may be. It may be at Balmston, or Ameriky, or the gowden Indies, it disna mak a bodle difference to the Brownie. Ah, my pretty leddy, he shows himsel whenever and wherever a Maxwell is about to dee; aye, an' mair forbye, he's been ken'd to show himsel when it has na' been a matter o' life an' deeth, but when there's been some great unseen danger threatenin' the house. Did I no look for his footsteps this blessed mornin' i' the snaw, but deil a trace could been seen; tho' I ken brawly, that no anither flake's fa'en to the grund sin' yesternight."

"Perhaps so, Donald; still it has only been your imagination. This fancied supernatural visibility might have been truly something of flesh and blood like yourself; and admitting, for argument's sake, that no snow has fallen since the evening of yesterday, you must confess, wise Donald, that the strong north wind which blew last night was sufficiently powerful to obliterate all traces of footsteps, had they been really there."

"Just sae," Donald answered, quietly. "Just sae. Ye winna believe in the Brownie, like yer ain feythor an' his forbears, but ye'll not only believe yersel, but ye'll gar ither folk believe a' the daft idle stories belangin' to this kintraside."

"And pray, Mr. Donald Spey," asked Flora, "what absurd stories am I accused of believing?"

"Why, did I no hear ye my ainsel telling Miss Hazlewood o' the Grange a' about the Lambton Worm just the ither day—a creepin' reptile, that twisted itsel three times round the Worm Hill? Certies, I wad as lief believe he coilt himsel three times round Painshey."

"I beg your pardon, Donald," said Miss Maxwell, with great stateliness. "I have a strong desire that you should be put right in this matter. I cannot say for myself that I do or that I do not believe in the Worm legend; there is most unquestionably a mystery - cloud hanging over this same story. Some people, Mr. Spey, very learned, and, consequently, very wise, account for it in this way. 'Once upon a time'—that's the way the old stories always begin, Donald—'once upon a time a fierce, lawless band of Scottish marauders had crossed the Border and made quite a successful foray as far south as the Tees. Returning homeward with their plunder, they were attacked by one of the Lambtons, at the head of a hastily gathered force. So fierce and determined was the onslaught, that this large band of Border thieves was totally destroyed, the men composing it being literally cut to pieces;' and on this incident, they — the same wise people, Donald—say the popular legend is founded. But whether it was really a monster worm, or merely an allegory, I cannot pretend to say."

"There's no muckle difference between the beasts," said Donald, sapiently, as though about to begin a learned disquisition on zoology. "There no muckle difference between the beasts. The worm, an' the sairpant, an' the allegory, an' the dragon, they're a' much of a kind."

Donald exhibited a considerable amount of surprise and annoyance when Flora went off into a convulsive fit of laughter on hearing this truly novel definition of an allegory; and he asked, with a severe look of offended dignity, "What had pit her intil sic a fit o' daffin?"

"Excuse me, Donald," the lady replied, making a powerful effort to restrain, or rather, to overcome the inclination to break out afresh, "but I really could not help laughing at the idea of an allegory being so closely allied to the genus reptilia."

"Aye, aye," said Donald, resignedly, "mak yer sport, mak yer sport, my leddy. For the Brownie, I believe in't, for I ken them that's seen it, an' what's mair, I've seen it my ainsel ; but as for your worm, or your allegory, or whatever else ye may please to ca't, I dinna value the truth on't sae muckle as that." And here he snapped his fingers contemptuously. "Then there's your Cauld Lad o' Hilton, an' yer Penniwell Ghost. Why, there's naebody wi' just a single grain o' common sense wad believe in them; an' there ye stand, an' winna believe in traditions o' your ain family—traditions that's been kenn'd in your ain house, an' handed frae ane til anither for hunders, nay, I might say for mair than a thousand year. An' now, Miss Flora, I've said my say, an' I'm ready to gang wi' ye."

"Very good, Donald; I will put on a cloak, and be with you immediately, then—hey for the mistletoe bough."

As Flora was skipping away, Mr. Maxwell entered the hall.

"Ah ! my child," he said, taking both her hands, and kissing her on the forehead, "I see you have a vast amount of work before you, and how is Donald Spey carrying out your ideas ? "

"Oh !" replied Flora, as she ran laughingly away,

"I have no reason to complain; whatever may be Donald's shortcomings—and I am sadly afraid their name is legion—he tenders a full compensation for his deficiencies in his great anxiety to please."

Kenard Maxwell, even at the age of forty-six, was a really handsome man, of the true manly stamp, and only that his hair was here and there besprinkled with the nipping frosts of time, and the equally keen and biting cares of life, he would have been deemed much younger.

"Oh, Donald," he said, as soon as his daughter had left the apartment, "did you observe anyone near the outside of the house last night?"

Instead of answering this question, Donald stood for a moment speechless, his old wrinkled face underwent a rapid change, and then, holding up both hands in dismay and evident horror, he exclaimed—

"Gude save us a'! Is it comin' peril or sudden deeth?"

"What mean you, Donald?" Maxwell impatiently demanded.

"Oh! dear, dear! Did your honour see him?"

"Who?"

"The Brownie!"

"Pshaw! No."

"Then I saw him, your honour."

"Indeed; and where did you see him?"

"In the garden."

" Ha! At what time ? "

" Why, let me see," Donald answered, reflectively ; " it wad be just about nine o'clock."

" How was he attired ? "

" He wasna clad as I expected to see him, your honour ; he had a horseman's cloak wrappit roun' him. Oh! wull-a-wins! what can it portend ? "

" Did you speak to him ? "

" Did I speak til him ? " echoed Donald, in amazement. " Did I speak til him ? Wad I hae the presumption, an' me no a Maxwell ! "

" Thank you, Donald, that is enough ; attend to Flora's wants, and see that she has her wishes gratified as far as possible."

" Deil a fear o' that, your honour ; she's keepin' the hale house, butt an' ben, in a parfite forment this blessed day."

Leaving Mr. Spey to his decorative work, Kenard Maxwell walked away. He was evidently somewhat disturbed, a solemn gravity having usurped the place of ingenuousness and cordiality.

When Flora returned to the hall, with cloak and hood, Donald said, exultingly—

" There now, my leddy, when I telt your feyther about the wraith he didna jeer, an' laugh, and flout, an' ca' me an auld fule body, and no muckle better than a whilliwha. On the contrair', he looked baith sad an' anxious."

" Now, Donald Spey," returned Miss Maxwell,

"I am quite sure that your wisdom is once more at fault. My dear father believes just as much in your supernatural Brownie as I do; but we will not discuss this matter further, for I am quite sure, if we were to continue the debate from this to next Christmas eve, I should be utterly unable to shake your foolish faith. No, sir, not another word, but come away to the heugh—wood."

Meanwhile Mr. Maxwell, on whom Donald's communication had really produced a deep impression, entered the library, and after seating himself, took out a letter, which he read again and again, his face wearing a thoughtful and troubled look.

"It is strange," he said, still holding the paper before him, "wondrous strange, how this same letter found its way into my sleeping apartment. Donald saw a man in the garden last night—of that there can be little doubt; but supposing this stranger to have been the bearer of this brief and mysterious communication, how could it possibly come within my walls unless the messenger was in league with some of my own household? 'Kenard Maxwell's loyalty to the House of Stuart is well known.' Aye, but to whom? 'Why does he sleep when he should be awake?' If there are friends to the royal cause in this neighbourhood, why do they not seek me openly in the face of day? The cause is by no means a happy one, if men are only to be wooed and won to its support by secret and mystic appeals.

Well," he continued, in a more cheerful tone, "time will show if there are friends of the king near. They will no doubt make themselves known, and Kenard Maxwell's sword will leap from its scabbard to aid an enterprise which promises a reasonable or probable chance of success."

CHAPTER VII.

"God bless the king, the faith's defender,
Nor is there harm in blessing the Pretender ;
But who the Pretender is, and who the King,
God bless us all, that's quite another thing."
—*Byrom.*

OWARDS the close of this same day—
the eve of merry, blythesome, gleeful,
jocund, jolly Christmas—a slight shower
of snow began to fall. The frost, which
for more than a week had been intensely bitter, was
now, if possible, sharper, and more keenly piercing
than before. The trees and hedge-rows, though
despoiled and robbed of their natural foliage by the
bleak autumnal winds, were now, in Lear-like
mockery, fantastically arrayed in pure white winter
blossoms, which, although chastely beautiful and
seemingly enduring, would soon, alas! like many of
the vain hopes and day dreams of poor visionary
humanity, droop, decline, and fade away without
bearing fruit. Not only were the ponds and gently
murmuring brooks bound fast in the icy embrace

of the chill Frost-King, but the lovely Wear itself, from Claxheugh rock to its source, far away through the wild glens and deep vales of Weardale, had its thick glacial covering.

It is delightful on such a night, and at this glad season of the year, to sit by a large sea-coal fire, and to see all around the happy, laughing faces of those we love; to hear the wintry wind whistle shrill without; to draw aside the curtains, and peer into the cold, pale moonlight; to see earth, trees, and shrubs shrouded in white; and while looking thus to say, "Ha! ha! this is indeed seasonable weather. Christmas without frost and snow would not be like Christmas at all." But, alas! there are two sides to everything and every question. On this memorable night, the eve of the anniversary day of the world's redemption, there were two poor Wear keelmen journeying eastward by the side of Pensher Hill, and they were honestly of opinion that frosts and snows, even at Christmas time, had their disagreeable disadvantages. They were ankle deep in the prose of the matter, and had no eye for its beautiful poetry. Poor fellows! at this festive season, when money was especially necessary to procure enjoyment, the ice-bound river cruelly forbade them to ply their honest, lawful, and legitimate trade on its breast.

"A nice neet this, Joaney, for ti' gan hyem ower-land in," said one of them, whose baptismal appellation

was Anthony, clapping his hands on his shoulders
for the purpose of restoring circulation to his
thoroughly benumbed and frost-pinched fingers.
" Aw tell'd the fitter the keels wad be all reet; but
like all cliver fules, he knaws far better nor onny-
body else. Sendin' a man up ti steith iv a day
like this, wiv a chance ti parish like a thowl afore
he gets hyem agyen; an' all for nowt, or else aw
wadn't care! Eff he had what he disarves, he
wad spend his Christmas i' the kitty, or else i' the
pun-fawd. But niver mind, Joaney," he continued,
breaking into a well-known chorus, " ' Keep up your
heart, and be ov good cheer, Prosparity will attend
upon the sons of the Wear.' We'll hev a quairt
of het yall an' a pot o' rum in't, when we get tiv
Offerton; eh, awd man ? "

"My canny fellar, so we will," his companion
replied, assentingly.

The thought of their apparently favourite beverage, and the near pospect of imbibition, served to
impart fresh vigour to their wearied legs, and the
two men proceeded onward at a rapid pace.
Crossing two or three fields by a narrow pathway,
known as " the Keelmen's track," they soon entered
Offerton. Half way through the ancient village,
and on the left hand, as you walked eastward, was
a house of public entertainment, which at the time
of our story—more than a century ago—laid claim
to a respectable antiquity. This venerable hostelry

is said to have afforded by no means unpleasant
quarters to Oliver Cromwell, when old Dry-
powder-Providence was marching in the rear of
that moral young man, Charles the Second. Noll,
as we know, overtook him at Worcester, and
Charles immediately afterwards went botanising on
the borders of Staffordshire, and for a short time
made an especial study of oak leaves.

On entering the large room or kitchen appertaining to the inn, our storm - beaten pedes-
trians were delighted to behold a blazing coal
fire, surmounted by a Yule log of considerable
size.

Several farm labourers and villagers were seated
on the rough benches, and to most of them the
two keelmen were apparently well known. After
shaking the snow from their habiliments, and
warming themselves for a moment before the fire,
Joaney advanced to the table and rapped loudly
with his knuckles. The summons was answered by
a stout red-faced girl.

"Beer a hand, hinney," he said, "an' bring us a
quairt o' het yall wiv a pot o' rum in't; we're
varry near foundered wi' the cawd."

"Dee ye want a spouted pot an' a glass?" the
maiden demanded, in anything but a feminine
voice.

"No, hinney," interposed Joaney's friend, somewhat hastily; "no, hinney, niver mind a glass.

Just bring'd iv a blin' pot;"* and turning to his companion, Toney continued, in a conciliatory tone, "a blin' pot's allus the best, Joaney hinney, eff a man on'y drinks fair."

When the coveted pot was placed before them, they were not long in paying their devoirs to its contents; and having filled their pipes, they were soon at ease, Toney taking a prominent part in the general and homely conversation, and ultimately, in response to an almost unanimous call, he agreed to sing a song.

"Now, mee lads," he said, by way of preface, "this sang what aw'se gawn for ti sing is just as true as onnything that iver happened i' the woruld. It's about a keelman that was comin' down the river, an' he had ti put his cable ashore at Cox-green for ti get the blacksmith ti put a link in't. Now, when he cam' away frae the steith he forgat all about it. They called the keelman Johnny Hossey; Bill Ellot, the offputher, married his dowter. Ye knaw Bill Ellot, Joaney?"

"Knaw Bill Ellot!" echoed Joaney. "Div aw nutt?"

"Now, lads," said Toney, "this is the sang;" and he at once proceeded with a tune compounded of many airs, "The Vicar and Moses" and

---

* A *blin'* or blind pot was a round earthenware vessel, out of which each drank in turn. The desire expressed by Toney for "a blin' pot" is obvious.

"King John and the Abbot" being the most prominent :—

> "Johnny Hossey's keel-cable it wanted a link,
>   Th' hanker and shackel between ;
> So he put it ashore at awd Fortin the smith's,
>   Near the foot o' the wood at Coxgreen.
>
> He ses, 'When at Law Lam'ton aw get the keel load,
>   Aw'll tak't in as aw'se comin' down,
> So that aw'll hev me hanker quite riddy ti drop
>   When aw get back ti Sunderland town.'
>
> Johnny slacked frae the steith at the top o' the tide,
>   Efter drinkin' the yall reythor free,
> An' about the keel-cable, at Fortin the smith's,
>   Not a mossel o' thowt then had he.
>
> He gat down below, about three-quarter ebb,
>   Tiv the place where the keel had ti lay ;
> But when he lifted the hanker ti tossed owerboard,
>   He swore an' he sed, 'Lack-a-day !
>
> 'Here's a hawful consawn !   Was there iver a man
>   Fand hissel' iv a pickle like me ?
> Aw hevn't nee cable ti bring the keel up ;
>   Aw wonder whativer aw'll dee ?
>
> 'Aw've offens heerd sed, biv the priest iv our church,
>   That nee matter where troubles may be,
> Eff ye on'y hev' faith, and iv Providence trust,
>   It's a thousand to one ye'll get free.
>
> 'Now the hanker aw'll tak', an' just pitch'd owerboard,
>   An' aw'll lay the keel's heed ti the tide ;
> An' just for this once try this syem Providence,
>   Ti see if he'll mak her ti ride.'

Now th' hanker he toss't, and he stood full ov faith,
  To see her bring up, so they say ;
But she went 'thwart the bows ov a collier brig,
  An' her ruther was carried away.

His set frae the coals ti the gunnel rowl'd off,
  An' then tummell'd ower the side ;
An' reet down the river, an' slap out ti sea,
  It went floatin' away wi the tide.

Johnny danc'd o' the Shuts, an' he cuss'd an' he swore,
  An' then he began for ti blare—
' Now, fine Master Providence ! here's a nice trick,
  What ! trust ye ?   No, niver nee mair ! "

As the sound of Toney's somewhat unmusical voice was dying away between the large oak beams running transversely overhead, a traveller, booted and spur-clad, and wearing the cape-coat of the period, passed through the kitchen, preceded deferentially by the landlord.

"Wee's that?" asked Toney of one of the farm servants who happened to enter the apartment at the same time as the stranger.

"It's a gentleman a-horseback, axin' for Squire Max'all o' Balmston," was the reply.

"They dee say," said another, seated near the fire, "that Squire Max'all's neether mair nor less nor a Jackeybite."

"Confushion tiv all Jackeybites!" exclaimed Toney, taking a long pull at the pot. "Aw'se for uphaddin' King George an gowlden ginneys; we winnot hev our tides paid iv brass money, an' we winnot wear wooden shoes, like them frog-eatin' Frenchers ; eh, Joaney ? "

His companion looked sternly into the pot, temporarily relinquished by Toney, and after noting the contents with evident disgust, replied—

" Niver ! "

" Well, my lads," said another, " I'll tell you what it is ; Jacobite or no Jacobite, Squire Max'all's a real gentleman, a true hearted landlord, and a good friend to the poor, and all I've got to say is this : I only wish I was under him. Every man, woman, and child on his estate, from the highest to the lowest, will be as merry as crickets this blessèd night."

" Aw'se for King George an' the Protersen Church," interrupted Toney ; " an' aw tell ye this, chaps, eff the riverlution briks out, as they say it will, ye'll see such a ridgement o' keelmen as the world niver saw afore, an'll niver see agyen ; an' wee can stand afront o' them. Why, neebody ! Here's to King George an' the Proter——" Here Toney stretched forth his hand for the pot, but, alas ! too late ; his companion, anticipating the attack, was placing it to his own lips.

The traveller at this moment returned to the kitchen, and placing his right hand on Toney's shoulder, he said, ironically—

" I wish all the supporters of King George may be like yourself, my friend."

Toney's self love was immensely gratified at this
remark, and he replied—

"Thank ye, sir; aw'se the man—Tonny Lawther's
just the chap—he's strite up, an' strite down—there's
nee mistake about him, nutt a bit. Now," he continued, "ye seem to be a man o' the reet sort ; aw
like the luck o' ye, an' aw sure aw'll be varry proud
to drink yer hilth."

"So you shall, my friend," said the traveller, "in
anything you like."

"A pint o' rum purl a-piece for me an' Joaney.
He's mee frind, ye see, sir. We allus tie when
we gan up ti steith ; an' we allus come ower-
land togither, just like two brothers. Dinnot we,
Joaney ?'

Joaney glanced uneasily at the now empty pot,
mentally measured in his mind's eye the respective
proportions imbibed by Toney and himself, and
having apparently come to the conclusion that the
brotherhood in question was something of the Jacob
and Esau character, he simply nodded his head.
The traveller, evidently amused, ordered the purl,
and a glass of brandy for himself, and when the
liquids came to hand, he said to Toney—

"Now, then, you must drink a toast with me.
Are you ready ? "

Toney, with the pot in his hand, fully prepared
for business, gave an affirmative nod.

"Well, then," said the stranger, holding his glass

immediately above a water jug on the table, " I'll give you the King." *

" Hooray ! " exclaimed Toney, lifting the still steaming pot to his lips ; and after drinking the best half of its contents, he added, " Aw'll uphad King George agyen the divil an' the Pope."

The traveller here threw down on the table some pieces of money, saying—

" Here, my men, it is Christmas eve ; drink my health." He then proceeded to the door, and having put some further questions to the landlord respecting the road to Balmston, he mounted his horse, and galloped off in the direction of the river.

* NOTE.—This was a secret way of giving a Jacobite toast at this period. It meant " The King *over the water.*"

CHAPTER VIII.

" We'll play the games, the merry games,
　Blind man and hunt the shoe ;
And kiss the lassies one by one,
　Beneath the mistletoe.
For Christmas joys come once a-year—
　To honour them combine ;
It was my father's custom,
　And so it shall be mine."

—Old Song.

THE traveller held his way at a rapid pace until the southern bank of the Wear was reached, and he could easily discern, in the clear wan moonlight, that the stream was covered with ice of a sufficient thickness to enable him to cross to the north side in complete safety. The rise and fall of the tide, in its ceaseless ebb and flow, had caused the glacious surface of the river to crumble away for a short distance from either bank. This difficulty was apparently of no moment to the traveller, for his steed clearing easily the open space between, came safely down on the slippery mass, although

7

in the act the noble animal slid almost down on its haunches. The horseman soon gained the other side, and could see on the rising ground immediately before him Balmston House, with the lights glancing and flashing from its illumined windows, thus giving unmistakable proof that the blithesome festivities common to the season were not forgotten by Kenard Maxwell. As the traveller slowly ascended the somewhat rugged banks, in the direction of the mansion, a man emerged suddenly from the shadow of the wood, and approaching the horseman, he said, in distinct though cautiously subdued tones—

"This is a surprise indeed, Mr. James! I certainly did not expect you here to-night."

"Pray excuse me," returned the other; "you are mistaken. This, I presume, is the residence of Mr. Kenard Maxwell?"

Not another word was spoken, and the traveller discovered, to his utter astonishment, that the man had disappeared as abruptly as he came to view. In deep cogitation he rode up to the house, and having dismounted, he ascended the steps and knocked lustily with the handle of his riding whip. The loud summons was speedily answered by a servant, and the traveller was informed that Mr. Maxwell was at home; and consigning the horse to the temporary care of one of his fellows, the man ushered the visitor into a private apartment, and departed to announce to his master the arrival of another guest. Throwing himself carelessly into a cosy-looking chair, he had scarcely begun a leisurely survey of the room when his host entered.

"Good even, sir," said the stranger, rising from his seat. "I am indeed sorry to trouble you on what seems a highly festive occasion, and am really afraid I ought to have timed my visit so as to harmonise better with your leisure and convenience."

"Nay, sir," replied Maxwell, as they shook hands, "do not say so. We are bound, in the remembrance of the Christ-God, whose birth in the flesh we celebrate with such rejoicings, to extend our hospitality to all ; and whatever your business may be, pleasant or otherwise, I hasten to assure you that you never could be more welcome to my poor house than at this particular moment."

"I thank you, sir," said the stranger; and then in a whisper he asked, "Are we alone ?"

"Perfectly," was the reply.

"No one within earshot ?"

"No one, I am quite certain."

"Good ; we will then proceed with the business I have in hand. I have arrived in this country from France within the last three days."

"Ha !"

"And I bear with me letters of introduction to

Mr. Maxwell from old friends 'over the water,' and am earnestly requested, during my short visit to England, to learn, if possible, if that gentleman's loyalty and devotion to the House of Stuart still bloom as freshly in his memory, and are as deeply rooted in his heart, as in the days of his earlier manhood? Here is a letter from a very old friend of yours, the Laird of Ross."

Kenard took the written message, and after perusing it he said, "This is indeed the hand of my old friend; it is many years since we met. Your name, I see, sir, is—

"Pierre Chedville, Comte D'Aubray," interrupted the other, bowing.

"Well then, Monsieur le Comte, we can say nothing about the business at present. Will your other engagements permit your making a home at Balmston until the birth of the new year? After that we can freely discuss the matter of your errand."

"Well, yes," Chedville answered, "my business may indeed be kept cool for so short a time, and I shall be proud to remain for so many days the guest of a gentleman so highly respected by those to whom he is intimately known."

"Agreed, then; but how shall I introduce you to my friends? You do not, I presume, being as you are engaged in a business of a somewhat critical nature, journey on your real patronymic?"

"*Pardieu!* no; that would be wooing danger with

a vengeance! You must make me known by my English appellation—Peter Thornton."

"Very good, Monsieur," said Maxwell, ringing a small bell; "I am sure you will find yourself at home. John," he continued, addressing the servant who had answered the summons, "conduct this gentleman to the strangers' room, and see also that his horse is well put up and cared for. You will find a fire in the apartment, and I believe everything you may require ; and I shall await your return here."

Chedville was conducted to a large and well-furnished chamber. A bright, rosy fire was burning cheerfully on the hearth. Performing his ablutions with an unusual degree of haste, he took from the saddle-bags brought to him by his attendant a few articles essential to the improvement of his appearance, and in a very short time was enabled to rejoin Mr. Maxwell.

The two gentlemen proceeded together to the large hall, where the mirth and fun were evidently "growing fast and furious." On entering this particular section of the Balmston mansion, our Gallic friend was agreeably surprised to behold so many truly beautiful faces, especially in a locality which he had hitherto pictured to himself as secluded, if not entirely isolated. He saw before him a goodly bevy of young ladies, the daughters of country gentlemen or substantial yeomen. There they were, in all the full bloom of high-class rustic beauteousness.

The keen eye of Chedville took in at a single
glance the male portion of the assemblage. He saw
they were mostly good-looking, robust young men,
attired as became the fashion of the day, but with
a clownish or countrified awkwardness ever attendant
on their various movements. Unlike himself, and
like poor Corin the Shepherd, they had " never been
to Court," and consequently " never saw good
manners."   When the host introduced his guest as
" his friend Mr. Thornton," bless you ! there was quite
a stir.   The gentlemen all bowed in a stiff, ungainly
style ; but the ladies—ah ! they curtseyed gracefully
down to their shoe-ties, and a whispered conversation
went round amongst them.

"Oh ! Jane, dear," said one, " did you ever see such
a handsome man out of a picture ? "

"Never, Mabel," was the reply. " What a carriage—
what a stately presence and commanding appearance !
Look you, he moves as though he were a prince. If
Flora Maxwell does not lose her little heart to him
to-night, faith I know who will.   Heigho !"

"How you talk, child ; he is perhaps a married man
already."

"Nonsense, Mabel ; a girl of your experience
ought to know better.   He doesn't look the tiniest
little bit like one."

This was a fairly general sample of the feminine
talk on the introduction of Mr. Maxwell's late and
unexpected visitor ; and those remarks would have

probably journeyed *sub rosa* round the room for some time longer had not Chedville unconsciously wandered underneath a bunch of mistletoe.   In a moment, to his utter astonishment, but certainly not to his displeasure, he felt, as it were, a vast multitude of plump, dimpled arms about his neck, and was rapturously saluted, almost simultaneously, on the cheeks, brow, ears, and mouth, by rich, rosy, velvety lips.   His surprise suffered no diminution when Mr. Maxwell, who was almost convulsed with laughter, pointed to the mistletoe overhead, and informed his guest that any gentleman bold and daring enough to venture beneath its shade rendered himself liable to be kissed by any lady present having an inclination to exercise a valid and time-honoured prerogative.

Chedville having submitted very quietly to this by no means distasteful penance, took up another position, and pointing to a similar emblem of Druidism, he said, smilingly—

" I assure you, ladies, that nothing but the fear of being considered over presumptuous prevents me taking my stand yonder, and indulging once more in a grand foretaste of Mahomet's Paradise."

Maxwell now favoured his visitor with a special introduction to his daughter ; and, after a few commonplace remarks, they stood up together in a country-dance.   The orchestra, limited to a. violin and flute, · struck up the lively old air of " Sir Roger," and off they went.

Dancing in those days was, physically considered, more an exercise than in our more degenerate times. To be sure, the prim, stately minuet was walked through in the more aristocratic circles, but at Balmston it was certainly unpractised, if not altogether unknown. After the dance was concluded, Chedville conducted his partner to a seat, and they were soon deeply engaged in an obviously interesting conversation. From the moment of their introduction, our French friend had continued to look on Miss Maxwell with undisguised admiration. Never, in his opinion, had he met with a lady so lovely and enchanting; and Pierre Chedville, Comte D'Aubray, the accomplished courtier—he, in faith, who had basked whilom in ladies' smiles, and had been often fanned by the perfumed breath of their gentle sighs—began to acknowledge himself more than half vanquished by the charming daughter of Kenard Maxwell.

"O ! 'tis love, 'tis love, that makes the world go round."

Dancing at length gave place to the merry, laughing games of "Blind Man's Buff" and "Hunt the Slipper ; " and last of all, to wind up the jovial amusements of the night, came the "Cushion Dance," prescribed by venerable custom for the termination of those festive gatherings. Degree was forgotten ; all class distinction and social rank were for a time put completely aside ; and the servants, hinds, and t tars came rushing *péle méle* from the kitchen and larder, where they had been hitherto regaling themselves to their hearts' content. Scramblingly they entered the hall, to participate, according to ancient custom and universal rule, in this last exciting dance.

At last, to the regret of everybody, the night's enjoyments were ended, and the guests, Chedville excepted, left for their several homes, some in conveyances remarkable mostly for dissimilitude. There were one or two *bona fide* carriages, but, as a rule, the sons and daughters of the country gentry had been conveyed to Balmston in vehicles resembling very closely our modern tax-carts. The scions or shoots of the more substantial yeomanry branches departed in old-fashioned gigs, whilst those in still humbler circumstances went joltingly away in the ordinary hay-carts. But what a party there, was at the door of Balmston House! All the young ladies saluted Flora Maxwell. Then again, those going east kissed those going west, and those going north kissed those going south, and *vice versa*. Then of course there would necessarily come a second edition of kissing when the young ladies arrived at their respective homes, and bade adieu to their swains; but this we are content to leave to the imagination of the reader.

Next morning Chedville rose early, considering it was nearly three o'clock when he retired to rest, and, although fairly tired with his journey and the night's amusements, he nevertheless for some con-

siderable time failed to woo the gentle sleep
"that knits up the ravell'd sleeve of care;" and
when slumber did at last condescend to sit on his
weary eyelids, Flora Maxwell was ever present in
his dreams. On entering the breakfast room he
was vastly surprised to see from the window a
number of men dressed in the most fantastic
manner, and bedecked with ribbons of the most
flaunting and gaudy colours. They were performing
a sort of mystic dance in front of the house, and
were all armed with short swords, each man grasping the point of the weapon of his *vis-a-vis* with
one hand while holding the hilt of his own rapier
with the other, and in this manner they danced
round and round in frantic glee.

Chedville was engaged debating with himself
the question as to who and what they were, when
Flora entered the apartment.

"Ah, good morning, Miss Maxwell," he said,
extending his hand, "I am so glad you have come,
as you will doubtless be able to enlighten me in
my poor ignorance. Pray, how do you name this
singular group I see from the window?"

"Oh! they are pitmen, or miners," the lady
replied, laughing good humouredly at Chedville's
apparent perplexity; "we call them guisers, or
sword-dancers. It is a customary thing for them
to go round in this manner at this particular
season of the year. See, their dance is now coming

to a finish, and they will shortly make a strong appeal to your benevolence."

As Miss Maxwell had predicted, the terpsichorean movements—which, by the way, were certainly not of the light fantastic character—ceased, and one tall fellow, with something in his hand resembling a tin dish, approached the window, and looking up to Chedville, while a loutish, good-humoured grin held temporary possession of his features, he shouted :—

"How there, man! thraw somethin' down for mee an' mee marrows! It's Chrisamis time, hinney."

Though an excellent English scholar, our Gallic friend was only enabled to comprehend the appeal for pecuniary remuneration by the ludicrous pantomimic action lent to the words, and taking from his pocket a coin, he threw it to the man. The miner caught the piece of money cleverly in the tin dish, and throwing it far into the air, captured it in the same manner in its descent. The sum evidently far exceeded the collector's modest anticipation, for he gleefully exhibited the coin to his friends, and they, with an unearthly shout, began another dance, apparently determined to give Chedville full value for his money.

Mr. Maxwell now entered, and after exchanging greetings, the trio were speedily seated at breakfast, the subject of conversation during the matin-meal being English customs at Christmas-tide.

CHAPTER IX.

"I,
Beyond all limit of what else i' the world,
Do love, prize, honour you."

—Tempest.

CHRISTMAS was undoubtedly a happy, merry era in "ye good olden time," and there is good reason to believe that its advent was invariably hailed by the humble toiler with unmixed pleasure and delight. Scott says :—

"'Twas Christmas broached the mightiest ale,
'Twas Christmas told the merriest tale ;
A Christmas gambol oft could cheer
The poor man's heart through half the year."

Sometimes we seem to have a sort of half regret that we did not live our individually allotted span at this particular period. But again, by exercising a little common sense, and going carefully back on our country's history, we have to confess to ourselves, perhaps a little reluctantly, that those "good old days" had their unpleasant drawbacks after all. The aspect of England in the fifteenth, sixteenth, and seventeenth centuries was not of the brightest. The wars of the Roses, Red and White, told heavily on the humbler classes of Britain. The change of religion and alternate triumph of creeds, with their attendant confiscations, persecutions, and strifes, were not calculated to make things pleasant. Then towards the middle of the seven- teenth century came the battle of battles and the strife of strifes—the great war between Freedom and Kingly Prerogative; then started into life Pym, Hampden, Eliot, and others—men characterised by Bishop Warburton as "a set of the greatest geniuses for government that the world ever saw embarked together in a common cause." To be sure, in 1745 things were looking much better; the Stuart curse was removed, and the very last relics of the feudal system appeared to have been swept away. The former, however, was yet destined to flicker faintly once more, before its light became thoroughly extinguished.

Chedville remained the guest of Kenard Maxwell until the birth of the New Year. During the interval between Christmas and New Year's day, D'Aubray spent the most of his time in the company of his host's charming daughter. Of course, being thus thrown, as it were, perforce into the society of each other, it is not a subject for wonder to find that a mutual regard, something very nearly akin to love, was quietly and almost imperceptibly engendered in the hearts of both. That Chedville was stricken was clearly manifested by his demeanour when in the presence of Miss Maxwell; but Flora, judging by outward semblance, seemed pretty well "heart-whole." She evidently enjoyed the company of the Comte, and being very young and quite inexperienced in the art of love, might have caught the ever-prevalent epidemic, and knowing none of the symptoms, might be suffering quite unconsciously from the malady.

On the last day of December Balmston House was visited by a few intimate friends of the proprietor, residing in the immediate neighbourhood; the party numbering something like a dozen, the sexes being equally represented. After the somewhat early dinner, according to Balmston custom, a proposal (emanating from some of the young people) for a walk along the river's bank secured the harmonious approval of the puerile portion of the company; and the young ladies, all befurred, and the young gentlemen, enveloped in their long cape-coats, went merrily away over the crisp snow. On their left hand lay the Wear, congealed to solemn silence by the keen, biting power of the brumal atmosphere.

Chedville, who had given his arm to Flora Maxwell, began at the outset (for reasons which

will doubtless explain themselves) to govern and
regulate the steps of himself and his fair companion in such a manner as to leave them in a
short time very much in the rear of the pedestrian
group. A few commonplace remarks were succeeded
by a lengthened silence; when Chedville said, in a
voice not altogether unmixed with emotion—

"I am sorry I shall be compelled to leave you
to-morrow, Miss Maxwell."

"Do you really go so soon, Mr. Thornton?" Flora
asked, in slightly tremulous tones, raising her dark
eyes timidly to his face.

"Yes," he replied, "I do most sincerely regret to
say that business of considerable importance imper-
atively prescribes the limit of my most agreeable
sojourn at Balmston House; and believe me when
I declare that the few truly happy days I have
spent here will be to me a sweetly cherished memory
for the rest of my life."

Flora was silent, and after a short pause Chedville
again spoke—

"You will, perhaps, think me somewhat premature
—nay, more, I am really afraid that I shall appear
to Miss Maxwell presumptuous and over-bold—in
saying what I am now about to utter; but in my
own justification I must plead the urgent necessity
for my sudden departure. Had circumstances kindly
permitted me to remain here for a longer period,
I might, nay, I would have kept my secret for

some little time still closely locked in my own breast. Miss Maxwell, I have to confess that since I entered your presence, just one short week ago, you have lived in my thoughts. From the dawning of my manhood up to that ever-memorable Christmas eve I had gone on my way unscathed ; but when we met, you kindled in my heart the pure flame of love, and hour by hour, and day by day that feeling, that passion—call it what you will—has grown in ardour and intensity, has, in fact, become a part of my existence, and as the time of my departure drew nigh, I found it was utterly impossible for me to leave Balmston without making this confession."

Not a single word from Flora. They were now standing together, and her tiny foot was tapping lightly on the snow; yet its fall, though ever so light, could be distinctly heard by Chedville in the solemn silence around them.

"You know me, Miss Maxwell," he continued, "merely as the guest of your father; but I may tell you that he is fully acquainted with my condition and true standing in the world. He knows that in fortune and lineage I am at least equal with himself. I mention this, Miss Maxwell, and plead my great love to justify myself, and to merit your forgiveness for the bold question I am about to ask —a question which, under circumstances of a less pressing character, might be deemed an impertinence."

Tap, tap, tap on the snow went the little fur-topped boot, just as lightly as heretofore, but a little, just a little, more unsteady in its fall.

"Oh, say, Miss Maxwell," pleaded Chedville, pressing her hand, "may I—may I hope?"

"Mr. Thornton," she replied, after a lengthened pause, looking up into his face, and speaking soft and low, "we have known each other but a few days, and—and—I pray you, pardon this agitation, which under the circumstances is but natural and maidenly. I have never to this moment even dreamt of marriage ; my days have been so happily spent with my dear father that I have never once looked into the world beyond. Believe me, I have but a very indistinct and imperfect idea of that love which, in order to ensure true happiness, should of necessity precede such an union. I know from the whisperings of my own heart that you are frank and sincere with me, and I will endeavour to repay you with the like frankness and sincerity. During your short sojourn at Balmston, I may confess that you have won my regard and esteem ; but before a maiden gives her love, wisdom and prudence would alike suggest a better knowledge of, and a more enlarged acquaintance with, the object on whom that affection is to be bestowed than I can possibly have of Mr. Thornton. But if I should become better acquainted with Mr. Thornton, and if Mr. Thornton—after gaining a full knowledge of

8

the many faults and various imperfections of Flora Maxwell—should still be of the same mind, why then, perhaps—perhaps—— "

" Heaven bless you for these words!" exclaimed Chedville, rapturously, as he kissed her half-smiling lips. " I could ask for nothing beyond this. I would not for the wide world ask you for a binding pledge until your dear father's full approval has been secured."

They now walked on slowly, and had not proceeded far when they were met by the rest of the party returning homewards.

The happiness of Chedville had evidently reached an indubious state of completion. His own individual cup of life's bliss seemed full · almost to overflowing.

At the tea table he sat next to Miss Maxwell, and when card-playing was introduced, Flora, in the cutting, fell to him as a partner; and this was considered by D'Aubray an excellent omen.

When it drew on towards midnight, the company, as usual in such cases, became musical. One jolly old squire, whose nasal organ had apparently arrived at the most perfect and complete condition of rubification, volunteered a hunting song, and the rough chorus was taken up by the male visitors, until the rafters rang again and again with " Tantivy !" " Yoicks !" and " Tally ho !"

Chedville sang a love song, and accompanied

himself on the spinet, or harpsicon. His rich voice took the company by surprise, and he was most deservedly applauded. The words of the ballad were simple and homely, and, coupled with the pleasingly flowing melody, afforded ample scope for an expression of deep emotion and true sentiment; and during the song he glanced furtively at short intervals into the sweet, though now somewhat pensive face of Flora.

> " See, proudly at our vessel's peak,
>   In wavy folds, the ensign fly ;
> The signal gun will shortly wake
>   The slumb'ring echoes where they lie.
> That sound will bid us part, my love ;
>   From home I go, and all that's dear ;
> But when o'er Ocean's paths I rove,
>   Then in thy heart's thoughts keep me near !
>
> " When, in the east, long streaks of grey
>   Are seen athwart the sun's bright face ;
> When howls the wind, and, crown'd with spray,
>   The wild waves hold themselves in chase ;
> When, at the solemn midnight hour,
>   The gath'ring storm awakes thy fear,
> In dismal wail, or madd'ning roar--
>   Then in thy heart's thoughts keep me near !
>
> " In the gay world of fashion's throng,
>   In rooms illum'd with golden light,
> Where music's strain, and beauty's song,
>   Wing fast the moments of the night ;

When in the mazy dance they move,
    If one should at thy side appear,
To hold thy hand, and whisper love—
    Then in thy heart's thoughts keep me near ! "

A transient mournfulness took possession of the company when Miss Maxwell sang, to a sweet plaintive tune, an ode to the departed year. Sad and sorrowful was the air, and as Flora's fingers swept the chords in the brief prelude, a sweet, silent, and painless sorrow crept slowly and imperceptibly into the hearts of the guests assembled at Balmston.

" Why look ye all so blythe and gay,
    So full of jocund glee ?
Why troll the song and roundelay
    In joyous ecstasy ?
Oh, can ye see the old year die,
    And drop no pitying tear,
But drown with mirth his dying sigh,
    Nor cry, ' Farewell, old year ?'
Say one farewell—yes, one farewell—
    To those we loved so dear,
Who smiled in health in thy brief time,
    Yet died ere thee, old year !

" Have ye not wept for kindred dear,
    Laid in the silent tomb,
Who welcomed in the dying year
    With music to their home ?
Yet still ye chant the merry lay,
    And welcome in the new,

Nor pause to think, ere its decay,
  Some friend may weep for you !
Say one farewell—yes, one farewell—
  To those we loved so dear,
To those who smiled in thy brief time,
  And died with thee, old year ! "

Did they remember ? Alas ! alas ! too well. Memory was busy bringing distinctly before the mind's eye the death faces of the dear departed ones—faces that were radiant with smiles, cheeks that glowed with the ruddy hue of health at their last New Year's gathering. Where were they now ? Some of them were lying in the peaceful sleep " that knows no waking," in yonder cold churchyard, under the snow. Ah me !

CHAPTER X.

" I now beseech you
To grant one boon, that I shall ask of you."
—*Two Gentlemen of Verona.*

CHEDVILLE greeted the early dawn, as it threw its first streaks of cold, misty grey over the high Wearland at Offerton Heugh, with a hearty "Bah!" because it heralded his departure from Balmston House, where he had passed some happy days, and within the walls of which he would leave his dearest treasure in life. Still, he was not the man to be led by feelings and impulses of love, however deep and however strong they might be, to·neglect or delay the performance of what he considered a duty; and springing lightly from his couch, he made a hasty toilet, and devoted some little time to the necessary preparations for his journey.

After a quiet breakfast for three—Maxwell, Flora, and Chedville—the two gentlemen adjourned to the library, and when they were both seated, Kenard began the conversation.

"Now, Monsieur D'Aubray," he said, "our festivities are over, and we can now settle quietly down to business. You have fully redeemed your promise to me, and I feel quite sure that your visit has been a source of pleasure to us both. Now you desire to know how Kenard Maxwell will comport himself should the King make a strong effort to get 'his own again.' If the rising is worthy the illustrious cause for which it is undertaken, you will find me there ; but mark me, Monsieur le Comte, and understand me clearly : I will not bind myself to render the slightest aid or assistance to some half-dozen loyal, hot-headed gentlemen in a mad enterprise, which must of necessity fail and come to nothing save confiscation and dishonourable death. If, on the contrary, the plot is fully organised, and there are moderately fair and reasonable grounds to hope for success, I know my duty to the House of Stuart, and will be found at the fitting time foremost in the ranks of those who now avow themselves the friends of Prince Charles."

"It is not—nor was it ever—in my nature to be too hopeful," answered Chedville ; "but I really do think we have good anticipatory grounds for a happy issue. The chiefs of many Highland clans are pledged to the cause, and they are expected to bring at least five thousand men into the field. His Majesty of France furnishes a limited number of men, and an unlimited supply of arms and ammunition; and besides, we possess the most reliable assurance of aid from the heads of many of the best and oldest families in England and Scotland. How we stand in the south and west of Ireland I need hardly tell you. Under the present circumstances I cannot see the slightest necessity for you to commit yourself in any way until we shall have entered Edinburgh. Lochiel, I hear, has undertaken to place the Prince in full possession of Stirling within a week of his landing on Scottish ground."

"It would be next to impossible for me to join the Prince in the Highlands with advantage to his cause. At Edinburgh, or perhaps Perth, I would be able to take up arms, with many other loyal friends residing in the Lothians, to whom I am well known, and over whom, I may say, I hold some influence. Believe me, I am glad to hear so hopeful an account of the fortunes of our exiled monarch."

"Then I may inform our friends 'over the water' that they may safely count on Mr. Maxwell's aid?"

"Yes, always under the conditions already stated. —But stay; I had forgot that there may be—nay, there surely are—other friends to the royal cause in my immediate neighbourhood. Read this; I found it in my sleeping apartment a week ago."

Chedville took the letter and perused its contents thoughtfully.

"It is strange," he said, "that a communication of this nature should have been made in a manner so mysterious. If those same parties are really friends to our cause, I should have thought they would have adopted a more straightforward and honourable course for the purpose of sounding your opinions."

"Those were indeed my own sentiments," Maxwell answered. "I thought it passing strange ; but I suppose it would be a waste of time to consider the matter further at present ; and now, having disposed of our business, I presume we had better go back to the breakfast room."

"Why, no," said Chedville, a bashful smile taking possession of his features. "I am sorry to detain you a little longer, but I have another matter of equal importance, as far as I am concerned. You already know my name and title, as my despatches clearly establish my identity ; but, in addition, I beg to inform you that I possess one of the largest estates in France." Mr. Maxwell's looks expressed surprise. "You are evidently astonished," continued Chedville, "at hearing me thus unbosom myself ; but I hasten to assure you that I consider it quite pertinent to the business in hand. I wish sir, to convince you, in the first place, that the position I hold in the world is at least equal to your own; and, in the second place, I have to confess that I have been most deeply impressed with the beauty and amiability of Miss Maxwell, and my present earnest desire is that you will—as you can easily do through your friends at the court of King James—institute an inquiry of the most searching character into my financial and moral standing. And when you have found, as you will do, that my honour is, and has ever been, untarnished; that I boast an ancestry of which any man might be proud; then I shall, with better confidence, ask Mr. Maxwell to permit me to pay my addresses to his fair daughter."

"This communication, Monsieur D'Aubray," said Kenard, after a slight pause, " does indeed take me by surprise, especially when I call to mind the fact that you have only been a short week under my roof."

" Long enough to know and esteem Miss Maxwell," interrupted Chedville.

" Perhaps so, Monsieur. I must confess I was not so long in the company of her dear mother—Heaven rest her!—before I was deeply in love with her; but I trust, nay, I firmly believe, that Monsieur le Comte has not for one single moment forgotten that he was the guest of Kenard Maxwell, and that he has been too honourable to exact a promise from my child."

" In that, sir, you do me but simple justice," said Chedville, hastily; and then, in a more composed tone, proceeded—" I am not a boy, Mr. Maxwell, to be led away captive by a momentary and slightly rooted fancy. I have spent my life, or rather the greater part of it, in courts and camps ; I have seen and conversed with some of the most fascinating and dazzling beauties in the courts of France and Spain, but their charms were lost upon me, for there was always a want of heart. In your daughter, Mr. Maxwell, I soon discovered that which a man seeking a life alliance should prize most—pure simplicity and truth, and true natural pride, without one touch of vanity. These are bright and sparkling gems in the crown of womankind, and meet and fitting companions for the rare and exquisite beauty possessed by Miss Maxwell. Feeling that my life's happiness was at stake, I gained from your fair daughter the knowledge that up to the present she was heart-free, and that no prior attachment existed. Had it been otherwise, no subsequent steps were necessary, and I should have left Balmston with a heavy heart. I have sought from Miss Maxwell nothing more than this : when I have succeeded in proving to your satisfaction my position in society, and in obtaining your full and free consent, she will then permit me to endeavour to make myself worthy of her love. I considered I was justified in ascertaining the sentiments of your daughter thus far, and I trust for my sake you will make the necessary inquiries at your earliest convenience. Miss Maxwell's answer, I may say, was worthy of herself : she knew but little of me, but admitted I was not totally indifferent to her; but she would leave all to time and her dear father's better wisdom."

"Monsieur D'Aubray," said Maxwell, earnestly, "understand me rightly. I do not for one moment question your honour; but in common justice to you, my daughter, and myself, I will make those inquiries, and if—as no doubt they will be—the answers are satisfactory, you shall have my full permission to pay your addresses to Flora. But mark this, Monsieur, I will not add even a feather's weight to the balance of her inclination: she shall be as free as air in her choice. And now, having disposed of this matter, as far as it can be disposed of at present, let us go back to the breakfast-room, where no doubt the poor child is sitting deep in conjectural meditation, putting down the whole of this long interview to her own account."

As they were about to leave the library, one of the servants announced "Mr. Marley;" and there entered to them a thin, spare man, apparently about forty-five years of age. His face was rather a crafty than an open one; every lineament seemed to say—"This is the shop for 'cuteness; pray mark the subdolus expression." His quick, ferret-like eyes were ever on the move; he had a straggling, reddish-brown whisker, which, like the sexton's beard in the "Taming of the Shrew,"

> " Grew thin and hungerly,
> And seemed to ask sops"

to promote its growth. He was partially bald, the small quantity of hair remaining on his head being of a still more fiery hue.

"Ah, good morning, gentlemen," said the visitor. "I really hope I don't interrupt you;" and here his eyes shifted quickly from Maxwell to Chedville, as though he would like to read their thoughts.

"O dear, not at all," Kenard answered. "Allow me, Mr. Thornton; this is Mr. Marley, land steward of Balmston, who, I suppose, has some business of importance with me this morning. Pray rejoin Miss Maxwell, and I will be with you shortly."

Chedville left the library, and as he proceeded through the passages leading to the breakfast room he muttered to himself—

"Marley, Marley! I am quite sure I never heard the name, and I am equally sure I never saw the face before; but the voice—I can swear to the voice; but for the life of me I cannot make out when and where I have heard it."

Chedville found Flora gazing with pensive face on the snow-clad hills of Pensher and Grimestone. The conversation in the library, so far as it related to the lady, was faithfully reproduced by the gentleman, embellished, as a matter of course, by sundry additional interlocutory observations, all bearing on the same delicious theme.

So thoroughly were the lovers engrossed in their agreeable conversation that they learnt from Mr.

Maxwell with surprise that Chedville's good steed had been standing ready saddled for more than a quarter of an hour.

Chedville proceeded at once to the entrance hall, accompanied by Mr. Maxwell and his daughter, and on reaching the steps leading down the lawn they heard Donald "high in oath," and saw him shaking his fist, apparently in ungovernable rage, at an old woman, gaunt and spare, with wild and haggard features. Her tattered garments, by their variegated character, gave to her a picturesque appearance of a kind that really possessed a charm in its very repulsiveness. Her linsey-woolsey petticoat was topped with a short ragged cloak of dunnest red; from beneath a shapeless hat of straw crept black straggling locks, lit here and there with thin streaks of grey, twisting themselves like writhing snakes about her wrinkled face; her withered right hand grasped a long forked stick, and she stood, a weird figure indeed, out there on the snow.

"Did it not come true, Donald?" she cried, in a shrill voice.

"Did it no come true, ye po-heeded auld deevil?" shouted Donald. "Aye, it did come true! it cam ower true! The verra day ye spaed my fortin', an' tell't me that a deeth lay near, was na' my ain sister's bairn drowned i' the Forth?—nae doubt dragged out o' the bonnie fisher-boat by your ain deviltries! Oh! gin I had ye on the ither side o' the Tweed—gin it were just your ain length, and that is na' muckle—I wad hae ye roasted for an auld witch ! "

Taking a hearty farewell of Kenard, Chedville, accompanied by Miss Maxwell, descended to the lawn, and at once attracted the attention of the old crone, who, ignoring the presence of the wrathful Donald, hobbled towards them, saying, as she approached—" Let awd Elspeth spae your fortin', my brave young gentleman."

D'Aubray looked laughingly at Flora, and gave the old woman a piece of silver, which she carefully consigned to an old leather purse, and then taking his hand, she bent her red, bleared eyes earnestly upon it.

" Ha, ha ! " she exclaimed, chuckling, " ye dinnot want for wealth, an' ye dinnot want for titles, no, no. Eh, but ye'll hev' a hard trial, and a big danger to gan' through ; but ye'll win through it all, an what's mair, ye'll prosper in what's nearest your heart at this moment ; the lines winnot lee, and ye'll aye crop the bonnie, bonnie flower o' Balmston. But it's not here ye'll mak her your bride ; no, it's far away, far away across the sea, among other folk that speak iv another tongue."

To say that Chedville was merely surprised would hardly convey the truth. He stood speechless, wrapt in astonishment.

Flora, however, knowing as she did her companion

only as plain Mr. Thornton, told the old woman blushingly, and with a slight laugh, that " she was all wrong."

" All wrang, my young lady !" Elspeth echoed, " all wrang ! No, no, the lines winnot lee—the lines winnot lee. Cross awd Elspeth's hand wi' a piece o' silver, an' let her spae your awn fortin', my bonnie miss."

" Come," said Chedville, giving the old woman money, " do permit her to try her skill in palmistry on you, Miss Maxwell."

Flora, after some hesitation, yielded her hand to the old spae-wife, and looking upon it even more keenly than she had previously gazed on that of D'Aubray, she said, after a long pause—

" Aye, aye, my pretty lady, you've never found out yet that the world is not all sunshine ; but ye'll ken that there's clouds and storms in life's sky before the year's out. Ye'll hev' a big, choking sorrow that'll go nigh to break your heart— dangers and perils, mair for others than for you, near an' dear though they'll be. But they'll pass away—they'll pass away ; and then there's a bright, calm future, peaceful and happy, right on to——No, no !" she screamed wildly, bowing her aged head closer down to the extended hand of Flora, and fastening her rheumy eyes earnestly on the open palm. " No, the lines winnot lee. Aye, it's there !" she muttered, abstractedly, "aye, it's plain to the eye ; but come it must. So young, so fair, to die so soon!" Flora, seemingly afraid, tried to withdraw her hand.

"Whisht, bairn, whisht!" the old woman continued, "it's not you the lines speak of. No, it's one just as young, aye, and fairer to the eye, than the dainty flower of Balmston. Fate is fixed, and ye mun e'en dree your weird, an' wade through her poor heart's best blood to your awn happiness. So young, so fair!—so young, so fair!"

Muttering thus, the old crone hobbled away across the snow-covered lawn, and disappeared in the forest pathway.

"Well," Chedville asked, after the departure of Elspeth, "what think you of your fortune, Miss Maxwell?"

"I hardly know what to think, Mr. Thornton," she replied. "I have never been at all inclined to give credence to fortune-telling; but old Elspeth was so earnest that I still feel half afraid. Do you think the future can really be foreshadowed this way?"

"Till this moment," D'Aubray answered, seriously, "I would have laughed at the matter, and looked upon it as an utter absurdity; but I certainly believe in the fortune-telling powers of Elspeth, for did she not tell me I 'would crop the bonnie flower of Balmston,' and I must believe that, since I so devoutly wish it to be so."

"Yes," said Flora, blushing deeply; "but do you

9

not think she might have ventured on that prediction simply because she saw us together ? "

" You heard her say I had no lack of wealth or
titles ? "

" Yes ; there she was wrong."

" Nay, there she was quite right. Now, moderate
wealth she might have guessed at, but there was
certainly nothing in my personal appearance to
suggest titles, and there she spoke truly."

Flora glanced at him in evident surprise.

" Then your real name is not Thornton ? " she said.

" It is not, Miss Maxwell," he answered ; " but
my true name was known to your father when I
came to Balmston, and in good time he will disclose
it to you. At present," he continued, laughingly, " it
is a secret, and I am somewhat of a mystery.
Farewell for the present. Believe me, we shall soon
meet again, when I trust we shall be still better
satisfied with each other. For my own part, I can
find neither faults nor imperfections in Miss Maxwell ; if they do exist, they are so effectually concealed by her many virtues that I am unable to
discover them. Farewell, and Heaven bless you ! "

He vaulted lightly to the saddle and rode away,
turning again and again to wave adieu to Flora,
who continued standing on the lawn until horse
and rider had crossed the river and disappeared
from sight.

CHAPTER XI.

"Our army is dispers'd already,
Like youthful steers unyoked they take their course ;
East, west, north, south, or like a school broke up,
Each hurries towards his home."
—*Henry IV., second part.*

THERE is now a wide and absolutely necessary gap in our story.

The Great Magician of the North, Sir Walter Scott, has already gone carefully, step by step, along the road we are about to travel, and the marchings and countermarchings of Charles Edward and his rebel army have been so graphically described in the pages of *Waverley* as to render recapitulation here perfectly unnecessary. This being so, we shall be content to briefly chronicle only such events in this truly disastrous campaign as apply to those individuals whose varied fortunes it is our duty to register.

On the 20th day of June, in the year 1745, a small party embarked at St. Nazaire, an insignificant Biscay port at the mouth of the Loire. Their vessel was an old partially used-up frigate, mounting sixteen guns, and named the *Doutelle.* The design of this brave little band was to raise a seditious revolt of sufficient magnitude to bring about a dynastical change in Great Britain. The attempt, at first sight, did indeed seem a foolish one—almost as mad as Louis Bonaparte's descent on Boulogne with his tame eagle. But again, Prince Charles Edward, the leader of this bold emprise, had with him in the *Doutelle* about five thousand pounds in money, and a large quantity of stores, while the *Elizabeth,* another old war vessel, was to join him at Belleisle, with two thousand muskets, six hundred French broadswords, and a quantity of ammunition; and, in addition, the young Chevalier built his hope of ultimate success on the attachment of a great portion of the British people to the House of Stuart. Charles had not proceeded far on his voyage when the old *Elizabeth* was unfortunately engaged by an English cruiser, and after being seriously battered and bemauled, she succeeded in getting back to Belleisle, where she may possibly remain to this day. The loss of so much war material was a very serious matter for the daring young Prince; nevertheless, he, together with his brave little band, kept on their course, and after a short time reached that part of the Hebrides known as the Long Island, from the fact that it appears at a certain distance to form a single continent, although it really comprises Lewis, Uist, Barra, and many other distinct islands.

The small party who had left the waters of Biscay to undertake a task so fraught with danger, disembarked from the *Doutelle* on the 19th day of July, in Lochnanuagh, a small arm of the sea dividing Arisaig and Moidart.

On the twenty-fifth all the stores were landed, and the frigate sailed away; and Charles Edward, the Marquis of Tullibardine, the Rev. M. Kelly, Thomas Sheridan, Francis Strickland, Æneas McDonald, the Paris banker, and the Comte D'Aubray were left at Borodale to mature their plans for the conquest of an empire.

Chedville was present when old Tullibardine unfurled to the wild breezes of Glenfinnen the large red silk banner with its centre of white, the standard of Charles Edward : carried forward for nearly two hundred miles on English soil, and back again, to be torn, rent, and blood-stained on the fatal field of Drumossie.

Kenard Maxwell joined the Prince at Edinburgh, and took part in the battle, if it may be so called, of Preston and Gladsmuir, where the army of Sir John Cope was so disgracefully routed.

Maxwell and Chedville, always attended by the faithful Donald, shared the fortunes of Charles Edward until the 4th of December, when the

Chevalier at the head of 7000 men entered Derby.
On the following day—the fifth—when the northward retreat was discussed, they strongly opposed
it; and the French Count even went so far as to
tell the Prince to his face, that on the very first
retrograde movement of the army his sword would
be returned to its scabbard, to be drawn no
more in the cause.

The young Chevalier, although wishful himself to
press on towards the capital, was unfortunately too
much under the influence of the Highland chiefs, and
they were by no means disposed to go beyond Derby.
They clamoured loudly for a retreat to the North for
winter quarters, and where, in the event of crushing
defeat, they could have their mountains and wild,
impassable glens close under their lee—havens of
shelter and quiet repose, as they had found them in
the "Fifteen." They cared but little for the poor
Lowlanders, who were entirely without these defences,
and had no means to shield themselves from the wild
fury and revengeful spirit of the thoroughly affrighted
Whigamores.

After a long, vociferous disputation, carried on in
English, French, and Gaelic, with a thin stream of
real Irish brogue perpetually meandering through it,
the tartans, as might have been expected, carried
their point, and the next morning the rebel army was
in full retreat back to the North.

Maxwell and Chedville, with a view to their own

personal safety, accompanied the main body of the retreating forces until the gates of Carlisle were nearly reached, when, bidding adieu to the unfortunate Prince, they, with the ever-faithful Donald, turned their horses' heads homeward.

The weather at this time was excessively cold, with occasional showers of rain and sleet. When some few miles from Carlisle, after crossing a stone bridge over the river Gelt, they came to a small hostelry, and here Maxwell and Chedville dismounted, and leaving their steeds to the care of Donald, they entered the house, and were served with refreshments by the landlady—a comely, buxom dame, smart, active, and garrulous withal. She told her guests that she expected her liege lord home in a " whupwhile." He had taken "the beast and the cwoley dog on to Brampton, tho' he wad fain ha' been at Carol market. But markets cudn't be thought after these days ; it was sic a sairy time, thur fightin's knock'd ivery thing out of joint ; the world was nae doubt gannin' wrang. Gibbie Armstrong had just gone by on the dapple powney, an' tell't her Brampton was chock full o' the petticoat men." While she was yet speaking the tramp of a horse was heard, and the landlord himself drew up to the door. The two travellers, fearing a surprise, rushed out at the first sound, and mine host casting an uneasy kind of a glance at the three jaded horses and their owners, appeared to take in the situation at once.

"Good day, gentlemen," he said, saluting Maxwell and Chedville respectfully.   "You'll excuse me; I don't wish to pry into no man's business or secrets ; but I take it you're Jacobite men, and, if so, there's great danger in the lonnon before you."

"Indeed !" exclaimed Maxwell in surprise ; then, gathering trust from the frank, honest face of the landlord, he continued—"Supposing, my friend, we were to admit that we have been associated with Prince Charles, or the Pretender, as he is called, how are we in danger by taking the road to Brampton ?"

"I will tell you," the host replied.   "Less than half-an-hour gone I passed a company of Hawley's Dragoons, camped at the Tarn side."

"The Tarn side !"

"Aye, Tawkin Tarn, about half-way between this an' Brampton."

"*Peste!*" Chedville muttered, shrugging his shoulders almost imperceptibly.   He knew that the horse under Hawley's command had been for days hanging persistently on the skirts of the rebel army.   "Is there no other way of reaching Brampton except by the main road?" he asked.

"Oh, yes," answered the landlord; "you can take away down by Geltside, but it is a rough bridle-path, I can tell ye."

"Rough or smooth, my friend," said Maxwell, "I am afraid it is the only route we can follow with safety."

"Then a little further on you will find a narrow pathway leading down to the river. Lead your horses down this, mount at bottom, and follow the course of the stream for about two miles. You will then come to a fair, open bridle-road leading up to the level; and then, just before you, on the right-hand, lies Brampton."

Following implicitly the direction given by the kind host, the three fugitives, together with their equine companions, reached the pathway marginating the Gelt—a pathway over-arched by trees; and although the bright leaves had withered and fallen away, there still remained a solemn beauty on the sylvan scene. The hoarse roar of the now swollen tributary of the Eden, as it rushed wildly on over its bed of red sandstone, effectually drowned the dull, sullen tramp of the horses on the sedgy pathway.

The rocks, towering skyward on either side, and casting their murky shadows athwart the deep glen, shed a weird-like gloom over the entire scene, and chilled the very soul with a deep sense of desolation.

After half-an-hour's ride the three fugitives reached a broader road, leading up to the high ground. Arriving on the fair level, they saw the small town of Brampton on their right-hand, distant about half-a-mile. They found the rebel forces drawn up on a green patch near the moot-hill, and in front of a quiet, unpretending hostelry, known now as the Sandhouse Inn. Chedville and Maxwell, being personally acquainted with the principal officers, were cordially welcomed.

The dauntless Balmarino was in command of the horse, while the small number of Lowland foot-soldiers were officered by Lieutenant Deacon and Captain Berwick, the Highlanders being under their respective chiefs. Deacon and Berwick appeared to be in capital spirits. "Come with us to the North," the former said, in jovial tones, extending a hand each to the new arrivals; "all will yet be well; the cause is bound to triumph. When we commence our spring campaign, we will march on to the great city without a stop."

Balmarino shook his head and smiled grimly. "The young," he said, "have always hope, while the aged easily despair; but young and old may see alike that this retreat is a fatal blunder, and destroys irretrievably the chances of the House of Stuart."

"In that we are quite agreed, my lord," Maxwell answered. "Our success depended on a forward march from Derby to London; the chance is lost, and not one of us here will ever march voluntarily in that direction."

Prophetic words!—In a few short months Balmarino perished on Tower Hill, dying, as he had lived, a brave, fearless man; and Berwick and Deacon were partially strangled, and disembowelled while yet alive, on Kennington Common.

While this conversation was going on, Donald

Spey, seeing an opportunity open for refreshment, of which he considered himself in great need, adjourned to the hostelrie with a tall Highlander whose acquaintance he had previously made. While imbibing the whisky, the retreat northward was freely discussed between the Lowlander and the Gael.

"Ah Tonal', Tonal'," said the latter, "if she'd no seen it, she wad'na ha' believed it. Your maister, ta laird's, no deein' ta canny thing by ta Prince, Got bless her! To leave her like this, just at ta maist warst moment of her life ; to leave her, as ta brown leaves of ta forest fall awa' frae ta trees in ta cauld November blast !"

"Hoot awa' wi' ye," interrupted Donald, "ye'se aye puttin' the saddle on the wrang beastie. It's just the ither way on ; the Prince is no deein' the canny thing by them that hae risk'd their fortins, forby their lives, to gie him a helpin han'. Where is he now ? Instead o' marchin' right on to London, and takin' the Dutchman by the lug, as a collie dog wad a sow that aye wants to gang her ain gait, what does he dee? Taks tent o' the talk o' a few puir Heelan' bodies, an' hies him back to the hills !"

"Aweel, Tonal'," answered the Highlander, after indulging in a deep draught, "she thinks ta Prince hes dune ta ferry best thing for hersel ; an' gin it were just left till Duncan M'Tavish, her nainsel wad'na pit a fit till the south for a sporran o' gowden guineas, for she hesna' had a drop guid whisky town her thrapple sin' ta tay she cam' ower Stirling prig."

"Aye, aye," said Donald, contemptuously; "it's a' verra weel for the likes o' yersel to talk that gait; when once ye've gettin' fairly among the hills, ye think ye can cover yer heeds an' yer hurdies with copsewood an' heather, sae that the varra deil himsel' wadna' speir ye out. But eh, man, ye're reckonin' unco fast! Ye gat quietly hame after the 'Fafteen,' but tak' my honest word ye'se no be sae lucky frae the 'Forty-five;' ye've been ower troublesome, and they'll no let ye sleep. King George's reed-coats will be up and ower the hills; an' hide where ye may, and skulk where ye can, they'll kittle yer quarters wi' their new fashioned bagonets. But eh, man," continued Donald, rising to his feet, "I maun awa', or the laird will be chafing;" and drinking off the remainder of his whisky, and shaking the brawny hand of the Highlander, he quitted the house.

The Gael was left to settle scores with mine host, which was indeed no difficult matter, for after proving his absorptive qualities by swallowing another half mutchkin of whisky, he squared accounts with the landlord by demanding and receiving "a piece of white money, just to tak' her on her way to Carlisle."

When their horses were well breathed and re-freshed, Maxwell and Chedville took leave of their friends, and with the faithful Donald resumed their journey.

Taking the most unfrequented paths, they passed near Bardon Mill, and fording the Tyne a little above Corbridge, they followed Watling Street for some distance. Leaving the old Roman road, they again took a bye-path, and crossing the Newcastle and Durham turnpike at Birtley, found themselves shortly afterwards on the Black Fell. When they reached the little village of Usworth their horses were sorely jaded, and being now within a mile of Balmston, Donald was sent forward to reconnoitre, with instructions to see Miss Maxwell if possible, on whose report alone they felt disposed to rely. They were naturally afraid to enter the village, as Kenard was so well known in the neighbourhood, and, pending the return of Donald, were compelled to remain unsheltered in the open country. A heavy shower of rain and sleet began to fall, and a keen, cutting wind blew strong from the north.

Chedville, despite all his firmness, could not help contrasting bitterly this last visit to Balmston with that made by him nearly a year before.

"*Pardieu! Votre Altesse,*" he muttered, shrugging his shoulders, "you have much to answer for. By your foolish conduct you have thrown away a kingdom fairly in your grasp, and destroyed some hundreds of noble gentlemen, not on the field, where it is an honour and a glory to die, but you have condemned them, by your own mad act, to the block and to the gallows ; bah ! "

After waiting for more than an hour, a dull, tramping sound assailed their ears, and through the now rapidly deepening gloom they saw indistinctly two horsemen approaching. Chedville's hand by a quick impulse sought his sword, but they were speedily reassured by a preconcerted signal from Donald, who now rode up, accompanied by the land steward of Balmston.

"How are all at home, Donald?" asked Mr. Maxwell, anxiously.

"Oh! fairly weel," replied Donald; "but Miss Maxwell, puir bairn, has been greetin' an' greetin' sairly, though she'll no confess. But, my certie, there's been bonnie wark! Your brother James has been at Balmston wi' mair than a dozen reed-coats, spiering after papers an' dockeyments."

"Aye, aye," said Maxwell, "I might have expected this ; false and treacherous to the last. No doubt he has already made terms with the House of Hanover for the broad lands in the north ; but, thank Heaven, Balmston is Flora's, and she has friends in power, able and willing to protect her interests, in despite of my false brother. Mr. Marley," he continued, addressing the steward, " when was this unwelcome visit paid to my house ? "

" Just three days since," was the reply.

Chedville started as though he had received a pistol shot, and walking his horse close up to the land steward, he peered anxiously into his face.

"Did they find anything of consequence?" Mr. Maxwell again asked.

"Yes, sir," the steward replied, "they found a document, signed by the Pretender, naming you to a command in the rebel army; and a letter from a certain Mr. Ross, having reference to the Count D'Aubray," and here Marley glanced maliciously in the direction of Chedville.

"This seems to me somewhat strange," Maxwell commented. "Those papers were most carefully concealed, and deposited in a receptacle, the secret being known but to you and me."

"They discovered it, however, sir, and so keen was their search, that nothing within the walls could have escaped detection."

"Well, it cannot be helped. Do you apprehend present danger from their return to the house?"

"I think not," the steward replied; "your brother said the rebels were in full retreat, and that you would doubtless go into Highland quarters with them."

"Good. I think we may find safe shelter at Balmston for a few days; what say you, monsieur?"

"Yes," replied Chedville, "under these circumstances I think we may; but perhaps some of those marauding dragoons may pay us a flying visit."

"I think it unlikely," said Maxwell; "we are a considerable distance from the main roads. But come, we can discuss the matter more at our ease inside Balmston House. My bones seem chilled with this awful weather."

And putting spurs to his horse, Kenard rode down the lane, followed by the rest.

CHAPTER XII.

"And if there be a human tear,
  From passion's dross refined and clear,
  'Tis that which pious fathers shed
  Upon a duteous daughter's head."
                    —*The Lady of the Lake.*

CHEDVILLE was deeply affected on witnessing the tender meeting between Mr. Maxwell and his daughter. Flora flung herself weepingly on Kenard's breast, while in a voice half choked by sobs she said—

"Oh, my dear father, how glad I am to see you once again; but oh, great God! what danger hangs over you even now!"

"Cheer up, my dear child," Maxwell replied, soothingly, while the big tears trickled down his manly cheeks; "let us put our trust in an all-wise Providence; all may yet be well."

Chedville took Flora's hand, and pressing it, he said, "Can you trust me, Miss Maxwell?"

"I can, Monsieur D'Aubray," she replied, returning

10

the pressure feebly; "you will do all you can for my poor father's safety?"

"I will save him, Flora," he said in a whisper, " or perish in the attempt."

Maxwell and Chedville retired for the purpose of changing their wet clothing, and soon returned again to the dining room, when the former having summoned Mr. Marley and the servants to his presence, addressed them as follows—

" I rely with confidence on the good feeling which has mutually subsisted between us hitherto, and do not hesitate to place myself entirely in your hands. I need hardly tell you—for you are already cognisant of the fact—that I have been engaged in an enterprise of which the existing Government of this country totally disapproves; and that the knowledge of my being here at Balmston, if carried to other ears, would immediately bring those who would remove me a prisoner, and lead me to the scaffold. If I can rest here for a few days, I shall in all probability be enabled to devise some means of escape; and when this sad affair has blown over, I will doubtless find an opportunity to negotiate with the Government, secure a pardon, and return to my home in peace. I therefore trust entirely to you, and hope you will be careful not to allow your tongues unwittingly to betray my presence here."

"On behalf of myself and the servants," said Marley, " I dare promise the most profound secrecy."

"Let ivery man speak for himsel'," interrupted one of the servants. "If I thowt my tongue wad betray the maister i' the mornin', I wad pull'd out by the ruts to-neet."

"An' so say I."

"An' I," "An' I," An' I," was echoed all round.

"My friends, I thank you," said Maxwell, visibly affected, "and will trust myself with every confidence in your hands."

The servants, led by the steward, left the room, and turning to Chedville, Maxwell said—

"I think they are all staunch and true ; what say you, Monsieur D'Aubray?"

"All but one," was the answer.

"Indeed! And which of them do you consider false?"

"Marley, your steward."

"Impossible! He is tried and faithful."

"I say he is a traitor! and you know enough of Pierre Chedville to be aware that he would not make a positive assertion save on positive grounds."

Flora looked alarmed.

"Oh, Monsieur D'Aubray," she said, "what do you know?"

"Answer me one question, Mr. Maxwell. On the night preceding the morning on which you made discovery of a certain paper in your sleeping apartment, was anyone in that same apartment with you?"

"Yes," replied Kenard, after a moment's pause; "when I recollect, I was slightly indisposed on that particular night, and Marley was with me for a few minutes."

"Good, I thought so; that letter was placed there by Marley, for the express purpose of inducing you to commit yourself to this unfortunate business."

"But there could be no motive, Monsieur D'Aubray."

"Oh, but there could be—a very clear motive. Listen! On the day of my departure from Balmston this gentleman, your land-steward, came into the library, and although his features were entirely unknown to me, his voice was strangely familiar. I could not, however, recall to my mind when and where I had heard it before, and only to-night have I been able to resolve the doubt. When Marley came up with Donald, and answered your first question, the time and place of our former meeting flashed back upon my memory. After crossing the frozen river on the night I first visited Balmston, as I approached the house, a man came towards me from the shadow of the wood, and in cautious tones he said, '*This is a surprise indeed, Mr. James! I certainly did not expect you here to-night.*' I told him he was mistaken, and asked him if the house before me was not the residence of Mr. Kenard Maxwell. I received no answer; the man disappeared as quickly as he came to sight. That man I will swear was Marley, your steward."

"In league with my brother! O Heaven! it cannot be."

"There is another proof which, in my opinion, clearly establishes his guilt. You stated to-night that the papers discovered were in a place the secret which was known only to yourself and this man. Now I happen to know from personal experience what great difficulty attends the search for papers in a house you have never entered before. When not concealed with more than ordinary care they are extremely apt to defy the most rigorous scrutiny ; and I am clearly of opinion that unless the place had been directly pointed out by Marley, those papers would not have been discovered."

"There is now no doubt in my mind," said Maxwell. "He is a traitor, and we are at his mercy."

"Not exactly," rejoined Chedville, quietly; "he thinks you are going to remain here for a few days, and will do nothing before to - morrow morning. A few constables would, he knows by the temper of your servants, be an insufficient force to effect a capture, and he cannot secure the aid of troops nearer than Newcastle. Your brother is doubtless in the neighbourhood, and with him Marley will first have an interview. Now I will go to Sunderland at once, and endeavour to arrange means for our escape."

"I am afraid there is great danger in your going there, Monsieur D'Aubray," said Maxwell; "and I cannot conceive how you would be able to carry out any plan successfully."

"Trust me," interrupted Chedville. "I have friends in Sunderland on whom I can rely most implicitly. I have carried a seaman's disguise in my valise through the whole campaign; this and a small boat is all I require. I will make my journey down the river to-night; water leaves no trail. The moon is nearly in her last quarter; it should be high tide here at about ten o'clock. I will prepare for a start immediately. By to-morrow night the soldiers may be here, and before that time we can be away. But about Miss Maxwell?"

"I will go with my father at all hazard," said Flora, in a decided tone.

"But, pardon me," Chedville observed, "should your presence interfere with the chances of his escape?"

"In that case I will remain here. But pray, Monsieur D'Aubray, do, if it be possible, permit me to accompany my father."

"Believe me, Miss Maxwell, I will do my best to meet your wishes."

About an hour after the above conversation had taken place, Chedville, disguised as a seaman, and

accompanied by Mr. Maxwell, left the house by a
private door, and, unobserved by the servants,
reached the side of the river, where a small boat
lay moored. Kenard brought out from a wood-
shed on the bank a pair of oars, and laid them on
the "thofts" of the little craft. The two men
shook hands in silence, and then Chedville, saying
in a low voice, "To-morrow I will be here with
good news," seated himself in the boat, and casting
off the painter, he let her drift silently down with
the tide for some distance, then shipping the oars,
he lent his full weight to the stroke, and sent the
frail little vessel flying over the water.

It was too dark to distinguish objects clearly,
yet could he see the high banks of Offerton heugh,
looming still higher in the intense gloom. Onward
went the boat, and the lights from the houses at
Hylton Ferry were reflected in the now rapidly
ebbing tide ; onward still, and the dark outline
of Claxheugh Rock rose in shadowy grandeur on
the left of the rower ; still onward, and he was in
the midst of the broad flat of Pallion, with nothing
visible on either side ; still onward, and the high
land of Suddick rose skyward on his port bow.
Plying his oars with unabated energy, he was soon
among the shipping in Sunderland harbour.
Threading his way carefully between the tiers of
the various craft lying at their moorings, he landed
at a place now known as Hardcastle's Slip. Fearing

that the boat, if made fast, might be recognised as belonging to Balmston, he placed the oars in her, and by a vigourous push sent her out into the middle of the stream, so that the ebb might carry her out to sea. Chedville then proceeded un-challenged and unquestioned up the long bank and along Warren Street, to the little public house where he was first introduced to the reader. Though "past twelve o'clock" (on the authority of the old watchman, whose husky voice could be heard at short intervals) the house was still open, and Chedville walked in. "Is Captain Jones in?" he asked of the landlady in the little bar.

"Yes," she replied, "he's in the parlour;" then observing her visitor more closely, "Why, bless me! it's Mr. Thornton," she said. "An' how have you been gettin' on?"

"Oh! I'm all right, Missus Ovingham, thank you. How do you and Joaney keep?"

"Just as well as could be expected these awful times. You'll find Captain Jones in the parlour. I believe he was just thinking of going to bed."

Chedville entered the room, and there sat Bill Jones with his glass and his pipe. On beholding Chedville he rose hastily to his feet, breaking his pipe, and flooding the table with the contents of his glass.

"My eyes!" he exclaimed, "what a fright you gave me! Blow me, if I didn't go for to think it was yer blessèd ghost! Give us yer hand, and tell us how yer last."

"Oh! quite well, Jones," replied Chedville, return-ing the Captain's hearty shake, "and I'm here to ask for your help immediately."

"Not to-night, Capytine Chedville?"

"Why, no, not exactly to-night. Where's the *Mary Ann* lying?"

"Low part of the harbour," replied Jones. "A bargin's a bargin ; she's been lyin' there this fortnite, accordin' to tarms. But I heern tell," he continued, sinking his voice to a whisper—"I heern tell that this affair o' yourn has sprung a leak, an' that all hands at the pumps won't keep it afloat ; and I also heern tell, this very day, that all wessels leavin' this ere port are to be searched, and that a custom-house officer has to stop aboard till she moves away to sea, whether it's foreign or coastways. This, d'ye see, Capytine Ched-ville, is to prevent these ere Jackeybites gettin' off shore."

"*Mon Dieu !*" exclaimed the other, "that is most unfortunate ; but *n'importe*, we must manage some other way. I wish to get a Jacobite gentleman and his daughter off to France ; and if you manage this, Jones, I will guarantee that you shall have as much money as will purchase the *Mary Ann*, and that I know is the extreme height of your ambition."

"Aye, that it is, Capytine Chedville, for the man that owns the *Mary Ann* owns the smartest little craft afloat on blue water.   But how is this 'ere matter to be brought about ? "

" Why," replied Chedville, " as the surveillance is so strict, there is only one course to adopt, and that is to get them safely stowed away in this quarter, and when the brigantine proceeds to sea, let her stand in after nightfall, and send the boat to the beach at such place as we may determine on."

" Aye, that's something like it, now.   Lor! Capy- tine Chedville, what a head you've got ; you're never at a loss."

" Yes I am, Jones," said the other, smiling ; " I'm at a loss now.   The gentleman and his daughter are five miles up the river, and I am afraid it would be exceedingly hazardous to bring them down in an open boat, or by land."

" Lor ! I can pilot you through that difficulty with a flowing sheet.   The man that keeps this ere house is a keelman, an' I heern him say as how he was goin' to staith to-morrow arternoon to bring down his keel. In course he will be down on the ebb, somewhere about twelve o'clock to-morrow night.   Now, he'll give them a passage, and stow them away in the stern-sheets.   All you've got to do is to take a keel- man's suit for the gentleman, and one of Patsey's coloured print gowns for the lady, and there you are, fair and square.   When they land from the keel, d'ye see, they won't cause no observations, cos why, there won't be nothin' particular in their looks."

"Can we see this man to-night?"

"Why, I do believe he's a-sittin' in the bar at this moment."

"There was a man in the bar as I entered. Is he true, think you?"

"As steel, Capytine Chedville; there's no fear of him."

Jones rapped loudly on the table with his knuckles and the landlady entered the room.

"Bring three glasses o' rum, Patsey," he said, "and tell your John to walk aft, if he hasn't gone to bed."

"You're just in time, Captain Jones; he's makin' ready to go upstairs."

"That's capital. Bring the glasses, and send him in, Patsey."

The glasses were brought, and after them, behind the little tray, came John Ovingham, the keelman.

"Now then, John," Jones began, "bring yourself to an anchor in that there chair—that's it. Now we wants to give you a real good freight, John, which won't do you no manner of harm, John, but contrarywise, good—a freight, John, that'll put a good round sum in yer pocket. We wants ye to bring a lady an' a gentleman down the water to-morrow night unbeknown to anybody, d'ye see; an' if so be you could take them aboard your craft, and land them safe at Sunderland, we won't mind standin' ten guineas, which aint to be picked up for next to nothin' every day."

"Aw see, Mister Jones, aw see," returned the keelman. "Its varry easy gettin' o' them aboard, but gettin' o' them ashore agyen'll be the warst."

"We'll manage that 'ere," said Jones. "We'll send a keelman's suit for the gentleman (my mate here will sail under somethin' like the same colours); your wife'll lend us a cotton gownd, and a Ingy silk han'kercher; and when that there lady has got that there gownd on her back, and that there han'kercher tied round her head, nobody'll go for to stop her an' ask her questions, d'ye see?"

"Aw'll undertak' the job, Mister Jones; an' eff the warst comes to the warst, aw cud say they ast for a passage an' aw gav' them one, but aw didn't knaw wee they war."

"To be sure," chimed in Jones, "there aint the least mossel o' risk."

"But where hev aw' ti' tak' them abroad?"

"You know Balmston, I suppose?" Chedville asked.

"Squire Max'all's?" said John; "nicely. Mony a good dinner aw've gettin' iv his kitchen, aye, an' mony a good stiff glass o' grog! Aw used to sweet-heart a lass there afore aw married Patsey; she knaws nowt about it though." And here Joaney indicated the partner of his joys, by jerking his thumb in the direction of the bar.

"Well then," said Chedville, "Squire Maxwell and his daughter are really the parties we want you to help, and if they have at any time done you a favour or shown you a kindness, you will be the more willing to assist them now in their great distress."

"Aye," answered the honest, warm-hearted keelman, "eff it's Squire Max'all, aw'll did without a penny reward."

"No, no," said Jones; "belay there! take a turn, John Ovingham! The labourer's worthy his hire, the sailor's worthy his wages, an' by consekens the skipper's worthy his freight; and when you've discharged your cargo 'cordin' to the tarms an' conditions of your charter party an' bill o' ladin', there's ten guineas'll be paid down to ye."

"Then maun aw bring up the keel at Balmston, an' gie them a hail?"

"No," replied Chedville, "certainly not; we must get them aboard without being noticed. But as there will doubtless be more keels coming down on the same ebb, we must have a signal agreed on. Can you chant any particular air?"

"What's a hair?"

"Can ye sing a tune of any sort?" said Jones. "What song d'ye know best, John?"

"Aw on'y knaw one sang."

"What is it?" asked Chedville.

"Bobbie Shaftie," replied John.

"Give us a verse," said Jones.

John Ovingham sang, in a low voice, and to a peculiar air, *sans* harmony—

> " Bobbie Shaftie's gyen to sea,
>   Silver buckles on his knee,
>   When he comes back, he'll marry me,
>   Bonnie Bobbie Shaftie."

" That will do," said Chedville ; " I will remember it. When you get a little below the Ford, sing this quietly, as if to yourself, and I will pull alongside, and when we are close to the keel, you must say ' Balmston ; ' then we shall be assured we are right."

" Aw see, sir ; trust to John Ovingham, an' he'll not disappoint ye."

" Now," said Chedville, " the next matter for consideration is where they can be concealed until we have an opportunity to get them safely aboard the *Mary Ann.*"

" Why, here," said Ovingham, " Ye cudn't hev a better place ; there's a little room upstairs, where they'll be as snug as a bug iv a rug."

" Right you are." Jones said, assentingly. " I don't know no place where they could be safer than in this 'ere house."

" Agreed," said Chedville ; " and now, Ovingham, can I have the loan of a boat in the morning ? "

" Yis," John replied. " Aw'll hev to gan away about ten o'clock to put the keel under ; we'll pull reet up to steith, an' efter it's dark ye can easily pull down to Balmston o' the second flood."

"All right! I'll meet you here in the morning about half-past nine o'clock ; and now, good night both," and saying this, Chedville left the house and walked rapidly on towards his old lodgings.

He soon reached the house, and knocking at the door, his summons was speedily answered by the bobbing out from an upstairs window of a deeply-bordered nightcap, a limited visible portion of the human face divine, and the celestial end of a nightdress—the apparition in sharp tones demanding to know who was there.

"It's me, Mrs. Willis," Chedville replied.

"Goodness gracious me!" she exclaimed; "why, if it isn't Mr. Thornton! Just wait a moment till I put on my gown."

Poor Mary, who was sleeping in the same bed with her mother, was also awoke by the knocking, and her heart beat quickly when she heard Chedville's voice.

The good woman soon opened the door, saying : "Laws-a-me! who would have expected you to-night. Come in, Mr. Thornton; I'll soon have a fire on, and I'll have a cup of coffee ready for you in a jiffy. Have you just come in from sea?" she asked, as she rattled away with the flint and steel.

"No," replied Chedville, "I have just come from Shields."

Mrs. Willis puffed at the tinder until she succeeded in persuading a brimstone match to ignite ; then, having lit the candle and set the fire going, she said—

"We were struck all of a heap like when Captain Jones called to tell us you'd joined another ship at Calais, and that we were to keep your room on all the same, and that he had orders to pay up, and likewise six months in advance. Both Mary and me considered this very kind of you, Mr. Thornton, and we were thankful to Captain Jones for the trouble he took. And is your ship at Shields now, Mr. Thornton ? "

"No," replied Chedville, dejectedly, "she's gone ashore on the Scotch coast, and is pretty nearly all to pieces by this time, and I'm back again to rejoin the old craft."

By this time the fire was blazing merrily, Mrs. Willis having manufactured an additional and powerful draught by placing above the fire-grate a large tea-board, on which a number of peacocks in unnatural gilt plumage were perpetually strutting.

"Now, Mr. Thornton," she said, as she put a cup, saucer, and a bread loaf on the table, "the kettle'll boil directly ; let me do you a rasher of bacon."

"No, thank you," Chedville answered, "don't trouble yourself, Mrs. Willis. I'll get nicely warmed, have a cup of coffee, and then I'm off to bed, for I am dreadfully tired, and I daresay it's getting on for three o'clock."

"Why, then," said the good woman, "I'll tell you what I'll do : while you're warming yourself and the kettle's a-boiling, I'll just slip up and make a weeny bit fire in your bedroom—for it must be kind o' damp, you know, though, mind, I've had the winder up whenever the weather was fine— and by the time you get your coffee, it'll be burnt up beautiful and bright."

Chedville nodded assentingly, and Mrs. Willis having first provided herself with the necessary fuel, went up the narrow staircase. She soon returned to the kitchen, and having prepared the coffee and handed it to her lodger, she bade him "Good night," and retired.

Sipping the steaming liquid without touching the bread, he then went to his room, where he found the prediction of his landlady fulfilled, for the fire had indeed "burnt up beautiful and bright." Without undressing, Chedville threw himself on the bed ; the eyelids, unclosed for four long days and four weary nights, gladly drooped, and over-taxed nature hurried him off into a sweet, sound slumber.

CHAPTER XIII.

"Though a' my daily care thou art,
    And a' my nightly dream,
I'll hide the struggle in my heart,
    And say it is esteem."

—*Burns.*

THOUGH tired and weary when he retired to rest, Chedville awoke thoroughly refreshed before eight o'clock; five hours of sound, healthful sleep had restored his body almost to its wonted vigour, and his troubled mind to an even serenitude. His toilet was quickly made, and going downstairs he found Mrs. Willis and her daughter in the kitchen, the breakfast preparations being just so far advanced as the uncertainty of the lodger's rising would permit. In a few minutes all was ready, and the three sat down to an enjoyable meal. Immediately after breakfast Mrs. Willis went out on some errand, and Chedville, hitching his chair to Mary's side, began at once to make her his confidante.

"Now, Mary," he said, "you're a woman, and,

despite that misfortune, I think you can keep a secret."

"Ah, Mr. Thornton," Mary answered, with a smile, "they say it is impossible for a woman to keep a secret."

"With most women it is so, but I believe you to be an exception to the general rule. But, Mary, dear, you must solemnly promise that you will not mention to anyone a single word of what I am about to say, not even to your mother, nor in any way betray the trust I repose in you. Do you promise this, Mary?"

"I do, Mr. Thornton," she replied, "most solemnly."

"Thank you," Chedville said, stealing his arm round her waist, and imprinting a kiss on her fair forehead. A thrill of exquisite pleasure ran through Mary's frame, and as she modestly adjusted herself on her seat, the thought of the dear little heart was—"Perhaps, perhaps, he may learn to love me yet!"

"And now, dear child," he resumed, "the statement I am going to make, will most conclusively prove the unbounded confidence I have in you. There is a gentleman of great wealth and high position in this county, who has, most unfortunately for himself, been engaged in this rebellion which you have doubtless heard so much about. He is now hiding in this neighbourhood, and if discovered

will assuredly die on the scaffold.   This gentleman
has a daughter just about your own age, Mary,
and they wish to escape together to France.   The
daughter, I may say, is in no personal danger, but
she will not consent to leave her father.   In France
they have many friends, and when they are once
there, they will be beyond the reach of those cruel
laws, which would condemn the father to a dishonourable and shameful death on the gallows, and
send the poor daughter broken-hearted to the
grave.   Now it is the intention of Captain Jones
to give them a passage in the *Mary Ann*, but as
all vessels are searched on leaving the harbour, it
is quite impossible to get them on board in that
way.   The only thing, therefore, is to bring up in
the roads after nightfall, send a boat ashore, and
embark them from the sea beach.   Now, Mary, I
want your assistance in this good cause, and I
know you will cheerfully give your help, for the
sake of the poor daughter who is so anxious to
save her father's life."

The bright tear drops were now glistening in
poor Mary's eyes.

"Oh, Mr. Thornton," she said, "do show me
how I can be useful to this lady and her father,
and I will be so happy!"

"Listen!   The *Mary Ann* will proceed to sea to-
morrow morning between ten and eleven o'clock.
She will keep a good offing till night closes, and then

stand in for the land. At eight o'clock to-morrow night you must go along to the little public-house kept by Patsey Ovingham, where you will find them. You will then conduct them by the most secluded and least frequented road to the sea beach just below the battery, and you will wait there under the shadow of the bank until the boat comes ashore. You know the spot ?"

"Yes ; but what must I say to Patsey? I don't think she knows me well."

"Say Mr. Thornton has sent you ; that will be quite sufficient. Patsey will give the young lady and yourself a couple of fish-trays, so that if you are met on the way it will be thought you are going to wait for the cobles ; and oh! Mary, dear," Chedville continued in deep, earnest tones, "fail not to perform this duty faithfully, for you hold the power of life and death in your hands."

" As I help them," Mary answered, looking upwards —"as I help them, may the good God so help me in my greatest need !"

Chedville gave no hint of his great love for Flora Maxwell. Was it because he had to some extent probed the secret lying deep buried in the poor girl's heart? Perhaps so ; we cannot tell.

"Now, Mary," he said, " I must go aboard. I expect to see you again to-night ; if not, you will not fail to perform the task you have undertaken."

" Trust in me, Mr. Thornton ; I will not fail you."

Chedville drew her towards him, and, kissing her again, he said, "God bless you, Mary! you have a feeling heart."

Widow Willis at this moment returned to the house, and Chedville, taking leave of mother and daughter, proceeded with rapid steps to the tavern of Patsey Ovingham, where he found Jones and the landlord waiting for him. After some conversation anent the important business in hand, Chedville donned one of Ovingham's short jackets, and placing on his head one of the peculiar hats worn by the keelmen of the period, he declared himself quite ready for a start. Bill Jones positively insisted that they should each drink a glass of rum—or "Jimmy Kay," as he jocularly termed the mellifluous compound—to the success of the enterprise. Chedville and the kindly, stolid John having assented, the drinks were brought in, and Patsey devoted herself to the task of making up the disguises for Maxwell and his daughter in a neat bundle. All being ready, Chedville and Ovingham proceeded to that part of the harbour known as the Mark Quay, where John's boat lay moored. It was about ten o'clock and nearly half-flood when they entered the little craft; the bundle was carefully stowed away in the stern-sheets, Chedville seated himself aft, and the keelman took first spell with the oars. When they arrived at Pallion, D'Aubray was enraptured with the beautiful river scenery, the banks of the Wear being thickly studded with trees on either side, excepting where the old castle of Hylton frowned grimly on the limpid stream from a well-cleared vantage space. Although the chill blasts of winter had perished the ornate beauty of its verdant banks, despoiled the trees of their lovely foliage, and wantonly whirled away the sere and yellow leaves, still Chedville could fairly imagine the especial loveliness of the Wear when Nature was at her best, and the glorious summer time reigned in golden splendour over all.

At Hylton Ferry Chedville took the oars, and Ovingham seated himself in the boat's stern. As the rower cleared the head of Offerton heugh and approached Balmston, he observed Miss Maxwell walking slowly to and fro on the river's bank. When directly in front of the Maxwell mansion Chedville's oar on the port side slipped from the rowlock, apparently by accident, and fell into the water, so that it was necessary to back the boat in order to regain it. When this was done the rower looked earnestly to the shore, the eyes of the lover and his mistress met, and the lady dropped her white kerchief on the grass. Chedville then resumed his rowing. The temporary loss of the oar and the fall of the handkerchief were preconcerted signals. As he rowed onward he could see that Flora continued to walk backward and forward for some time, and then leisurely bent her steps towards the house. After proceeding about a mile, Ovingham requested

Chedville to pull ashore in front of a little public-house standing alone on the northern skirts of Cox-green wood. They landed, secured the boat, and entered this seemingly isolated hostelrie.

The only occupant was a woman, who appeared be very old, although she still retained some vestiges of hardy vigour. In reply to a whispered question from Chedville, Ovingham said, " She's far above a hunder'd, but how much aw dinnot knaw ; she disn't ken hersel, an' there's neebody round here awd enuff ti tell her. Aw've knawn her for mair than thirty year, an' she disn't luk a day awder than when aw fust ken'd her." The old woman brought in the quart of ale ordered by the keelman, displaying a briskness and alacrity which would have become a woman fifty years younger.

" That's somebody aw dinnot knaw that's wi' ye the day, Joaney Ovin'ham," she said, looking keenly at Chedville.

" Aye," returned the keelman, " he's a nevey o' mine, Mally. He's a sailor, an' he's out ov a ship, so he's gawn i' the keel a bit alang wi' me."

This answer was apparently quite satisfactory to the old woman, and after a lengthened pause she said—

" How's the war gettin' sattled, Joaney ? "

" Why," replied Joaney, " biv what aw can hear, its gawn deed ageyn the rabbles, Mally."

" They say Squire Max'all's amang them. Did ye hear that, Joaney Ovin'ham ? "

"Why, yis, Mally, aw did hear't, but aw dinnot knaw for truth."

"He's a nice man, Joaney."

"There's nee mistake about that, Mally."

"Aye, an' so was the Edens afore him."

"Aw suppose see, Mally. Ye wad knaw awd Eden, aw'se warn't?"

"Which Eden did ye say, Joaney Ovin'ham?"

"Mister Max'all's wife's father aw mean, Mally."

"What!" the old woman asked, contemptuously, "Ruth Eden's father? Aw ken't Ruth Eden's gran'-fath-er," and here old Mally laughed triumphantly. "Aye, Joaney, aw was a gay big lassie gleanin' i' the harvest field, an' my mother shearin', when word cam' that Eden was killed at the battle o' Woster. Aye, lad, there was sair, sair greetin' beyth up an' down the watterside that day; for there was mair than Ralphy Eden went to their last account. My mother's awn brother fell alang wiv him, side by side, Joaney Ovin'ham."

"Fighting for King Charles?" Chedville asked.

"Deed war they nut," answered Mally, quite indignantly; "they were fightin' for the Parleyment and the country."

"That's a long time since, Mally," Ovingham said in conciliatory tones.

"Aye, so it is, Joaney," she answered proudly; "aye, so it is, but lang as it is aw can mind on't— aye, an' what's mair, aw can tell ye beyth the day

an' the year. That battle was fowt, Joaney, o' the
third o' September 1652."

"More than ninety-three years ago," said Chedville;
"and you can remember it?"

"Aye, aw remember the news comin' to Painshaw
as weel as eff it was on'y yesterday—better," she
added, "for now aw cannot remember some things
that happen fra' day to day."

Chedville's thoughts turned as it were instinctively
to the present campaign. What was its aspect?
Blacker and more dismal than the route of Charles
the Second's army at Worcester!

"*Mon Dieu!*" he muttered, "what a blighting
curse has rested on the House of Stuart since the
death of James the First. His son doomed to the
scaffold; his grandson exiled for years, and only
restored to make greater the fall of the Second
James. Then the noblest and best blood of the
land poured out like water to replace them, and
no success; and even now the same ill-fortune is
treading fast on the heels of Charles Edward.
Should he fail to leave the British shore, he will
meet the same fate as two of his race, Charles the
First and *La Belle Marie.* Truly they are a
doomed people. Retribution! maybe so; on the
seed of the man who clasped in friendship the red
hand of his mother's murdress!"

After sipping their beer, and partaking of
some bread and cheese, produced by Joaney

from a capacious wallet, the keelman said, in a whisper—

"Aw'll gan up ti the steith, an' ye can either stop here, or, if ye like, ye can walk down biv the side o' the wood an' see how the land lies at Balmston. Leave the boat here, she's all reet; an' dinnot ye cross ower ti the north side, cas' the grund's oppen, an' ye'll mevies be seen." Giving those wise directions, Joaney left the house, and proceeded briskly up the river to the Low Lambton Staiths.

Chedville sat for about a quarter of an hour after the keelman's departure, and then leaving the house, he walked slowly down by the side of the Wear, taking care to keep well within the shadow of the wood. As he approached the more open ground, he observed a man walking rapidly along the north bank of the river, and as he drew nearer, Chedville had no difficulty in recognising Marley, the land-steward of Balmston. With a half joyful exclamation, D'Aubray rapidly regained the shelter of the wood, and cautiously watched the movements of the steward. Marley halted directly opposite Chedville's place of concealment, and after looking carefully round about him, he entered a little boat which lay moored among the rushes on the northern bank, and casting her loose, rowed slowly over to the south side.

Marley landed on a little stone quay about fifty

yards below the spot where Chedville lay hid, and having made the boat fast, the latter saw him disappear behind a clump of dwarf trees, and then, with a cautious, stealthy tread, prepared to follow him. Chedville soon found himself on the narrow beaten pathway pursued by the steward, and at length saw him standing near a little water spring, oozing lazily from the moss-covered rock. Marley was evidently waiting for some one, as he was peering anxiously into the dark wood. Dropping on his hands and knees, Chedville crawled noiselessly through the thick undergrowth until close to the spot where the other stood, and there he lay holding his breath, but with his keen, piercing eyes fixed constantly on the steward. After some time he heard footsteps, and looking in the direction from which the sound proceeded, he saw a man coming with hasty tread down the pathway leading through the wood. As the man approached nearer, Chedville had no difficulty in recognising in the new-comer a likeness to Kenard Maxwell, and had no doubt that the person before him was the apostate brother. Had there been the least shade of uncertainty in the mind of D'Aubray, he would have remained but for a short time in a state of dubitation, for Marley exclaimed, with evident delight—

"I am glad you have come, Mr. James; when did you receive my message?"

"Only two hours since," replied the other, "and

I have ridden hard to Offerton. Your news surprised me vastly. How long does my brother purpose staying at Balmston ? "

" For a few days," Marley answered ; " but under the most favourable circumstances he would have had to wait until an opportunity for escape presented itself, and I really see no chance of that at present."

" Good ! You say there is another gentleman with him, and that he is the same person who paid a lengthened visit to Balmston about a year since, and that you heard my brother address him as Monsieur. This is doubtless the Comte D'Aubray, a Frenchman the Government have a particular desire to see. Indeed, so anxious are they for a personal interview, that they offer two hundred guineas reward for his apprehension. Marley, Marley, you have the devil's luck ! Is he still at Balmston ? "

" Yes, and likely to remain."

" Better still. I sent off immediately for twenty dragoons, as resistance might be offered. They will arrive at Balmston from Newcastle by seven o'clock in the morning, so that we are sure to take the birds on the nest—eh ! Marley ? " and here James Maxwell laughed like a fiend.

Marley, however, did not seem at all mirthfully disposed, and drawing from his pocket two documents, neatly folded, he handed them to his companion.

" There, sir," he said ; " I have written out the two

agreements, which we should sign at once. You, by one of these papers, guarantee to pay me two thousand guineas if I deliver up your brother, and the undertaking holds good whether he be convicted of treason or not."

"I hardly see the necessity for such a document," interrupted Maxwell, somewhat haughtily. "I should have thought my word of honour would have been sufficient for you, Mr. Marley."

Chedville could with difficulty suppress a contemptuous exclamation; here was a man betraying a brother to the scaffold, and talking of honour!

Marley evidently estimated James Maxwell's rectitude and high principles at their proper market value, for he went on, heedless of the interruption— "The other document I have already signed. If, by your aid, I succeed in becoming the husband of Flora Maxwell, I agree to give you, as soon as possible after the performance of the marriage ceremony, a legal charge on the Balmston estate for four thousand guineas, this sum to be paid over to you, and the charge voided within a period of three years."

Chedville, in the extremity of his rage, moved in his hiding-place, and thereby caused a slight rustling in the underwood.

"Ha! what is that?" Maxwell asked, timorously.

"Nothing to disturb us," said Marley, reassuringly. "It's only a bird, sir."

Chedville saw his danger, but was only able to subdue his almost ungovernable passion by gnawing his nether-lip until his fine teeth became purple-hued.

"You have a pen and inkhorn I suppose?" James Maxwell said, after a careful perusal of the papers handed to him by Marley.

"Yes, sir, I have," the other replied, producing the writing materials.

"Well, give me the pen; I will sign this paper, and although I could easily have my brother arrested without your help, you will not find me backward in carrying out what I have promised."

James Maxwell, after placing one of the papers in his breast, took the pen, and assuming a half-kneeling position, he rested the other document on his right knee until his signature was affixed; and handing it back to Marley, he said, "There is my agreement to pay you the two thousand guineas when my brother is safely captured."

"Thanks," the steward returned, taking the paper with an exultant smile; "but you fully understand, Mr. James, that I must not be seen in this affair. You must keep me clear altogether, so that in the event of your brother's acquittal, I may still retain my office at Balmston."

"As you will, but there is no fear of my brother being acquitted. The Duke of Cumberland would not pardon his own brother were he but half so deeply steeped in treason as Kenard Maxwell. But

we must also have this same Comte D'Aubray in
our net, for between ourselves I have an idea that
he has already proposed for Miss Maxwell.   Ah,
ha! you start at that, Marley!"

"How know you this?"

"Why, one of the letters we discovered with so
little trouble—thanks to you—was from the Laird
of Ross, and was evidently a reply to a searching
inquiry made by my brother into the character and
financial standing of the Comte—an inquiry which, in
my mind, could only be instituted on this account."

"Ha!" exclaimed Marley, "I almost thought as
much a year ago, when I saw them talking so
earnestly together on the river's bank.   He shall
never marry her, and may the foul fiend fly away
with me if I allow him to escape."

"Bravo, Marley! I like to hear you; you have a
spice of the devil in you, and no mistake; but I
must get back to Offerton, where I have left my
horse.   Keep your eye on Balmston, Marley, and if
they move, follow them carefully, and mark them
down."

"No fear of their changing quarters," said
Marley; "your brother believes all in his house to
be trustworthy, and the dragoons will just arrive
in time to give him an appetite for breakfast.   By
the way, I wish you had arranged for my arrest as
a suspected person; it would have made the thing
look better, and would have averted all suspicion."

"Truly, a clever device," remarked the other; "why did you not give me a hint when you sent your message? It's too late now, my friend. Keep your eyes open ; and now, good-bye."

They separated, Marley walking down towards the river, and Maxwell proceeding leisurely through the wood. As soon as he felt it prudent to do so, Chedville started to his feet, and, keeping still among the underwood, he cautiously followed James. When they had reached the heart of the small forest, Chedville stepped boldly on the pathway, and called out in a voice loud enough for the other, who was considerably in advance, to hear—

"James Maxwell, traitor, stay!"

The gentleman appealed to turned sharply round, and, judging from his pallid face, he seemed by no means delighted to behold a stranger to whom both his name and character were evidently known. He thought of calling aloud for help, but soon abandoned the idea, for Chedville, drawing a pistol from his breast, and pointing it at the head of Maxwell, said slowly, and with a truly unpleasant emphasis on each word—

"Your cry of alarm will bring you no friend. Take my advice and do not attempt it. If you do, I will send a bullet through your coward heart!"

"Who are you, fellow?" James demanded, assuming with great difficulty an air of boldness, which sat upon him something like a sailor's pea-jacket on the captain's monkey—a decidedly bad fit.

12

"Fellow me no fellows," Chedville answered, sternly; "I know you, and that is sufficient. You have denounced your brother as a traitor to the House of Hanover, and are now doing your best— or rather your worst—to send him to the scaffold, so that you may inherit his broad acres. In taking up arms in the cause of Prince Charles Edward, your brother has done what he considered his duty, actuated by a loyal feeling, spurred on by a high sense of honour—to both of which causes you are an utter stranger—and for this he must die! And shall you, a traitor to all laws divine and human ; a Cain—with your brother's blood on your hands ; a Judas—with the price of that blood in your pocket, in the shape of the title deeds to his estates —shall you go scathless? No, James Maxwell! Traitor!—coward!—villain! hear me! One of us will leave this wood alone, and whether it be you or me, Heaven's justice will decide."

"What! will you murder me?" cried Maxwell, turning deathly pale.

"No," replied Chedville, "I am no murderer. If I were I would shake hands with you, and call you friend and brother. I could have shot you unseen ere you left this place ; but not to save the lives of those I love best in the world would I play the assassin. Here are two pistols ; take your choice of them, for this duel is to the death."

"A duel!" returned the other. "No, I cannot

fight with you—with you I have no quarrel; and besides, your attire does not show you to be a gentleman."

"A gentleman, forsooth!" Chedville exclaimed, laughing bitterly. "The most despicable villain—nay, the lowest, meanest, vilest wretch that crawls the earth—would conceive the condescension his own, in consenting to meet James Maxwell in fair and honourable strife. A gentleman, quotha!—aye, in truth, a better gentleman than George of Hanover, whom ye serve! The best, the noblest blood of Normandy flows in the veins of Pierre Chedville Comte D'Aubray."

Although Maxwell had half guessed the individuality of his opponent, he started back as the name and title of the Frenchman fell on his ear.

"I refuse to fight with you," he said, in evident trepidation.

"But you shall do so!" Chedville sternly answered. "Come," he added, extending the butts of the two pistols we saw in his possession at the opening of our story; "come, sir, make choice of your weapon, or I will shoot you down as I would a prowling fox!"

"What quarrel can I have with you, a stranger utterly unknown to me until this moment?"

"If a poisonous snake crosses my path, shall I permit it to go unscathed, to envenom and destroy, because I never met it before? Make choice of your weapon, I say."

" I will not."

" We shall see."

Stepping close to Maxwell, Chedville smote him on the cheek with his open hand, so heavily that the finger marks were for a moment seen in their blanched lividness. This insult was too much for the craven-hearted James.

" Give me the pistol," he cried, hoarsely.

" Choose," said Chedville, extending the weapons as before ; " choose, but first listen to me. We will step back each man five paces—eye to eye, for I know and will not trust you—and while we are doing so, the muzzle of each pistol must be pointed to the ground ; if you make the slightest attempt to bring your weapon to the level before the distance is reached, on that instant I will fire."

Maxwell took the pistol, trembling more with rage than with fear, and the two men stepped backward in a cautious manner, their eyes fixed keenly on each other.

" Now," said Chedville, when the space had been carefully measured, and each man stood on his ground, " if there is an advantage I wish you to have it. Although the contest is unequal (your worthless life is alone at stake, whilst I am risking three lives in this quarrel), you shall give the word to fire, one—two—three ; at two we raise our weapons, at three we fire."

Maxwell looked at his pistol, saw that it was full

cocked, and then, in an unsteady voice, proceeded to count.

"One!" a lengthened pause.

"Two!" As he uttered the word, James Maxwell raised his pistol and fired at Chedville. The latter felt a twinge in his left arm near the shoulder, as though it had been suddenly cauterised with a red-hot iron.

"False and treacherous to the last!" he said, hissingly, as he pointed his pistol with deadly aim at Maxwell, who now stood trembling in every limb. "I might have expected this."

The entire frame of the miserable man seemed now to be working in irrepressible agony. His eyes sought anxiously the stern face of Chedville, but no signs of mercy could he see depicted there; and realising his position in all its fulness, the vile wretch threw up his hands imploringly, and with a despairing shriek was in the act of falling backward, when there was a bright flash, a sharp crack, and the bullet from Chedville's weapon was lodged deep in the coward heart of James Maxwell. Chedville gazed on the body of his opponent until assured that life was extinct, then, taking the pistol recently discharged by the dead man from the ground where it lay, he sat himself down on a fallen tree, quietly drew from his pouch a supply of ammunition, and proceeded, in a truly nonchalant fashion, to reload both weapons.

CHAPTER XIV.

"To you I give myself, for I am yours."
—*As You Like It.*

THE fleecy clouds in the eastern sky were changed, and had begun to deepen to gloom, and to indicate the approaching close of the short winter's day, when Chedville returned to the little riverside inn.

Ovingham was waiting for him, and was seated near the fire in the kitchen.

"Ye've been a lang time away," he said, in a low tone; "hev ye seen onny thing?"

"Nothing of importance," Chedville answered. "When it is dark, Ovingham, I will take the boat and row down to Balmston. By eleven o'clock, or a little after, we shall look for you. You remember the signal?"

"'Bobby Shaftie.'"

"And the password?"

"'Balmston.'"

"All right. And now, what say you to a glass of something hot and strong? We must be careful

not to take too much, Ovingham, to-night; it is
absolutely necessary that our heads should be clear
and our wits keen and astute."

"Niver fear me," the other answered, "awl be
up ti the mark, aw'se warrant ye."

The old woman was summoned, and two glasses
of rum ordered with hot water and sugar, and by
the time they were emptied it had become quite
dark. After some further conversation anent the
business in hand, Chedville and his companion
left the house; with a hearty handshake they
parted, the keelman taking his way up the river
side to the staith, and Chedville getting into the
boat to row down to Balmston.

The flood tide was now making, and Chedville
rowed as close as possible to the bank, for a double
purpose—to keep well in the dark shade, and to
avoid the strong current. After rowing some
time the lights of Balmston burst on his view, and
he saw them one by one mirrored and dancing in
the gently rippling stream. A little further on
his keen eye observed the dark outline of a man's
form on the north bank, and dropping his right
hand oar noiselessly in the water, he sheered the
boat in towards the land. As the little craft
approached nearer, the man came close down to the
water's edge, and asked, in good lowland Scotch,
"What's o'clock?"

Chedville, by a rapid left hand stroke, sent the

boat stem into the bank, and placing the oars fore and aft the thofts, he seized the painter and sprang ashore.

"How are they at Balmston, Donald?" he asked, anxiously.

"O! fairly weel," answered that worthy, for it was indeed himself, "but the puir bairn's kind o' waefa', an' it's no to be wondered at; she has ower muckle reason to be sad."

"I agree with you, Donald," said Chedville. "Poor young lady, I hope another day will see her more at her ease. You can manage a boat I suppose?"

"Hoot, awa!" returned the other contemptuously, "I've been amang boaties syne I was the height o' a thristle; gie me haud o' the painter, Count, for ye maun be sair forfairn."

"There you are," said Chedville, placing the small chain in Donald's hand, "and, Donald, you must stop by her until I relieve you; should she be taken away or get adrift by accident, we shall be in an awkward predicament."

"A' richt, your honour; trust her to me. I'm unco waukrife, an' I'll sit in her as fast as though I were fastened to the thoft wi' a rape. Sae now, Count, there's the key o' the little door at the end o' the house. Ye ken the road, but aye keep keekin' round as ye gang up the bank, an' tak' tent 'ye're no seen. Ye'll find Miss Flora and the laird in the little room at the heed o' the stair."

"Good, Donald! And now hand me that bundle out of the stern sheets."

"Here it is, your honour," said the old man, handing Chedville the package containing a portion of the wardrobe of John and Patsey Ovingham.

After ordering the faithful Donald to row cautiously down under the shelter of the wood, the Comte proceeded in the direction of the house, and going to the east, or lower end of the mansion, he applied the key given him by Donald to a small door, which opened easily. Entering the building, and carefully locking the door on the inside, he ascended a flight of stone steps, and tapped thrice at the wall. A secret panel was immediately drawn back, and Chedville entered a small room, neatly furnished, and lit up with an antique lamp, where he found Kenard Maxwell and his daughter. The former grasped him by the hand, saying. "Welcome, Monsieur D'Aubray; I can see in your face that you are the bearer of good tidings."

"I am indeed," Chedville answered. "I have arranged the plan of our escape, although not without some difficulty. There is, most unfortunately for us, a disagreeable surveillance exercised at Sunderland at present, all ships leaving the harbour are strictly searched; and the customs authorities have a man on board each vessel until she sails. Nor does the inconvenience cease here: by a special proclamation no vessel is permitted upon any pretence whatever to leave the port between sunset and sunrise."

"This is, indeed, a serious matter, Monsieur. And, pray, how have you managed to get over those apparently insuperable difficulties ? "

Chedville having carefully examined the apartment, and satisfied himself that there were no listeners, detailed the whole of his plan to Mr. Maxwell and Flora ; and producing the bundle, he said—

" Here are your masquerading habits, but it will not be necessary to don them before ten o'clock."

" O ! Monsieur D'Aubray," said Flora, "we can never repay you for the interest you have shown, and the great peril to which you have so willingly exposed yourself to aid my poor father."

" Yes," rejoined Chedville, taking her hand and drawing her skilfully to one corner of the room, "yes, Miss Maxwell, you can amply repay the debt for both. Promise me, Flora, dear Flora, that when your father is in perfect safety you will give me this hand for my reward."

Miss Maxwell bent down her head, as though she had become deeply interested in the peculiar pattern of the tapet work which covered the floor of the apartment. At length she raised her face, on which a smile, a blush, and a tear were most earnestly engaged in a contest for supremacy, and looking full into Chedville's eye, she said — " I promise this, Monsieur

D'Aubray, and I am glad you only asked for the hand."

" Indeed ! " Chedville exclaimed ; " and why ? "

" Because," she answered with a low, sweet, musical laugh, "because the heart was lost in the snows of last winter. I did not miss it then, but I discovered the loss long before the leaves came back to the trees."

For this naive and ingenuous reply, Chedville rewarded her with a kiss.

When Flora left the room, taking with her the different articles of feminine apparel brought by D'Aubray, the latter said in an undertone to his host—

" I have a painful communication to make to you, Mr. Maxwell, and whether you condemn or applaud me for the deed, I cannot repent it. I am—I feel thoroughly satisfied of my own conscience, and sure that I have acted according to the most honourable impulses of my poor nature."

Chedville then related the particulars of the interview between Marley and James Maxwell. When he touched on the proposed marriage for Flora, a red flush overspread Kenard's face, and he muttered through his fairly clenched teeth, " The villain ! " As Chedville narrated the circumstances attending the duel, Maxwell listened with the most ardent and intense interest, and as the manner of the treacherous shot was recounted, he said slowly, and in a low voice, as if to himself, " False, false !—ever false ! "

"And now," said Chedville, "do you blame me for the part I have played in this tragedy?"

"No man can blame you, Monsieur D'Aubray," Kenard answered, as he took the hand of the other in a firm grasp. "Had you shot the traitor from behind a tree, it would have been simply an act of retributory justice; but your action in this matter fully confirms the report of my old friend Ross, that you 'were known in Paris as the soul of honour and the Prince of Chivalry.'"

"Here," said Chedville, handing the undertaking of Marley to James Maxwell, which he had not neglected to secure, "just examine this instrument of villainy."

"The scoundrel!" Maxwell exclaimed, on reading the document; "a charge on Balmston for four thousand guineas! But for your admirable penetration, Monsieur D'Aubray, this villain would have led me on to the scaffold—me, whose bread he has eaten for years. Ungrateful forgetfulness of benefits bestowed is bad enough, but this double villainy can surely have no parallel in crime."

"Give me the paper," said Chedville, taking it from Kenard and consigning it to his pocket. "A settling day with Marley will come, and I may want this."

The night wore on, and the time for their departure began to draw nigh. Chedville consulted his watch; it was ten o'clock within a few minutes when Flora re-entered the apartment clad in Patsey Ovingham's garments, her only head covering being the silk handkerchief suggested by Jones.

"What think you, Monsieur D'Aubray," Maxwell asked, "would there be any harm in making the servants acquainted with our departure?"

"There might be none," Chedville replied, "but in my opinion it would be unwise to do so. I believe that, with the exception of Marley, they are all staunch and true ; they will know to-morrow that you have escaped, and will be glad of it when they see the dragoons at fault."

In this arrangement Maxwell acquiesced, and having retired to a small ante-room, he shortly returned in the disguise brought for him by Chedville.

"Now," said Chedville, rising and preparing to leave the apartment, "give me five minutes to get the boat ready, and then do you steal out cautiously to the river ; " and making his exit by the panelled door he proceeded in quest of Donald. After walking down the Wear, Chedville whistled, and was answered by the light dip of oars, and the faithful old man soon reached the bank.

"All right, Donald?" he asked, when the other was sufficiently near.

"A' richt, yer honour," replied Donald ; "but ch, my certie," he added, " it's a raw cauld nicht for the puir bairn ! "

"It is cold indeed, Donald," said the other. "But pardon me, I had forgot; what are we to do with you?"

"Wi' me, count! An' what wad ye dee wi' me? I maun e'en gang alang wi' ye, an' the laird, an' Miss Flora." Donald said this in the most decisive manner, as though the matter did not permit of the least possible doubt.

"But there will be so many of us that our numbers may awake suspicion."

"Weel! weel! dinna run the laird intil ony danger for the sake o' Donald; guidness kens I value his life far abune my ain. But oh! Count dear, if ye can manage it ony way, dinna leave me ahint! I've never left his side, fair weather or foul, for mair than forty years, an' I wadna' like to do it now, mair especially when he an' the bonnie bit lassie are gannin' far away intil a foreign country, amang folk maybe little better than wild savages!"

This remark was certainly the reverse of complimentary to Chedville, but that gentleman only noticed it by a smile, and after considering a moment, he said—

"Well, Donald, there seems no other way than this: you must embark in the keel with the others, and we must go into a committee of ways and means while on our passage to Sunderland."

The boat was now lying close to the bank, and as D'Aubray ceased speaking, Kenard Maxwell and his daughter came down—the latter carrying a small bundle, which Chedville promised to convey on board the *Mary Ann* before she left the harbour.

When they were seated, Donald gave the boat what he called "a shog," which sent her clear of the bank and well into the stream, and Chedville, taking the oars, rowed quietly down under the shelter of the wood, its tall trees, although leafless, still being able to cast a shadow of thick darkness over a portion of the water. Chedville and Donald now held the boat safely moored by means of the long thick rushes which grew luxuriantly by the river's bank, and the conversation was carried on in low whispers. The wind was now westerly and blowing a tidy breeze ; Chedville was glad of this, for he knew the keelman could utilise his clumsy square sail, and thus shorten their passage to Sunderland by at least an hour.

After some anxious moments Donald called their attention to a keel looming large through the gloom, and when nearly abreast of them Chedville prepared to shove off, but the preconcerted signal was not given, and the unwieldy craft held onward and disappeared in the night. Another and another followed with the same result. Could Ovingham have forgot? Chedville became impatient ; again his quick eye detected the outline of another keel approaching, and before it reached the place where they lay concealed the rustling noise of the haulyards gave them notice that the sail was being lowered to ease the way of the vessel; and immediately afterwards the inharmonious ditty came floating over the water—

> " Bobbie Shaftie's gyen to sea,
> Silver buckles on his knee."

Never was an audience more delighted with a melody since music had its birth. The boat left the friendly shelter of the dark wood, and as Chedville placed her alongside the keel, the man came to the port gunwale, and in a low voice gave the word, " Balmston ! "

"All right, Ovingham," D'Aubray said, as he sprang lightly from the boat and proceeded to assist Miss Maxwell on board. Mr. Maxwell and Donald followed, and the little craft was dropped astern, and made fast to the tack-pin. Ovingham showed them the way into the stern-sheets from the main hold. The appearance of their quarters was, if possible, rendered more dismal by the aid of a glimmering oil-lamp, which the kind-hearted keelman had provided for their use.

When Miss Maxwell, her father, and Donald had succeeded in stowing themselves carefully away, Chedville shook Ovingham by the hand.

" Several keels have already gone down," he said, " and I was really afraid yours was among them."

"Didn't aw tell ye," the other replied, "didn't aw tell ye ti hev' nee fear o' me. But, aw say, there's one mair than aw expected ; wee's he ?"

"He is an old faithful servant of Mr. Maxwell's," said Chedville, "and having accompanied his master to Derby, he is in the same danger. I did not think of him when we made our arrangements, but we must get him off to the *Mary Ann*, if possible."

"Why, let me see," Joaney rejoined, ruminating, "let me see. It wad be onnything but seyf for him to land to-neet ; but eff he stops i' the keel till tee moan neet, aw could fetch him out efter dark, and get him off wi' the tothers."

Chedville thought this most decidedly the best plan, and going at once to the stern-sheets, he made Ovingham's scheme known to the faithful Donald.

"The keelman will bring you food in the morning," he said, "and I am sorry indeed to subject you to this close confinement ; but the safety of Mr. Maxwell renders this course absolutely necessary."

"Dinna say anither word," interrupted Donald. "Gin it wad help the laird, or mak' him mair safe, I wadna object to gang intil the river, an' lie droukit a' nicht."

The breeze holding good, and keeping the clumsy square sail full, the keel soon reached Sunderland, and was safely moored abreast of the "dark entry," as it was then called. Mr. Maxwell and his daughter, accompanied by Chedville and Ovingham,

13

went ashore, leaving Donald to coil himself up behind the towline, in the darkest corner of the murky
cabin. After landing, they proceeded leisurely along
the Low Street to the foot of the Long Bank,
and succeeded in reaching Patsey's welcome tavern
without attracting attention.

Good fortune seemed still disposed to smile on
the fugitives, for there was no one in the house
but the buxom landlady and Captain Jones. The
plump, comely dame had a cosy room provided
upstairs, with a bright fire burning cheerfully in
the grate. There was an old-fashioned press-bed
in it for Mr. Maxwell's use, and a small room
leading from it was set apart for Flora's accommodation.

It was now about two o'clock, and after taking
some slight refreshment, more to oblige the landlady than from actual need, Miss Maxwell retired to
rest. Shortly afterwards a knock came to the door,
and Kenard having opened it, Chedville entered.

"Ah," he said, speaking in a low tone, "Miss
Maxwell, I see, has retired to rest."

"Yes," Kenard answered, in the same subdued
voice, "but I fear not to sleep, poor girl."

"I would have come up sooner to bid her good
night, but I have been having my arm dressed."

"Your arm, Monsieur!" Maxwell repeated, in
astonishment; "have you injured it?"

"A little," said Chedville, quietly; "I forgot to

mention it before. I was slightly wounded here by the treacherous shot ; it is only a flesh wound, and not of the least consequence."

"Well," returned Kenard, smiling, "you certainly do take things coolly, Monsieur D'Aubray ! "

"Well, perhaps you are right, sir, and this same coolness of disposition has stood me in good stead more than once ; but I must bid you good night. The chances are I shall see you no more until I come ashore for you to-morrow, or rather let me say to-night, for it is now well into morning. You will trust yourself entirely to the guidance of the young woman who will come here to conduct you to the place of rendezvous. Good night."

"Good night, Monsieur D'Aubray," said Maxwell, as they shook hands.

Chedville now descended the stairs and entered the little parlour where Jones and Ovingham were seated. To the latter he paid the ten guineas agreed on, and having arranged with him to bring Donald to the house after nightfall, and promising to meet Jones on board the *Mary Ann* at eight o'clock, he left the house and proceeded to. his lodgings. He did not knock at the door, but being furnished with a key, he let himself quietly in.

He found the fire burning brightly in the kitchen, and his supper standing on the oven shelf; and sitting down by the former he did ample justice to the latter, and then taking his candle went off to bed.

CHAPTER XV.

"Adown the glen rode armèd men,
　　Their trampling sounded nearer."
　　　　　　　　　　　　　　—*Campbell.*

CHEDVILLE jumped from his bed just as the clock was striking seven, and dressing himself with amazing alacrity, he went downstairs and found his breakfast quite ready. While doing full justice to the morning meal, he informed Mrs. Willis that the *Mary Ann* would proceed to sea about mid-day, and that his bag on board contained sufficient apparel for the voyage.

The communication anent the clothes gave a sense of relief to the good widow, who saw no chance of her being able to do up two or three shirts, and wash and dry a couple of guernseys, on so short a notice.

Bidding the widow good-bye with a hearty hand shake, he beckoned Mary into the passage.

"Remember, Mary," he said earnestly, " Patsey

Ovingham's at eight o'clock, and then to the beach, immediately below the battery."

"Trust me, Mr. Thornton," Mary answered, "I will not fail."

"I am sure you will not, Mary. God bless you, kind-hearted little girl! We will meet again to-night; till then farewell."

And kissing the sweet face, Chedville hurried away from the house, and was soon standing on the deck of the brigantine. To his delight he saw the little vessel was not more than half load. "This is capital," he said; "Jones is always alive to duty. Should we fall in with any of those English cruisers, it will be no easy matter to overhaul the *Mary Ann* in this trim."

An official of the customs was walking the deck with the proud bearing which he considered the dignity of his office demanded. This gentleman regarded Chedville with an inquisitive, if not suspicious look, when he came on board; but seeing him take upon himself his mate's duties, and hearing him issue his orders to the men in true nautical style, the officer's distrust speedily vanished.

By half-past ten the anchor was aweigh, and the wind being west-north-west, and a middling breeze at that, the jib was set, the topsail shook loose, the customs official landed, and the *Mary Ann* sailed over the bar.

Chedville perceived Mary Willis on the pier. As

soon as she caught his eye, she fluttered her kerchief in the breeze, and he returned the salute by waving his hat.

" Now," said Jones, when they were fairly over the bar, " it's my opinion, d'ye see, that the wind'll draw round to the nor'-west, or maybe the nor'-nor'-west, so we'll just let her go off nor'-east, and then, d'ye see, we'll fetch that there battery easy."

The *Mary Ann* stood off in a north-easterly direction, and soon became to the observers on shore a mere speck on the horizon.

.   .   .   .   .   .

Great was the consternation and panic of the faithful servants of Kenard Maxwell, when, at seven o'clock on this same morning, they heard the measured tramp of a body of horse, and saw some twenty dragoons coming at a rapid pace down the road leading from Usworth to Balmston. They easily divined the dread object of this early visit, and one of them rushed frantically to the bedroom occupied by their master since his return. Knocking loudly at the door, and receiving no answer, the loyal fellow considered this no time to stand on idle ceremony, and dashed at once boldly into the apartment. Mr. Maxwell was not there, and, to his surprise and unbounded delight, he saw the bed had not been slept in.

Beaming with joy, he descended to the hall and communicated the glad news to the other servants ;

and their bewilderment was still further increased when Miss Maxwell's maid informed them that her young lady could not be found, and that her room had not been occupied during the last night.

By this time the detachment of dragoons had surrounded the house, and the officer in command— a dashing young fellow—dismounting from his steed, ascended the stone steps in front of the Balmston mansion, and plied the knocker with nervous vigour and scant ceremony. The door was speedily opened by one of the servants, on whose face exultation and lingering doubt appeared to be somewhat equally blended.

"Now then, my man," said the officer, "I have come to arrest Kenard Maxwell of Balmston, Pierre Chedville, otherwise the Count D'Aubray, and one Donald Spey—all three accused of treasonable practices against the person and throne of his most gracious Majesty King George. Resistance is useless, and escape utterly impossible. Kindly tell those gentlemen that I have every desire to perform my most unpleasant duty in the least painful manner, and that I sincerely hope they will neither waste my time nor exhaust the slender patience of my troops."

"Not one of the persons you ask for are to be found in this house," was the answer to the officer's demand.

"Right, my good fellow," returned the trooper,

with the utmost *sang-froid;* "quite right! I do not
blame you for perverting the truth ; the cause is a
good one, and would justify more than lying ; but
allow me to observe that prevarication and delay
are alike useless.   I happen to know, on the best
possible authority, that those gentlemen are in or
about this house.   I want them, and I must have
them, even though I have to pull the building to
pieces and overhaul it stone by stone.   Here, Corporal Hughes, take half-a-dozen men with you, and
search the place from roof to basement ; knock
down all slight partitions, and break in wherever
you can detect a hollow sound."

At this moment Marley, the land-steward—whose
house the dragoons had passed on their way to
Balmston—arrived on the spot, apparently in great
terror and dismay.

"Oh, dear ! oh, dear !" he exclaimed, addressing
the officer in tones of well-affected grief, "have you
come to arrest my poor master ?"

"I have come for that purpose," said the other,
"and have sent six of my men to search, but your
fellows say he is not in the house."

Marley turned pale at this information, but on
second thoughts he considered this merely a *ruse*
on the part of the servants, and turning his eyes
heavenward he ejaculated, with well-seeming thank-
fulness, "God be praised !" and then seeing the
officer turn sharply round on him, he continued, in

whining tones, " Far be it from me, sir, to say I approve his fault. No! no! As a true and loyal subject of His Majesty King George—Heaven bless him!—I cannot do that ; but, sir, he was a good, kind-hearted master, and I cannot be otherwise than glad if he has escaped. Poor, unfortunate, misguided gentleman ! "

The officer, who was a man of sterling honour and integrity, was in nowise displeased to hear Marley utter those apparently kindly sentiments.

The steward mounted the steps, and taking one of the servants aside, he said, in a winning whisper—

" I trust you have them safely hid away, John."

" I don't know, Mr. Marley," answered the man ; " I don't think they are in the house at all. Mr. Max'ell's bed hasn't been slept in ; no more hasn't Miss Flora's, an' she wouldn't have gone into hidin' about the house. The dragoons ain't come after her, I expect ; she ain't been doin' no traitor work."

" Eh, what ! " interrupted Marley, gasping for breath, and turning red and pale alternately, " eh, what ! You think they have escaped? "

" Indeed I hope so," the man replied.

The six troopers, with Corporal Hughes, now returned from their fruitless search, and the latter announced the fact that they " could find nobody."

" Take six additional men to assist you," said the officer ; " begin at the bottom, and re-rummage every hole and corner till you come to the roof. My

instructions are to take them, and if they are here, I
will most assuredly do so."

Marley was almost beside himself.   He waited in
the most horrible suspense, hoping to hear the soldiers
announce their success.   Minute after minute went
slowly by, the noise of destruction kept going on,
but no trace of the fugitives could be found.   The
secret chamber and private staircase were in turn
discovered, and on the latter was found a small
golden brooch, which one of the female servants
declared to be the property of Miss Maxwell.

"Aye," said the officer, examining the trinket, "I
see how it is : they have had an inkling of this
morning's business, and have cleverly anticipated
us by decamping last night."

Marley was furious, and losing all presence of mind,
he exclaimed—

"My life on't, if you search the wood yonder you
will find them."

"Why, heyday, my man, what is this ? " exclaimed
the trooper, looking at the steward in utter astonishment.   "A few minutes ago you were praising God
for their escape, and now, methinks, you would gladly
chant a *Te Deum* for their capture."

Marley saw now that he had fatally committed
himself, but the two thousand guineas, and Flora
Maxwell's divine form, were only before his eyes.

"It is no matter, sir," he said, boldly, "what you
may think ; you are here, I take it, to do your duty."

"You are right," replied the officer, "and I am reminded that I have strangely forgot my duty as a soldier, in permitting my gallant fellows to become bricklayers' labourers."

"I tell you," shouted the steward frantically, "if you search the wood below, you will find them."

"Now, out upon you for a base, treacherous villain!" exclaimed the trooper, indignantly. "My instructions state that the information is on good authority, having been furnished from Balmston ; and I verily believe you to be the betrayer of your master, whether for the sake of the Government reward, or for the better concealment of your own peculations, is best known to yourself. Sergeant Sim," he continued, "take ten men and scour yon wood from end to end;" and calling for a light, he began to walk cooly before the front of the house smoking a cigar. In about half-an-hour Sergeant Sim and his troopers returned from the wood, after—as the reader already knows—an ineffectual search. Marley noted their arrival, and his features were now livid with rage and disappointment.

"Well," said the officer, "no success, Sim?"

"Not any, Cap'en," replied the man, touching his hat in military fashion.

"They've gone to Sunderland," said Marley, "and if you follow them up you will most assuredly capture them."

"My instructions," returned the Captain, with cold

dignity, " were to come to Balmston, and arrest three
persons on a charge of high treason.   I am thoroughly
satisfied those three persons are not in this house, nor
yet in the immediate neighbourhood, and my duty
having been faithfully discharged I now go back to
Newcastle.   But," he continued, as he vaulted lightly
on his steed, "there is one other thing, I should like
to do before my departure."

"What is that?" Marley asked, a pale gleam
of hope darting across his face.

"Why," replied the officer, "it would have
afforded me unlimited satisfaction to have had
the pleasure and the power of being able to string
you up to the highest branch of the tallest tree
in yonder wood for a dastardly traitor;" and
with a merry laugh he rode away, followed by his
company, leaving Marley stamping and shaking
his fist in ungovernable rage.   How long the
steward would have continued standing thus,
we cannot say, but on turning round he saw
slowly approaching him the whole of the male
servants belonging to the house.   Marley's first
idea was that they were coming to him for instructions, under their materially altered circumstances; but this notion was quickly abandoned
when he saw them form themselves into a crescent,
evidently with the design of overlapping both
his flanks.   They came towards him slowly yet
surely, and before he had time to think or act, he

found himself in the centre of the ring. Not a word was spoken by the menial band ; the whole of their business had an obvious pre-arrangement. Marley was lifted from the ground and carried— despite his struggles, threats, and imprecations—to the rear of the house, where he was properly soused over head and ears in the duck-pond, and left to scramble out as best he might.

Blinded alike by rage and muddy water, Marley struggled to land, and shaking himself after the manner of a Newfoundland dog under similar cir- cumstances, he held up his fist, while in a voice rendered hoarse by cold and passion, he cried out, " You scoundrels, I'll make you pay for this ! "

This intimation of the steward's kind intentions was received with groans and hisses, and one of the men cried out, "Come on, my lads, let's give the ugly traitor another duck !" The suggestion was received with a cheer, and Marley, seeing them advancing towards him, took to his heels, and never once relaxed his speed until his own door was reached. Muttering curses loud and deep, he proceeded to divest himself of his dripping raiment, and having procured a dry suit, he ordered out his horse.

"Fate is dead against me," he exclaimed, "but I may save myself yet. If I can effect their capture in Sunderland, where they have surely gone, I can still claim the Government reward for the French Count, and the two thousand guineas from James Maxwell."

James Maxwell! He little dreamt that the wintry sun, peering earthwards through the white, misty morning clouds, was at that same moment shedding its dim watery rays on the cold death face of his co-partner in treachery, lying still and lifeless in the heart of Coxgreen wood.

CHAPTER XVI.

"Was not this love indeed?"

—*Twelfth Night.*

AFTER watching with eager eye the good ship *Mary Ann* until her topmasts alone were visible from the pier, Mary Willis returned to her home. After a scanty dinner (for her appetite had deserted her) she took up her needle and began to ply it actively; but though her fingers were quick and nimble, her thoughts were more active still. They turned naturally to the fugitives she had promised to aid, and anon fastened themselves on the memory of Chedville.

Her meditations were indeed pleasant: her maiden fancy was most industriously engaged in airy architecture, and upreared a lovely castle, bright hope the foundation, and Peter Thornton the crown of the superstructure.

Imagination was still busy in the depiction of a happy future for poor Mary, when a loud knock, came to the door—so loud that mother and daughter were alike startled.

"Goodness gracious me!" Mrs. Willis exclaimed; "why, whoever can it be, Mary?"

"I'm sure I don't know, mother," Mary replied.

The widow, on reflection, came to the conclusion that the mystery might be effectually cleared up by answering the door, and after adjusting her cap, she undid the latch, and started back in astonishment, for there on the threshold stood five men, four of them evidently officers of justice.

The widow was too much amazed to speak, but Mary, who had followed her mother to the door, asked them politely what they wanted. The leader of the party, who was none other than the land-steward of Balmston, did not vouchsafe an answer to Mary's question, but turning to his companions, he said—

"Walk in, gentlemen, and then this young lady will find out what we want."

Acting on Marley's invitation, the posse entered the widow's kitchen, the steward locking the door after them, and coolly placing the key in his pocket.

"Now then, young woman," said one of the officers, "we'll tell you what we want. We're here in the name of the law. You've heard of 'the law and the prophets;' alongside the law, young female, the prophets is nowhere. In the name of the law we come here to look for traitors."

Mary Willis turned pale, and said, faintly, "You will find no traitors here."

"But, you see, we think differently, young woman," Marley observed, in his sternest manner, "and we are here to institute a strict search——"

"In the name of His Most Sacred Majesty King George, the Duke of Cumberland, and all the Royal Family—God bless 'em!" the officer interposed.

"Just so," said Marley; "we are here in the king's name. You have a young man by the name of Peter Thornton lodging with you, have you not?"

"Yes," Mary answered; "but he's not here. Thank Heaven! he has gone to sea."

Marley saw the red flush which for a moment overspread the girl's face, and, chuckling to himself, he muttered—

"So, so, I didn't expect this; I've got a master key to open the closest lock." And turning to the girl, he said—"Yes, my dear, that is so. We find he went to sea to-day in the *Mary Ann*, and also that he went alone. The companions of his flight from Balmston we find, on the best authority, were not with him in the vessel. It is a pity the villain has escaped!"

"You lie, sir!" exclaimed Mary Willis, the rich blood again suffusing her cheeks, and her eyes proudly flashing in anger. "You lie, sir; Peter Thornton is no villain!"

"Poor girl! poor girl!" said Marley, in well-assumed

14

tones of deep commiseration, "do you know who this Peter Thornton is?"

"Yes," answered the girl, "he is Peter Thornton."

"You are wrong; he is not, and has no claim whatever to the name. He is a very wealthy French Count, and a Jacobite, and has been in arms for the Pretender from June until within the last few days; and the Government now offer two hundred guineas for his apprehension." Mary grew pale; this was indeed something like truth; she had not seen him once in all that time.

"And what is more, my dear," Marley continued, fastening his eyes on the girl's pallid face, "he has been aiding and abetting the escape of another Jacobite—one Kenard Maxwell. We know they left the house of Maxwell last night, and that they were accompanied in their flight by Mr. Maxwell's daughter and servant. Their intention is to escape to France, and should they succeed in getting clear off, this same Count D'Aubray, *alias* Pierre Chedville, *alias* Peter Thornton, is to marry Miss Maxwell, and——God bless me, my dear young woman! what's the matter?"

He might well ask the question. Mary passed her hand across her brow, gazed wildly round the room, and sank in apparent lifelessness on the floor. The widow lifted the slight form from the ground, and placing her in a chair, she soon succeeded in restoring her child to consciousness.

"Now, my dear," said Marley, soothingly, when she had partially recovered, "don't take on like this, I beg of you. When it suits you to hear me, I will go on with my story. But don't hurry, my dear ; take your own time, and tell me when you are ready."

After a few moments Mary motioned with her hand for Marley to proceed.

"Well then," continued the steward, availing himself at once of the permission silently accorded, "as I was about to observe before this unpleasant interruption, this Thornton, or rather this French Count—that's a great title, my dear, almost equal to a duke in this country—came to Sunderland last night, or early this morning, in company with Kenard Maxwell, his daughter, and a Scotch servant, one Donald Spey, a rank born rebel. Now, we have seen the customs officer who was doing duty on board the *Mary Ann*, and this man gives us a full and true description of this same Thornton or Chedville. The officer confesses that at first he had some suspicion, but the Count gave his orders to the men in such a thorough seaman-like manner, that the man was completely deceived. Now, my dear, this officer most emphatically declares that no other person or persons proceeded to sea in the vessel, and the important question we are now called to solve is simply this—Where are Kenard Maxwell, Flora Maxwell, and Donald

Spey to be found? Now, my dear young woman, to the person able and willing to give me this information, I am prepared to pay the sum of one hundred guineas ; yes, my dear, one hundred guineas, in good and lawful money of Great Britain."

"Which aint to be grabbed every day for next to nothing, young woman," observed one of the officers. "Lor' bless you! a hundred guineas 'll bring the sweethearts buzzing round ye like honey bees round a full-blown flower on a summer's day."

Poor Mary Willis! what were her feelings as she sat in that chair!

"All hope is fled," she whispered to her poor, sad heart; "the dream of my life is indeed gone; heaven help me in this strait, and guide me aright! Aye, it is so—for the life of the father he will receive the hand of the daughter. But the father is in my power, his life is in my hands! If I give him up, how then? The daughter can never be his, for did he not assure me she would die of a broken heart? Do people die of broken hearts? I hope it is so, for there is calm, quiet rest in the grave. Shall I deliver up the father? No! a thousand times no! He loves this girl, and Mary Willis would give her life to save even a dog that Peter Thornton loved!"

She rose from her seat; her face was indeed pale, but calm and placid, like the waters of the lake when the wind, which erstwhile sent' the ripples dancing over its breast, has sunk down in peaceful slumber behind the hills.

"What you have told me," she said in quiet tones, addressing herself to Marley, "I have certainly listened to with great surprise, for Peter Thornton was known to me only as a poor sailor, earning his daily bread on the water. He came here to sleep last night as usual; he brought no one with him, and he left this morning to go to his vessel. You are at liberty to search the house."

Marley had been deceived; his master key had failed him at the first lock.

"Well," he said, "in spite of what you tell me, I do believe you know something of their place of concealment, and we must search the house. If it is found that you are in any way aiding and abetting their escape, I warn you, young woman, that you will be severely punished."

"The rooms are open; you can search where you will," the girl coldly replied.

"Yes," said Mrs. Willis, who now found her tongue, "you can search, and search, and search. We don't conceal no traitors here, and if you was to go down on your bare bended knees, and tell me Peter Thornton was a traitor, I wouldn't believe you; no, not if you was to take your Bible oath on't! There!"

Rooms, closets, cupboards, a press bed, and a

wardrobe were severally explored by Marley and his party.

"Well, they're not here, young woman," the steward admitted at last; "that fact cannot be denied. But if you do know where they are to be found, here in this bag are the hundred guineas, which I will put into your hands at once, if you will guide us to their place of concealment."

"If you were to give me a thousand I could not do it," she answered, "so that it is useless to talk further," and she turned coldly away.

When Marley and his companions were again outside the house, he said—

"I'll tell you what it is: in spite of all she says, I firmly believe that little girl knows more than she chooses to tell, and it would not be a bad idea to leave one of our men on the look out. If she leaves the house, let him follow her unobserved; and if he sees her in suspicious company, let him run at once to the Life Boat public-house, where we will wait him. If nothing happens after an hour's watch, you can send another man to relieve him."

.   .   .   .   .   .

Before the appointed time Mary Willis left the house, without shawl or bonnet, her head being simply covered with a silk handkerchief, and proceeded towards the house of Patsey Ovingham. It was now quite dark, and the girl, although she looked at intervals carefully round, was quite unconscious that her steps were closely followed by one of the officers placed on the watch by Marley.

When Mary entered Patsey's the man continued to walk slowly to and fro before the house.

"There aint nothin' suspicious so far," he said to himself, "but I'll see what sort of company she comes out with, and then I'll mark them down for a grab."

Meanwhile the girl went up to the bar, and said to Patsey in a whisper—

"I have been sent here by Mr. Thornton."

The landlady eyed Mary keenly and somewhat suspiciously for a moment, but there was something in the face of the girl which effectually banished her distrust; and saying, "All right, hinney," she preceded her up the stairs, and pointing to the door of one of the rooms, she added, "Go in; you will find the young lady there."

Mary opened the door indicated by Patsey's index finger, and stood for a moment on the threshold. Miss Maxwell was seated in a chair. Though still clad in Patsey's cotton gown, the peculiar head-dress worn by her on the night of their escape from Balmston was removed, and her long dark hair hung loosely down over her shoulders. Mary gazed in silent admiration on the beautiful girl before her, saying to herself, "No wonder! no wonder! how could he help loving her?" She then glided quietly into the room, and addressing Flora, she said,

"You are Miss Maxwell, I suppose?" Flora started; but gaining confidence by óne quick glance at Mary's frank face, she answered in the affirmative, and placing a chair, requested her to be seated.

"You have come," she said, "to conduct us to a certain place, and your name is Mary Willis?" Mary nodded her head. "Mr. Thornton," Flora continued, "places the greatest confidence in you, and from what he has told me, I have no hesitation in trusting in your hands what I love dearest and best in all the world—the life of my father."

"I am here to aid you, Miss Maxwell, and will sacrifice my own life for his safety if necessary. But I want to speak a few words to you on another subject. When you are safe in France, you will marry Mr. Thornton : is it not so?"

Flora's look expressed surprise and alarm.

"Who told you this?" she asked.

"A man who, with four others, was searching our house to-day for your father, and offering a hundred guineas reward for his apprehension. I nearly made up my mind to betray him."

"Oh, Heaven! for the reward?"

"No, lady, you do me wrong. I would never have touched it."

Flora looked at her in amazement.

"Listen to me, Miss Maxwell!" Mary continued, impressively. "From the first day Peter Thornton came to our house, I felt I loved him—aye better,

far better than he will ever be loved by you, though
I doubt not for one moment that you love him well,
and will make him happy; but I could have braved
even death itself to have had him put his arms
around me and say, 'Mary, I love you!' In wishing for his love, I was not presumptuous, lady. I
regarded him as a poor sailor, and as such, no unequal match for a lowly girl like myself, and I still
had hope that one day he might learn to love me.
Judge then of my dismay—picture to yourself, if you
can, the anguish of my poor heart—when I found
to-day that Peter Thornton, the poor mariner as I
thought him, was a French nobleman of great wealth,
and that he was pledged to you—that the gift of
your hand was the price of your father's liberty!
Oh! then, at that moment, when the bright hopes
so long treasured had fled, and I was left alone in
despair—then I saw in you a rival, and some demon
whispered to me, 'Betray the father, and the
daughter will never wed Peter Thornton.' "

"But," said Flora, kindly, "your better angel came
to your aid, my poor girl."

"No," replied Mary, "not so. I said, those who
love truly and well should think only of the happiness of those to whom their love is given. If he will
be happy with Miss Maxwell, it is my duty, by the
love I bear him, to secure that happiness—to suffer
bravely, to sacrifice contentment, bliss, and even life
for love."

Flora threw her arms round Mary's neck, and kissed her tenderly. "Those sentiments are truly noble, my poor girl," she said. "But did Monsieur D'Aubray ever give you reason to suppose that he entertained for you that affection which——? You know what I mean, Mary, better than I can express myself."

"No, no! I tell you, kind and tender as a brother might be to a sister has Peter Thornton been to me. If there had been one single spark of love glowing ever so dimly in his heart's core, I could have discovered it. When you are his wife, and are sitting with him by your own fireside in the far-off country to which you are going, you will tell him how he was loved by poor Mary Willis. There will be no harm in telling him this, for before that time the early spring flowers will be gently waving over my grave."

"No, no, my poor girl!" said Flora, the tears hanging like pearl-drops on her long, dark lashes; "you will yet live to be happy."

"Never, Miss Maxwell, never! You cannot love him as I do, or you would not speak thus. Come, lady," she added, with a strong attempt to be calm, "come; it is time for us to go. On my knees, while I have life, I will pray for you both; and when in yon bright and better world, I will pray unceasingly, for then I shall be nearer to Him whose mighty hand is all powerful to help. Come, lady, let me assist you." Saying this, she gathered in her hand the long tresses, and bound the handkerchief round Flora's head. They then proceeded down the stairs, and taking from the passage two fish trays placed there by Patsey, the two girls went out into the street.

The man by whom Mary Willis had been followed to the house was standing near the door, and as they passed him he peered keenly in the face of Miss Maxwell, while his own features were lit up with a truly gratified expression.

In utter ignorance of the man's presence, they went on for some short distance, and then came to a halt near the Fisherman's Row, and in a few moments they were joined by Mr. Maxwell and Donald, and the four proceeded in the direction of the sea-beach.

"Now," said Mary, in a low tone, "you must permit us two to walk on first, and if we should meet with anyone, do you leave us to encounter them, and do you get into shelter until they pass by, for should you be spoken to your voices would betray you at once."

They continued walking on until they reached a narrow road lying between two hills, and leading down to the sea-shore, when they heard voices, and the sound of footsteps evidently approaching them.

"They are fishermen just landed from their cobles," whispered Mary. "Keep close under the shadow of the bank, and leave them to me;" and the girl began to sing a verse of a well-known ballad in a clear voice—

> "Fower Colliers lay in Hendon Bay,
>   At anchor for the tide."

The two remaining lines were at once taken up by the fishermen, and came back to them on the breeze—

> "The *Saucy Jane* and the *Eden Main*,
>   The *Fox* and the *Rover's Bride*."

"Now, lasses, tak' care o' yoursells," said one of the men in passing.

"There's nee fear for us," Mary answered, with a laugh ; "wee dinnet get drunk like ye, Mattie Oliver."

This retort was evidently appreciated by the rest of the men, for their laughter could be still heard in the distance.   Maxwell and Donald came from under the bank, and followed the girls down to the beach. They arrived at length on the spot pointed out by Chedville, and taking their stand under the bank where the old battery frowned above them, they waited in anxious expectation the arrival of the boat from the *Mary Ann* which was to bear two of them to liberty.

They waited but a short time before their ears were saluted with a sound caused by the regular dip of oars, and Mary, after whispering to them to keep close, walked down to the water's edge. In a few minutes she returned.

"All right," she said, "the boat is ready. Come quickly."

The whole party moved down over the shingly beach, where they found Chedville waiting them on the strand, and the boat lying a few yards from the shore.

"Thank God, Miss Maxwell!" he said, taking Flora's hand, "a few minutes more will see your father in perfect safety."

"We owe you much indeed, Monsieur D'Aubray," Flora returned in whispered tones.

Chedville, with his usual forethought, had taken an exceedingly wise precaution in bringing the boat of the *Mary Ann* to the sea margin ; he had discreetly provided himself with a small kedge, and about twenty fathoms of two-inch line. The line being made fast to the kedge, the latter was thrown overboard some forty yards from the shore, and the small craft then carefully backed in to the beach. Even to those uninitiated in the mysteries of seamanship, the utility of this sage arrangement must be obvious ; for in the case of a sudden surprise, the boat could be quickly hauled out through the shore breakers into comparative safety, without shipping the oars. Flora took an affectionate farewell of poor Mary Willis, and was then carried by Chedville through the surf, and seated in the stern of the vessel. Kenard Maxwell and the faithful Donald waded out, and were assisted on board by the crew. The whole party, with the exception of D'Aubray, were now embarked, and the latter was standing close down to the water's edge, bidding a last and final adieu to the girl who so fondly and truly loved him, when his eyes were for an instant dazed by two bright musket flashes on the bank, just underneath the battery; and ere the loud reports were borne to his ear, Mary Willis had fallen seemingly lifeless in his arms.

"Great Heaven!" he exclaimed. "Mary, speak! are you hurt?"

"Yes, yes," she answered faintly, "to death; and it is best so; I can die happy now."

Chedville knew that the poor girl spoke the sad truth indeed, for he could feel the warm life blood streaming over his hands, and growing thick, clammy, and even cold between his fingers.

"O Mary! my poor girl," he muttered; "how dreadful!"

"Fly, Mr. Thornton," she said, yet more faintly. "Fly, and save yourself."

It was time indeed. He could now plainly hear the rapid fall of approaching footsteps; and a voice he knew to be Marley's cried out—

"On, my lads! Fifty guineas more if you take them alive."

The drowsy senses of the poor girl drank in the sounds and understood their meaning. Releasing herself by an almost superhuman effort from

Chedville's grasp, she stood for a moment upright and unsupported.

"Away!" she cried, pushing him from her, "away at once! My life for yours; you can not, you shall not let me die in vain!" As she uttered these words, she fell lifeless to the ground. Chedville knelt beside her, and placing his hand on her breast, knew that all was over. He rose, his teeth firmly clenched; then drawing forth a pistol, he looked towards his pursuers, and exclaimed, "Now to revenge thy death, my poor girl!" Then shouting to his crew, he said, "Haul out, my lads, ten yards further, and ship your oars."

Marley heard the voice, and cried, "Faster, faster! that's the Frenchman! On faster, or they will escape."

Chedville retreated slowly, with his face to his foes, till the coming wave washed his feet. The men were now close upon him—he could distinguish the outline of their figures in the darkness.

"Seize them," shouted Marley, as he bounded on, closely followed by another man, "seize them in the King's name."

Chedville allowed them to approach almost within arm's length, so fearful was he of throwing away his shot, and then exclaiming: "Die, villain, the death you have so long merited!" he raised his arm rapidly and fired. The ball crashed through Marley's skull, and the treacherous villain fell without a groan. Turning with the activity of thought, he hurled the now empty pistol with such terrific force and unerring aim at the other, that the man fell senseless to the ground ; then dashing into the water, he struck out for the boat, and laying hold of her stern, he shouted—

"Haul on the line, quick, hand over hand! So, that's well. Now, cut from the kedge, and pull for your lives !"

The morning sun, red as the blood shed on the past night, rose slowly above the blue line of ocean, as the *Mary Ann* held on her southward course. The "look-out," with hand-shaded eye, was standing near the knight-heads ; the helmsman's hand grasped the tiller, moving it slightly to starboard or to port at intervals. But stay, there are two more figures on the deck of the little craft. Chedville and Flora Maxwell are standing there on the weather side, away off the main rigging ; his arm encircles her slender waist, and her head reclines on his breast. Hist ! what do they say?

"Banish all fear, dearest Flora ; your father is now as safe as though he stood on French soil."

"Yes, Pierre, I feel that it is so, but another mighty grief gives birth to these tears ; old Elspeth spoke truly—'Fate is fixed, you must even dree your weird, and wade through her poor heart's best blood to your own happiness !'"

TALES AND BALLADS OF WEARSIDE,

SOMETHING ABOUT THE OLD WEAR KEELMEN.

IN the year 1855 I was a young man, just turned one-and-twenty, my hat covering my family and responsibilities. At this particular period of my life I was not, as now, the owner of a good little wife and six substantial pledges of her affection. At the time of which I write my home comforts were as pleasurable as those of most young men. I lived with my mother, who was a widow with a moderate competency, and being an only child, ruled supreme in the maternal household.

Coming home from business one evening in the month of June, in this same year of grace 1855, and sitting down to tea in our cosy back-parlour, my mother said—

"What d'ye think, Tom? Here's a letter from your uncle Andrew; he's coming down here for a fortnight."

This was indeed a surprise. Uncle Andrew was

the eldest brother of my maternal relative; and being principal owner of a large London coal-wharf, and in a good pecuniary position, he was, as a matter of course, looked up to with respect, intermingled with awe, by the rest of the family. Uncle Andrew, although a native of the banks of the Wear, had not visited the scenes of his youth and early manhood for more than thirty-five years; and to find that he had taken this fancy into his head was certainly a matter of surprise both to my mother and myself.

In his earlier days my uncle held an office of trust and importance at the Low Lambton Staiths, in the immediate neighbourhood of which he first saw the light. This office he relinquished for a situation in London, his employer being a coal merchant of some position. After a few years had passed away, his diligent attention to business was rewarded with a partnership in the concern, and now he was, at the age of seventy-two, the principal owner of a large coal-wharf, and the envied possessor of a large sum of money.

Three days after that on which my mother received his letter, Uncle Andrew arrived in Sunderland, and expressed his surprise at the changes since the time he had walked its streets in the flush of life and the prime of manhood. The docks, the harbour, and the town improvements occupied his attention for nearly a week. One evening he said—

"Thomas, can you spare a day from business—say to-morrow or next day?"

"I can spare to-morrow, uncle, if you wish it," I replied.

"Well, I do, then," said he. "There's a full moon

to-day, and the tide will flow about four o'clock to-morrow afternoon on the bar; and as I hear you're a bit of a hand at boat-rowing, I want you to get a small boat and row me up as far as Lambton Castle. I haven't seen the upper reaches of the river, Tom, for nigh forty years."

Next day, about quarter-flood, we both started away from Hardcastle's Slip in a handy little boat. At the commencement of our voyage my uncle began to regard the altered appearance of things in no very pleasant light. Saw-mills, chemical works, iron works, sending forth from their chimneys sluggish, lazy-looking columns of dense smoke; the incessant ring of the caulking-mallet, accompanied by the more decisive tap, tap of the maul, seemed to fill Andrew's soul with disgust.

"Ah, Thomas, my lad," he said seriously, "what a change is here! Why, I remember when from the upper part of Deptford to the Bird-and-Bush, a distance of seven miles and a-half good, there wasn't a single manufactory, and only one or two small ships building about Hylton; and now here's nothing but noise and smoke as we go along. By-the-way, Tom, just where we are now brings to my mind a story about a keelman. He had come down from the staith, and had his full allowance of beer before he left Chater's Heugh. When he got down here to the low part of Pallion, his senses were rather beclouded with the liquor; and it being a still night, with a nice gentle air of wind from the south, the dead bell at Bishopwearmouth Church began to toll. Joaney Patchet—that was the keelman's name—heard the first sound distinctly, and thinking it was the church clock, and being anxious about the time, he began to count the strokes.   He counted up to seven-and-twenty, and then exclaimed in amazement—'Why, bliss my sowl and body, aw've niver been o' the watter at see much a'clock since aw went iv the keels!''

I laughed heartily at this, when my uncle said—

"Ah, look, Tom, there's Hylton Castle seems to be going pretty much to ruin.   That was no doubt a grand place, Tom, when the barons were all in their glory.   They were like monarchs in the olden time ; each of the barons used to keep a fool, a fashion with our old nobility, Tom, but it's gone out of use— not that there's any scarcity of fools ; heaven knows they're plentiful enough !   You see that clump of trees down beside the river's edge ? "

" Yes," I observed.

" Well," continued my uncle, " one day one of the barons was walking among the trees, and the fool happens to come down to the water-side.   The baron saw the fool, but the fool couldn't see the baron, because he was hidden by the leaves and the thick growth of underwood.   So the baron cries out, in a feigned voice, " Holloa ! "   Then the fool looks round, and he says, " Holloa ! "   Then the baron cries out again, " Whose fool are you ? "   To which question the fool replied : " I'm Baron Hylton's fool ; whose fool are you ? "

The recollection of this old story seemed to afford Andrew the greatest satisfaction.   When we had rowed on a little further, something ahead caught the watchful eye of my uncle.

" Pull away, Thomas," he exclaimed, " there's the

tide keels going through Stotten ; three, four, five—as I live there's only five of them ! Why, I've seen a hundred and twenty keels going up in one tide, all in cluster, like a swarm of bees. Ah dear me ! what a falling off! So much for railways and the march of intellect."

" You seem to forget, uncle," I observed, " that even your one hundred and twenty keels of eight chaldrons each would be of very little service with our present coal export. Why, sir, only last week a large American vessel, called the *Minihaha*, was load with nearly one hundred keels of coals in less than two days ; and she was only one of more than a dozen load in the same time."

" True, Thomas," he answered, " I grant you all this ; but if, like me, you had known the keelmen in the heyday of their prosperity, you would be inclined to drop a tear to the memory of their departed glory. Why, sir, in 1800 the keelmen were everybody. They were, in fact, the Missis Grundy of Sunderland social life. And if the grocer meditated a rise in flour, the greengrocer an advance in the price of potatoes, or the butcher had an intention to put up the price of beef, the question was, 'What will the keelmen say?' sometimes, however, varied by the still more important question 'What will the keelmen do?' Why, I remember on one occasion when the butchers advanced the price of meat, the infuriated keelmen almost totally destroyed the shambles, which at that time stood in Sunderland High Street."

We now passed Hylton ferry, and were gliding smoothly along between the high wooded banks of Offerton Heugh; this spot being left, even in 1855, undisturbed by the foot of commercial enterprise, seemed to afford the greatest pleasure to my uncle, chasing away the dusky clouds which had hitherto obscured the long past.

"You see those three houses, Tom, at the top of the heugh on the south side?"

"Yes," I answered.

"When I was a young man, the occupants of those houses made their living entirely by *hailing*."

" By what ? "

" By *hailing*."

" And what's *hailing* ? "

"Why, you see, when a string of keels were coming up rather late in the tide, or when the wind was northerly, or north-west, and blowing down this ratch, the keelmen took *hailers*."

" And what did the *hailers* do ? "

" All the keels were made fast together, and a long two-and-a-half or three inch line was passed ashore from the first keel, and men, women, and children laid hold on't with both hands, and letting the rope lie over their right shoulders, away they went like a jolly long team of canal track horses; and on some occasions they would *hail* the keels in this manner right up to the Low Lambton staith."

"Rather a laborious employment," I remarked, " especially for women and children."

"Very," replied my uncle, " but in those days a very profitable one. But casting the coals from the keels into the ships at Sunderland was about the most laborious work I ever saw. Eight men would go into a keel, strip off every article of clothing excepting their flannel drawers, stockings, and shoes, and from the commencement to the finish, each man's shovel would be in full play.

"I remember a man—his name, I believe, was Tom Baxter. On this occasion he had commenced to cast at two o'clock in the morning, and by half-past seven he had assisted to discharge three keels. At eight o'clock another keel was ready to start with, and Baxter was again going in with his gang, but just before commencing, another man who had not worked at all that morning suggested that, as Tom had already been in for three casts, he should lie out, and allow him (the man) to go into this keel. Tom, who was a greedy fellow and remarkably keen for money, strongly objected to this, and began to cast again like a steam engine. When the keel was about half discharged, Tom was observed to stagger, and fall back on the coals; the others immediately went to his assistance, lifted him up— and found him dead."

When my scientific rowing, considerably aided of course by a strong flood tide, had taken us past Cox-green to Low Lambton, we landed, and at a small public-house recruited and cheered our inward man with a bottle of stout.

"You see No. 1 spout, Tom, my boy?" This after the first glass of stout.

"I remember a good joke one of my fillers, John Watson, once played there. You must know there was a standing rule at the staiths—first come first served. As the keels arrived up, they came on turn in the same order, unless there was what was called a tie, that is two keels tied together, one towing astern of the other, and the two keelmen using their sets on the port and starboard gunwales of the first keel; when this occurred, there was then a toss-up for turn.

"Well, one day a man known by the name of Bobby Gowlan' comes puoying his keel up a little before high water, considerably in advance of the others; and mooring her under No. 1, he comes ashore and says to John Watson, in his own peculiar phraseology, 'Aw say, Joney, giv a luck ti my keel wi' the hand, an' see that neebody gets my turn, till aw gan an' get a quairt.'

"Now Bobby's keel had been foul of a vessel in the harbour some time previously, and the upper portion of her stem had been partially knocked away. Bobby was either too poor, too greedy, or too indolent to get it repaired, and it was a distinguishing mark by which his keel was known all over the river.

"As soon as Gowlan' was gone, John Watson, my filler, who was always a bit of a wag, poor fellow, slips down into the clay-hole, and coming back with a large lump, he goes on board Bobby's keel and proceeds to repair the stem. After it was built up quite perfect with the clay, Watson sprinkled it well with coal dust, and the appearance of the craft, as may be expected, was very much altered for the better.

"The other keels came up, and those who arrived first secured the vacant berths, while the remainder dropped their anchors off-side.

"By-and-by Gowlan' comes walking down the quay, with his pipe in his mouth, and his hands in the pockets of his short jacket. Seeing a keel under No. 1 spout without the characteristic feature his eyes had been so long accustomed to look upon, he ejected from his lips a volume of tobacco smoke and an ugly oath at the same time.

"'Wees gettin my turn?'" he exclaimed. 'Here's a consawn, shovin' my keel out an' puttin' his in! Aw niver heard tell ov such a thing since aw was boan o' my mother; its piracy o' the high seas, nowt better—nowt better! Why it's far warse—stealing a man's turn iv open dayleet! Eff he thinks aw'se a fule, he's a lang way wrang, aw'll seun let him knaw!'

"Bobby was now bankrupt in words, and proceeded to express his indignation in deeds. Rushing to the spot where the shore ropes were made fast, he cast them off, and looked on, with that fiendish sort of joy which gratified revenge always engenders, at *his own* keel drifting away down on the ebb tide, and bumping against all the obstacles that lay in her way."

"I remember another keelman, who was at the same time in our work," resumed my uncle, lighting his pipe; "his name was Cuddy Taylor, and a queer eccentric fellow he was. If anybody told a wonderful story, Cuddy was always able to overtop it.

"I remember a conversation amongst the keelmen at staith one day, about a large turnip which one of them had seen. After listening, Cuddy observed that 'the turmot was nee dout a big un; but it was nowt like the Waldridge turmots. When aw was a bit of a lad,' he continued, 'Squire Eden had on'y three turmots iv a five yacker field, an' the middle one grew that big it shoved the t'other two clean ower the dyke!' Cuddy being once too

late from staith to save water down to Sunderland,
intended to bring up at the top of Offerton Heugh,
and accordingly let go his anchor; but the keel
having considerable way, and the cable coming
suddenly taunt, it snapped, and Cuddy's anchor was
lost. He glanced at both sides of the river and on
the south bank he observed a cow quietly grazing.

"'Aye,' he muttered to himself, 'that's a good
mark; the hanker's reet abreest o' that cow, an'
varry near the middle o' the river. Aw'll get it easy
temoan.'

"Next day, at low water, Cuddy was up to look for
his anchor, but to his surprise and consternation his
mark was no longer there; the cow had evidently
migrated to fields and pastures new, and poor Cuddy
sustained a loss, although he at the same time gained
a certain amount of worldly wisdom, for he swore on
the spot that 'he wad niver tak' a mark biv another
cow as lang as iver he lived.'"

After we had disposed of two large bottles of stout,
and finished our pipes, we re-embarked in the frail craft,
and passing under the Victoria Bridge up by Pensher
Staith, Biddick, and Fatfield, finally arrived at Lambton Old Bridge, where we had an excellent view of
the castle. During the passage up every object of
interest was carefully noted by my uncle, and the
sight of the Worm Hill behind the Biddick Inn
procured for me a recital of the famous legend.

"I'll tell you what it is, Tom," said my uncle, as I
lay on my oars taking a survey of the magnificent
building and grounds, "there's very little water here
now-a-days."

"You're right," I replied; "there's hardly enough

for a small boat at spring-tides in some places. Was there a greater depth in your younger days?"

"Was there? I should think so. Why, I remember when I was a young man there were coal-staiths at Picktree, a great deal further up than this, and keels used to go up regularly to load."

"Indeed!" I said.

"Oh, yes, it's a fact, Tom. You've heard of Picktree? that's where Elsie Marley lived."

"Elsie Marley?" I asked. "What Elsie Marley?"

"Why," replied my uncle, chanting—

'The wife that sells the barley, honey;
That lost her pocket an' all her money,
Abacker the bush i' the garden, honey.'"

"Pooh! nonsense," I said; "Elsie Marley was a Scotchwoman."

"A what?" cried out my uncle; "a Scotchwoman! Who told you that?"

"Sir Walter Scott," I replied.

"Sir Walter Scott be blowed!" he returned, contemptuously. "Why, she kept a public-house at Picktree; my grandfather used to frequent it regularly when she was alive."

"Nay, nay," I said, mildly, "that cannot be. Scott introduces the ballad of Elsie Marley in the *Fortunes of Nigel*, and puts it into the mouth of one Richie Moniplies, an eccentric Scotch servant; and the incidents recorded in this same book are supposed to be in the reign of James the First, and this wise monarch left the world, very much against his will, in 1624, two hundred and thirty-one years since. Now, sir, do you think that a man like Scott would have introduced this particular ballad into this particular book unless he had some good solid reason to suppose that it was as old as the time of which he wrote?"

"I don't care a single pin about Sir Walter Scott. I know where Elsie Marley lived, and when she died."

"But, uncle, Richie Moniplies, while excusing himself to Nigel for having indulged in 'potations pottle deep,' says—'I crushed a quart with that jolly boy, Jenkin, as they call the 'prentice; and that was out of mere acknowledgment of his former kindness. I own that I moreover sung the good old song of Elsie Marley so as they never heard it chanted in their lives—

> 'Oh, de ye ken Elsie Marley, honey;
> The wife that sells the barley, honey;
> For Elsie Marley's grown sae fine,
> She winna get up ti feed the swine.'"

Here my uncle broke in with—

> "An' lies iv her bed till half-past nine;
> Oh, lazy Elsie Marley."

"I tell you, Tom," he continued, "as I said before, I don't care what Sir Walter Scott supposed, nor what he didn't suppose. Elsie Marley is a purely local character, and kept a public-house at Picktree, chiefly patronised by the Lambton pitmen. Why, sir, the ballad itself bears out the fact—

> 'Elsie Marley wore a straw hat,
> But now she's gettin' a velvet cap,
> An' she may thenk Lambton's cheps for that.'

What does that mean, sir? what does that mean?

Is it likely, think you, that any Scotchwoman, living before the time, or even in the time, of James the First, would get a velvet cap out of Lambton's cheps ? I tell you, Tom, Elsie Marley was born at Picktree, lived all her life at Picktree, and coming down the water-side from Chester, when she—

'Was na fou but just had plenty,'

she fell into the river, and was drowned near Picktree, on the fifth day of August 1768. There now, I know it and can prove it."

Putting our boat's nose down stream, we came to Biddick, and going ashore at the inn there, we stayed a short time ; the strong ebb-tide assisted our progress considerably, and we arrived at Sunderland about nine o'clock in the evening.

While passing down the Rack, my uncle called my attention to a particular spot.

" There, Thomas," he said, " that's where the first coal staiths were erected at Sunderland. They were put up by Mr. Nesham, a large coalowner, in 1815 ; but the keelmen and casters, resenting this innovation, assembled *en masse* on the 22nd of March, and pulled them to the ground."

Late at night, when we were sitting together smoking our last pipe before retiring to rest, my uncle said—

" Thomas, do you know, I feel as if I had discharged a duty to-day. Visiting the scenes of my boyhood has had a wonderful effect on me ; pleasant memories have awoke within me as it were from the dead, and I have felt myself nearer to my departed kindred and friends than I have ever been since the time I followed their mortal remains to Pensher churchyard. When your own hair, Tom, is silvered over with the frosts of three score and twelve years, you will understand this feeling better. It is a pleasant thing for an old man, after an absence of many long years, to stand on the spot where he gambolled, an innocent child; to think of the playmates of his youth, and the friends of his early manhood, gone before on the long, long journey, and to be able to say with a fervent, thankful heart, 'The time of our re-union is drawing nigh;' to feel no terror at the approach of Death, but to almost wish for his coming; to look upon himself as a well-ripened sheaf, ready and willing to be gathered into the great garner, there to await the advent of the Lord of the Harvest."

AUNT TICKETTY.

ONE fine morning in the month of June, a good many years ago, when the rising sun was darting his glad rays on the water, causing the placid bosom of Hendon bay to sparkle with golden light, a collier brig was seen approaching Sunderland harbour. The brig was under the charge of a well known pilot, who could handle her like a toy, and she was brought safely over the bar, and up as far as Hardcastle's slip, where she was moored to the buoys. While the vessel was being made fast with the hawser chains, the pilot was asked in the customary manner, by the skipper, to step into the cabin for the twofold purpose of receiving his pilotage-money and refreshing his inner man with a drop of "something short." Pocketing the foy, and lifting the glass to his lips with "Thank ye, sir, here's yer varry good hilth," the pilot proceeded to gaze with wrapt attention on an old-fashioned and curiously-made chair which stood in the cabin. After regarding it for some time with the deepest attention, he said, "That's a queer awd chair ye've gettin' thare, maister."

"Yes," replied the skipper; "that chair is about two hundred years old."

"Bliss us all! ye dinnot say see."

"Oh, yes," returned the captain, "it's quite a fact, I assure you. It's one of the Louis Quatorze pattern. I bought it in Hamburg especially on account of its *antiquity*."

"Indeed, sir," said the pilot, as he finished his glass, slightly mystified rather than enlightened by the captain's lucid explanation, and proceeded to quit the cabin, having been told to send down his partner, who was doing duty in the coble, to get a glass.

The invitation given by the pilot savoured more of pantomime than of words : it consisted of "Geodie," and an expressive jerk of the left thumb over the left shoulder in the direction of the cabin. This was as plain or plainer to "Geodie" than the most elaborately-worded invitation would have been, and he was up the side, along the deck, and into the cabin in a jiffey, while the pilot walked forward to see that the crew had made the hawser chain properly fast to the buoy. As he came aft again, he saw with marked astonishment his mate " Geodie " emerging from the companion with the old-fashioned chair in his possession.

" Halloa!" the pilot exclaimed, "what are ye gawn ti' dee wi' that?"

" Aw'se gawn ti tak't tiv the maister's house."

" Where?"

" Ti the maister's house iv Dee Arcy Tarrace ; he's gien us a shillin' for ti tak't up."

" Ye've meyd a mistake, Geodie ; it hesn't ti gan tiv his house. Ye'd better ax him ageyn."

" Nut mee," replied Geodie ; " he tell'd us plain enough, wiv his awn mouth."

" Varry weel, my man," continued the pilot, sententiously, "dee yer àwn wey; but aw tell ye, ye're wrang. He tell'd me quite a different story iv the cabin ; he said he'd bowt it iv Hamburg, frev a chap they call Lewis Catall Patten, an' he gat it spesshally for his Aunt Ticketty ; an' that's where it'll let te gan, ye'll see eff it hesn't."

THE PILOT POET.

FROM all branches of our native industries poets, rhymesters, and ballad makers have from time to time emerged.

" Good old Jeff" (Chaucer) was a lawyer in 1350. We really do not know whether the law was considered a profession or an industry in the middle of the fourteenth century, but this we can say—it is unquestionably one of the most industrial industries in Sunderland at the present moment. Christopher Marlowe, born 1564, at Canterbury, served some little time learning to make shoes. William Shakespeare, who was born two months after Marlowe, was a wool-comber or carder. " Rare Ben Jonson " was a bricklayer ; Herrick, his companion, was a goldsmith's apprentice before he " bore up " for the church. Matthew Prior was a waiter in the house of his uncle, " The Rummer Tavern," Charing Cross. Mark Akenside assisted his father, a butcher, in Newcastle. James Hogg was a shepherd. Wither, Beattie, Burns, and Bloomfield were farmer lads. But why go on ? It is left for us, and on ourselves alone devolves the pleasing task of bringing forth from a long obscure repose some of the unpublished lines of the only poet ever known to spring out of the ranks of that hardy, daring race—the Sunderland Pilots. The poet (whose name we forbear to mention, in order that his descendants may not become vain of his accomplishments) carried his rhyming propensities into his every-day life, and even his business conversation was not merely garnished with, but absolutely carried on in rough, ready, and uneven-metered versification.

The divine spirit of poesy slumbered in the brain of the pilot for some time, and was only called into active life by a certain event—or rather double event, for his wife (who, by the way, was the mother of a fine little daughter) went a little out of the usual course the second time, and presented her husband with two fine healthy boys at once.

When the result was communicated to the father,

16

he ran out of the house, through the Hat Case into Silver Street, and rushing into the room occupied by one of his married sisters, exclaimed—

> " The Lord forgie me all me sins !
> Our Bessy's browt ti bed wi' twins."

This was his first known attempt at rhyme ; the poetic shell had burst, and from that day forward the nine sister goddesses took him under their own especial care.

One day this original fell athwarthawse of a west-country skipper, who also, by a remarkable coincidence, proved to be an inveterate rhymer. It happened (as Arty Ward says) "thusly":—A small brig was seen at a considerable distance standing in for Sunderland roads, and the tide being at the flood, the poet-pilot and his partner entered their coble, and rowing down over the bar, proceeded with a long, measured stroke in the direction of the vessel. After some considerable time the brig was reached, and putting the coble alongside, the poet was soon on deck, while the frail craft in which his partner remained was made fast with a line, and dropped astern. To the boy standing at the gangway the disciple of Homer put the following question—

> " My little man, just tell to me
> What yer maister's name may be."

The boy having replied that it was Gowdy, the pilot-poet, walking aft, addressed the captain, who was steering, and the following rare and racy rhythmical dialogue began—

PILOT:

> " Now, ye're a man aw'se proud to see !
> Mister Gowdy, what's the foy to be ? "

SKIPPER:

> " Well, pilot, if you had your way,
> What would your conscience let you say ? "

PILOT:

> " One pund one is all aw wish,
> An' a bit o' beef iv the cobbel dish."

SKIPPER:

> " Fifteen shillings, you'll understand,
> Is all I give for Sunderland."

PILOT (pleadingly):

> " Fifteen shillings ! disn't thou think sham,
> When we've rowed see monny miles frae hyem ? "

SKIPPER (with dignified firmness):

> " Fifteen shillings ; I'll pay no more ;
> If you don't like it, go ashore."

PILOT (indignantly waving to partner):

> " Haul up the cobbel ; we winnot stop,
> But we'll row tiv suth'ard till our hands they drop."

SKIPPER (looking over port-quarter as the coble is going away south):

> " You'd better change your mind, old boy,
> And take the fifteen shillings foy."

The PILOT-POET (holding up his hand by way of emphasis):

> " Eff others likes ti tak't they may,
> Aw'se off ti suth'ard, so good day ;
> Aw'se nut like Esau, Mister Gowdy,
> Ti sell my buthreet for a crowdie."

THE SILK UMBRELLA.

SUNDERLAND shipwright took unto himself a wife, but, alas! like the Moor of Venice, he "loved not wisely, but too well." The lady he saw fit to endow with his name and worldly goods was passing fair and truly virtuous—two estimable qualities in a woman ; but to the sorrow and extreme regret of the husband, he found she either knew nothing of the duties of a housewife, or didn't care two straws about performing them. Poor Alick (his godfathers and godmothers had given him the name of Alexander) saw he had made a mistake before the honeymoon was half over ; badly cooked victuals, a slovenly house, and an utter —nay, almost studied—neglect of his work-day apparel, induced him to the belief that, by the exercise of ordinary judgment, he might have done better.

One evening, after his tea, he dressed himself in his best, and before going out he said to the partner of his somewhat equivocal joys—" Jinny, aw'se gawn tiv the lodge to neet; an' while aw'se away aw wish thou wad set some buttons o' my fustain trousers ; aw've telled ye about them till aw'se fairly tired, an' aw've had them tied up all day wi've pieces o' spunyarn. Now, Jinny, aw've myed my mind up, eff them buttons isn't on ti neet, aw'll just gan ti wark iv the morning wi my best black suit;" and with this he marched out of the house in manifest wrath. Next morning his trousers were just in the same condition —not a button sewn on, not a stitch put in. Alick threw them from him with an oath, and proceeded leisurely to don his Sunday suit of superfine black, omitting nothing, from the patent leather boots to the " long-sleeved hat." After being thoroughly dressed he awoke his wife. " Now, Jinny," he said, " aw tell'd ye what aw wad dee, an' aw intend ti di'd. What hev ye to say for yersel ?" Jinny was probably something like the famous parrot, if she thought a great deal she said nothing ; and Alick marched forth to his daily labour ; but when half-way down the stairs his steps were arrested by the sound of her voice—" Alick, come back !" " Ah, ah !" he ejaculated ; " aw thowt this dodge wad fetch ye, awd lass ; ye're coming tee, are ye ?" He went back into the room with a triumphant smile on his face, a smile which would have becomingly illuminated the features of the Macedonian conqueror whose name he bore. " Now, then," he exclaimed, as he entered the room, " what d'ye want now, eh ?" The wife of his bosom suffered her eyes to fall upon him for a single moment ; then pointing languidly to one corner of the room, without so much as raising her head from the pillow, she said, in a voice which, for even calmness and placidity, drove him almost to madness, " Alick, thou's forgettin' thy silk umberella ! "

A HEAVENLY RACE.

TOMMY S. was by birth a Yorkshireman ; Tommy S. in business was a vendor of coals in the streets of Sunderland, some forty years since ; Tommy S. in religion was a prominent member of the Free Church, or Tabernacle folk, having joined that body immediately after its exodus out of the bonds of Wesleyanism. Tommy's horse seemed to have been reared in the school of saintly piety, for its attenuated appearance indicated spiritual rather than bodily existence. Tommy, unlike a vast number of the "unco guid an' rigidly righteous," did not doff his religion with his Sunday clothes, but carried his piety round about the town with his coal cart; and he has often been heard chanting a revival hymn and pausing between lines to recommend his wares to the general public, thus :—

" The gospel ship has long been sailing—(*Coals !*)
   Bound for Canaan's peaceful shore—(*Coals !*)
Thousands now are sailing in her—(*Coals !*)
   Yet there's room for thousands more."—(*Lambton Primrose !*)

Tommy was remarkably fond of scripture quotations, and his prayers were sometimes made up by a string of them, not, however, always accurately rendered. One favourite quotation of Tommy's was from the First Corinthians : "If after the manner of men I have fought with beasts at Ephesus ;" but to the last day of his life he persisted in giving it thus : " If after the manner o' men I've fou't wi' beasts an' elephants."

On one occasion Tommy was riding his horse up Durham Lane, one fine evening in the month of June, and on the day preceding that on which the "cup" was to be run for on Newcastle Moor. Tommy, who was taking his horse out for the express purpose of indulging this representative of the Rozinante family in a gratis grass feed by the road-side, was met by a wag to whom he was apparently well known.

"Halloa!" he exclaimed, looking critically at the bag of bones bestrode by Tommy, "are you going to the races?"

"I'se allus at the races," Tommy replied, with severe dignity; "I'se allus at the races. I've been runnin' a race every day for't last twenty years; but it's nut for a gowlden cup—no, no; nor yet for a silver waggon. Praise the Lord! it's for a crown o' glory, an' it's hingin' o' top o't winnin' post for me, as seun as I get in; an' if I indure ti' the end, I'll win't an' weer't. Hallelujah! gee up, meer"—and Tommy, to borrow a phrase from old John Bunyan, "went on his way rejoicing."

DIVN'T YE KNAW HE'S IV OUR BOX?

THE permanent good resulting from the formation of friendly societies is incalculable; they have been the means of infusing a spirit of thrift and providence into the minds and hearts of by far the major part of the working-men of this country, and Parliament has not been slow to recognise this as an incontrovertible fact, although at the same time it may be said, with a great deal of truth, that legislation has not done so much for friendly orders as might, or rather should, have been done.

Many years ago, when Forester, Oddfellow, and

Druid societies were almost unknown in this locality, the want of them was inadequately provided for by what was called " The Yearly Box." This was invariably held at a public-house, the landlord kindly acting as treasurer in consideration of a certain amount being deducted from each member's subscription for drink. It was a matter of little consequence to the landlord whether the whole of the members attended the meetings or not; those who failed to attend forwarded by some means their box monies, and if twenty subscriptions were paid, and there were only five members present, the five had the glorious privilege of imbibing the entire quantity which would have been consumed by the whole twenty members under other circumstances. Thus, as may be seen, a man had the chance of being able to get himself blissfully intoxicated on his own threepence; and this not unfrequently happened where the majority of the members were seafaring people.

The yearly box was (and is yet, for I believe that one or two still drag out a miserable existence) an insecure investment. It terminated yearly, and if there was any balance after the sick, death money, and other expenses were paid, this balance was divided amongst members in equal proportions.

A new box was then commenced, but if, as it often did happen, the box had been, to use the common term, " heavily laid on " during the past year, a lot of the younger members would back out, and the remainder being unable to carry it on by themselves, it would of necessity collapse; and in this case it would not be without the bounds of possibility to suppose that a member who had made his regular payments for a period of six or seven years previous to its finally smashing up, might find himself on a bed of sickness the very next week, with the bitter knowledge forced upon him that his six or seven years' contributions to the yearly box might just as well have been throwh into the sea. The payments out of this fund ran something like five shillings per week sick money, one pound on the death of a member's child, two pounds on the death of his wife, and three—sometimes four—pounds on the death of a member himself.

Many years ago, when the antiquated yearly box was more the rule than the exception, a mason and a shipwright went off into the roads in a small boat to fish. Returning to the harbour, they encountered two or three rollers on the bar, and the boat unfortunately getting athwart, was upset, and the two piscatorial adventurers were thrown into the water. Having a slight theoretical knowledge of swimming, they struck out in opposite directions.

A pilot standing on the pier hailed a pilot coble just coming to the bar, and directed the attention of the man on board to the men in the water. He began to pull vigorously towards the mason, when he was hailed by his friend on the pier with—" Nut him, Geodie, nut him ; save the tother one fust."

Geodie rested on his oars for an instant, and looking up to the pier, exclaimed—" What matter dis't mak' which one aw save fust ? "

" What matter!" shouted the other almost frantically —" it mak's all the matter iv the wurld ; divn't ye knaw that carpenter chap's iv our box ! "

VIRGIN MARY SOUP.

SOME forty years ago, when the Inquisition was all-powerful in Italy, a Sunderland brig was discharging a cargo of coals at the port of Leghorn, and there being a holiday, the whole of the crew, with the exception of the mate and the cabîn-boy, had shore liberty. They wandered up and down the streets, and through the squares of the city ; at length, late in the day, they entered a large church or cathedral, and while examining the inside of the building their attention was attracted to a small image of the Virgin in pure gold.

" By gox ! " exclaimed one of them, " what a lot o' sovereigns that wad mak'."

" Let's tak't away," said another ; " there's not a liven' soul about."

A hurried consultation was held, and the lady finally accompanied them on board their vessel without her consent being asked. At the evening service in the church the Virgin was missed from her pedestal, and the more ignorant of the people assembled were under the impression that she had walked off in displeasure for some cause unknown to them. The monks and priests, however, upon whom the superstition of religion had but a feeble hold, came to a very different conclusion, and a search for the missing Virgin was instantly instituted.

" From information received," to quote Bobby XY, No. 22, the visit of the sailors to the church was known to the officers of the Inquisition, and next morning every vessel in the harbour of Leghorn was thoroughly rummaged.

The boat going from ship to ship with a number of armed men on board was soon perceived by the crew on board the brig, and they speedily came to the conclusion that the Virgin Mary was being earnestly inquired after, and they were in an awful state of consternation.

" If they find the image aboard of us," said one of them, " we'll niver see nayther wife nor bairns nee mair."

" Oh, gie'd ti me," cried the cook, " an' aw'll put it amang the soup, an' aw'se sure they'll niver find it there !"

The Virgin, carefully rolled up in a piece of repairing canvas, was handed to the cook, and was speedily consigned to the bottom of the steaming copper, without benefit of clergy.

By-and-by the boat containing the officers of the Inquisition arrived, and after a rigid but fruitless search they departed.

The master soon afterwards came off to the ship for his dinner, knowing nothing whatever of either the abduction of the golden lady or of the inquisitorial visit to his vessel. He sat down to dinner alone in the cabin, being waited on by the boy, and the following conversation ensued :—

" Boy, gie's a drop mair soup."

" Yes, sir."

" The soup's fust-rate ti-day."

" Aye, so it owt ti be, sir."

" So it owt ti be ! What for then ?"

" What for ?—aw'll seun tell ye what for. Ye winnot get soup for yer dinner ivery day wiv the Virgin Mary boiled in't ti gie'd a flavour !"

A NEW WAY INTO SUNDERLAND
HARBOUR.

TONEY JOBLIN', a pilot, was as well known to the inhabitants of Sunderland and Monkwearmouth, half a century ago, as his namesake Toney Fire-the-Fagot in the *Kenilworth* of Sir Walter Scott is now known to the general public. Eccentricity and Toney walked hand in hand together through life; and many stories, in which he sustained the part of hero, are still as "familiar as household words" round the hearth-stones of old Monkwearmouth residents.

Toney at one period of his life "went in the keels," as the employment of Wear keelmen was generally termed, and while engaged in this particular line of business had the misfortune to lose a set; he however succeeded in finding it, having had the forethought to get a learned friend to cut or burn his initials into the wood. On recovering it, he held it up in his hands in triumph, and exclaimed, with infinite delight—

"Luck there, lads! W. X. for Toney Joblin'. Eff aw hadn't been a good scholar, aw wad lost mee set!"

Toney on another occasion started for "Law Lambton Staith" a little too late. The flood having waxed, and there being some fresh in the river, he was unable to proceed further than the lower part of Coxgreen; and after mooring his keel, walked back "ower land" in high dudgeon and in the dark. When he arrived home he began to bewail the unfortunate fate which entailed on him the cruel necessity of proceeding again early in the morning, for the purpose of getting his keel up to the staith. His conversation being pretty freely interseminated with oaths, at length compelled the interference of his better half.

"Oh! dear me, Toney," she exclaimed, "divn't gan on iv that way; ivery body livin' hes their trials an' troubles; remember Job, hinney."

"Job!" returned Toney, with a smile of extreme contempt for the Patriarch of Uz; "what had he ti put up wiv compaired ti me, aw wad like ti knaw? Job was niver skipper ov a keel, ye daft awd wife!"

But it is with Toney as a pilot, and not as a keelman, that we have to deal. On one occasion, while acting in the former capacity, he was put on board an Ipswich schooner off Blackhalls, the vessel being bound to Sunderland.

The captain informed Toney that he had never been in the Wear before, and that this was in fact his "first voyage to the north." Toney at once began to eulogize the port and the people, and soon succeeded in producing on the mind of the Ipswich skipper a favourable impression.

"Are there any particular amusements in the town?" the captain asked of Toney, as he stood at the tiller.

"Why, nut just now," replied the latter, "'cept at Fair times; we used for ti hev bull baits o' the Moor, but that's all deun away wiv."

"Have you no comedians at Sunderland?" was the master's next inquiry.

"Why, no, sir; aw divn't think there's onny about

us," was Toney's answer. "There's plenty o' them growin' a bit farther tiv the north, atween Whiberin an' Mawson Rock."

"I suppose you have good anchorage here, pilot?" the captain said, after a few moments pause.

"Fust rate, sir," was the reply.

"What are your shore-marks here for the best anchoring ground?"

"The varry best grund, eff iver ye hev ti bring up," said Toney, "is ti tak Sunderland Church an' St. John's Chapel; an' when ye get the church an' chapel tail ower end, iv ten faddoms watter, leg o yer anchor. It's all fine blue clay, an' ye'll ride there till the day o' judgment."

As the vessel drew near the port, the shades of evening began to fall, the coming darkness being considerably increased by the aid of a dense fog, so thick that poor Toney, in attempting to grapple his way into the harbour, put the schooner ashore behind the north pier. The sea was fortunately as smooth as a mill pond, and there being but little wind the vessel came gently to the beach—as Toney afterwards observed, 'she wadn't ha' brocken a hegg shell.'

It being ebb tide, she soon fastened herself, and Toney was for a moment or two in a frightful state of agitation.

"Hiven bliss us all!" he piously ejaculated under his breath, "the ship's ashore; an' eff aw cannot get out o' this mess, aw'll loss mee brench altigither."

Toney, however, proved himself quite equal to the occasion, for after a brief inward converse he

went boldly up to the captain and said, with all
the sincerity that pure inborn innocence might be
supposed to command—

"Now, sir, ye're all reet ; the tide's ebbin', an' ye'll
seun be fast agrund. When the watter leaves ye, just
run out a line frev the starbut bow an' another frev
the pote quarter, an' ye'll lie as snug as a bug iv a rug,
an' fust thing iv the moanin' Sir Hedwith's cairts 'll
be down for yer ballass'. And now, sir," continued
Toney, "as aw hev a little Scotchman for ti tak ti
sea this tide yet, an' as ye nee doubt knaw yersel,
neebody can afford for ti let nowt gan past them
these times, aw wad thenk ye for the pilotage an' a
put ashore ; siven fut an' a half at fifteen pence."

Toney was paid his pilotage, landed by the ship's
boat on the beach, and speedily vanished in the
darkness.

Early next morning a large number of people
covered the sands to the northward of the harbour,
drawn thither by the at all times startling report of
"a ship ashore ;" and the poor captain found, to his
horror and astonishment, that instead of his vessel
being, as he expected, safe in a harbour, she was
lying on a main beach, and that a stiff breeze from
eastward for six hours would knock her into more
pieces than Toney's pilotage would represent when
changed into half-farthings. Neither the captain nor
any of his crew were able to speak positively as to
the pilot, and it was not until some years after
that Toney consented to take credit for this famous
exploit.

BOB THE RIGGER'S CHRISTMAS TURKEY.

TOLD BY HIMSELF.

E knaw Captin Hooper, sir? Aye, aw thowt see. Now he's a fine man, eh?—ivery inch a sailor, an' a parfit gentleman. Two years this varry Chrisamas he was superintendin' the outfit of a big iron barque, built for a Liverpuil form. Aw had the contrack for tee put the stores abord, load her up, bend the sails, an' mak' her ready for sea. O' the day afore Chrisamas Day, about eliven o'clock i' the foreneun, he says to me, "Robbit" says he (he allus called us Robbit), "Robbit," says he, "aw's gaun for tee mak' ye a Chrisamas prisent."

"Thenk ye, sir, varry kindly," says aw.

"Weel, Robbit," he says, "ye've had some extra wark aboard," says he, "an' ye've had to move the ship once or twice mair then ye participated when ye meyd the contrack; an' aw've meyd my mind up ti make ye a prisent of a fine live turkey for yer Chrisamas dinner."

"Aw's varry much obliged tiv ye, Captin Hooper," says aw.

"Varry weel, then, Robbit," says he; "gan up tiv my lodgings iv Olive Street at once, an' my lan'lady 'll gie ye the turkey."

Off aw starts alang the Ropery, up Cousin Street, past Coxon Field's skule, and up the Back Lonnin. When aw knock'd, the lan'lady cam' tiv the door. She knaw'd me weel eneugh—aw used tee gan up iv a neet ti see Capin Hooper about things.

"Oh, Robbit," says she, "ye'll hae come for the turkey?"

"Yis, ma'am," says aw.

"Come through intiv the back yaird," says she, "an' ye'll get it."

Through the passidge aw gans, efter aw wipes my feet o' the mat; an' when aw gets intiv the yaird, there he is, walkin' about as proud as eff he had five hunder'd a year comin' in frev shares i' the Watter Company: a grit big bird, twice as big as the biggest coachin-chiner. When aw went up tiv him, he walks up ageyn the rain tub, an' when aw tried to tak' haud ov him, aw'll be blist eff he didn't show fight.

"Holloa!" says aw, "nyen o' that, now!" an' aw clicks up a busom shank that was lying i' the yaird, an' maks a sweep at his legs, when down he drops like a widder's pig. Aw mittens him, pops him under my airm, out o' the back door, and off towards heym. Aw went down past the Orphan 'Sylum, across the moor, an' intiv the Rig, wiv about twenty bairns efter us.

When aw went intiv the house the wife says, "Good gracious, Bobby! what's that thou's bringin'?"

"What's that!" says aw, quite proud like; "it's a live turkey for our Chrisamas dinner. Ye'll be the varry fust one out o' your family that iver sat down ti get yer dinner off a live turkey. Isn't he a noble bird?" aw says, puttin' on him down o' the floor; but aw'd hardly getten the words out o' my mouth when he flees reet up on to the top o' the desk-bed, where the wife kept all her bit fancy things, an' afore aw could get near hand him he gies one flacker, an'

17

down comes the chcency and the chalk onyments like
showers o' snaw ; then he turns round an' sees his-sel
iv a nice bit luckin'-glass we had above the chimla-
piece, and he gans slap at that, an' down it comes on
tiv the floor iv about a hunder'd-an'-fifty pieces, some
on them not as big as a thrippenny bit. The wife she
screams, an' the bairns all runs out.

"Oh, dear! Bobby," she says, "tak' that awful
turkcy away."

"Turkey!" says aw ; "it's niver a turkey i' this
good world : its somethin' that's not human, aw's sure
o' that." Just as he was kind o' mak'in his mind up
to hev some mair fun, aw fetched him one wi' the
poker, an' he laid down for to consither a bit ; but aw
didn't give him the chance, for aw collars him, pulls
him out intiv the yard, an' afore he had time for to
knaw where he was, aw shoves him intiv the coal-
house, an' aw fastens the door.

When aw gans back intiv the house, the poor wife
was trying to mak' a bit decent selvidge out o' the
cheeney, and the room luck'd for all the world like a
wreck abacker the pier. We had a nice chalk image
o' Moses as he was comin' down frev some mountin,
wi' the law printed upon a big flagsteyn, an' there was
poor Moses lyin' wiv his head off, an' the ten com-
mandments broken all ti bits.

"How are we gaun ti get that awful beast ceuk'd ?"
aw axes her.

"Ceuk'd!" says she ; "aw wadn't try to ceuk't ; an'
eff it was ceuk'd, aw wadn't eat a bite on't, eff ye wad
gie me a soverign for ivory mouthful."

"Then, what'll we dee wi'd ?" says aw.

"Aw's sure aw divn't knaw," says she.

"Aw hev'd," says aw, as a thowt struck my mind. 'Aw'll slip down tiv our butcher, an' get him ti tak't an' give us the vally on't iv beef." Down aw gans, an' he was iv the shop.

"Mister Moir," says aw, " there's a gentleman aw've been workin' for meyd us a prisent of a real live turkey for our Chrisamas dinner, but our wife disn't care about the trouble o' makin on't riddy ; an' besides, we divn't care much for holler meats iv our house ; so aw just thowt ye mevies wad tak' the turkey, an' give us the fair vally on't iv a nice roastin' piece o' beef."

"Aw'll dee that, Bobby," says he, "an' aw'll gan up wi' thou and luik at it."

Up we gans, an' aw opens the coal-house door, and there he was lying coil'd up iv one corner.

"Isn't he a noble bird, Mister Moir?" says aw, gettin' behint the butcher, for aw was expectin' he was gaun to mak' another spring.

"Aye, it's a fine turkey, Bobby," he says; "aw'll tak' him, and ye can trust ti me ti send the beef."

"All reet," says aw; an' he pulls him out o' the coal-house wiv a bit of a struggle, an' off he gans ; an' ye may depend, sir, it was a big relief tiv me when aw saw that awful beast clear o' the house. Off aw gans ti the ship, an' Captin Hooper he's stannin' at the gangway as aw'se gaun aboard.

"Robbit," says he, "where have ye been?"

"Where hev aw been!" says aw; "ye may ax that." An' aw tells him the whole story, just as aw've tell'd ye, sir, an' he jumps about the deck laughin' till aw thowt he wad a meyd hissel varry bad ; but that wasn't the warst on't. He tell'd the story all ower Liverpuil, aw knaw he did ; for when aw meyd the

Keungepore ready for sea last year, Captin' Toft, the owerlucker frev Liverpuil, when he settled wiv us, said—

" There, Robbit, there's a sovereign extra for yoursel, an' if it had on'y been a bit nearer Chrisamas time," says he, " aw wad a meyd ye a prisent of a real live turkey."

A queer turkey ! Aye, sir, ye may say that—aw call him a reg'lar Bulgarian atrockity.

CHARTERED BIV THE SECK.

IN the time now gone by, when our old colliers were subjected to no Board of Trade supervision, and when our hardy tars were not afraid to stand a long spell at the pumps, an old brigantine-rigged vessel, noted for her invariably leaky condition, left Sunderland with a cargo of coals for St. Brieuc, a small port in Brittany, to the westward of St. Malo. After a passage of six days, during all which time the principal duties of the crew consisted in relieving each other at the pumps, in every watch, she arrived at her port of destination, and proceeded to deliver her cargo. Owing to the great rise and fall of the tide at St. Brieuc, the vessel lay the best part of her time high and dry aground, and the pumping process was—to the great relief of the crew—for a short period abandoned. On the day when they were working out the last portion of their coal cargo, the captain, who had been ashore, came off to the ship about dinner time, and accosting the mate, who was working the basket at the gangway, he said—

"Geodie, aw've fixed the ship."

"Fixed the ship?" queried Geodie, elevating his eyebrows; "fixed the ship; where for, then?"

"For Lunnon," replied the skipper, in a dignified manner.

"What are we gannin' ti load then?" again asked the mate.

"We're gannin' for ti load a full an' cumpleat carga o' flour."

"Carga o' flour!" echoed Geodie, all aghast; "is't for a stairch factory?"

"Stairch factory be hanged!" returned the master; "we're gannin' ti load a full an' cumpleat carga ov the varry best flour iv secks, an' aw've chartered for two franks an' twenty santeams a seck."

"Varry weel," said Geodie, "ye owt for ti knaw best; but aw'll tell ye what it is, eff we hev onny bad weather o' the passage ye'll hev ti report her at Gravesend loaded wiv a big crowdie."

The coals were discharged, and in a few days the vessel had completed her outward lading, and cleared from the port of St. Brieuc with the first dry and perishable cargo she had held in her belly for many a long year. Fortune was propitious, and with the exception of a stiff breeze from the north-north-west when off Cape La Hague, which lasted about three hours, the vessel had a moderately fine passage to the Downs, and was at length safely moored in a discharging berth in the Thames. To the great delight of the captain, and to the utter astonishment of the mate and crew, the flour was coming out in good order and condition, there being scarcely a perceptible dampness on the outside of any of the sacks. The master seemed as he walked the deck to have had at least an inch added to his boot heels, but the mate was heard to mutter in a prophetic tone, and with a significant head-shake, " Aye, aye, it's all varry fine, but stop till we come tiv the grund tier."

The " grund tier" was at length reached ; but alas for the poor skipper ! a change came over " the spirit of his dream." The salt water had been been playing freely fore and aft in the bottom of the vessel as high as the turn of the bilge, and the bottom of every sack in the ground tier was completely rotted away.

The mate was below in the hold hooking on, and having made the first sack in the last tier fast, he gave the usual signal " How-way !" to those on deck. Up went the sack, leaving the flour standing up on the ceiling of the flat like Lot's wife on the plains of Sodom.

The master, who was standing on deck, seeing with amazement and horror the empty sack appear above the combings of the hatchway, shouted down to the mate—

" Holloa ! what's the matter now ? "

" What's the matter now !" replied the mate ; " nowt's the matter."

" Why, what's this ye've sent up ? "

" What's that aw've sent up ! Why, it's a seck."

" Aw knaw it's a seck, ye fule," exclaimed the now thoroughly exasperated skipper ; " but where's the flour ? "

" Where's the flour ! Why, it's down iv the hould

here ; what d'ye want wiv the flour ?   Annit ye chartered biv the seck, two franks an' twenty santcams ?
What mair dee ye want, eh ? "

RUNNING THE BLOCKADE OFF THE
ELBE.

FIFTEEN years ago, or thereabouts, Prussia
and Austria combined to plunder Denmark,
and wrested from her Schleswig and
Holstein, two of the most fertile and fairest
portions of her territory.

England and France at this time looked calmly
and with singular indifference on the cruel and
wanton despoilation of the property of a brave little
man by two big bullies.   To be sure the Danes
did not believe in Mahomed, but worshipped the
same God, and held the same faith with ourselves ;
and this may account for, although it in no way
excuses, the apathy of England.   Had they been
Turks instead of Danes, they would doubless have
been cheerfully assisted by our sink-each-other
ironclads and self-exploding guns :   but being
Christians, you see, they could not reasonably expect
help from us, for we hold a fixed belief that Christians
are, or should always be, able to take care of
themselves.

It has been said that "when rogues fall out,
honest men get their own," but Prussia, or rather
North Germany, and Austria gave this old-fashioned
proverb the lie direct, for when the two robbers

fell out about the spoil, and at Koniggratz, in June
1866, the weakest thief went to the wall, the strongest
still retained the plunder.

Although the Danes, after efforts and exertions
almost superhuman, were compelled to succumb to
the vastly superior numbers of the enemy on land,
they nevertheless—with the blood of the old Vikings
still warm within them—continued to hold the
supremacy of the sea till the very last, and were able
to blockade, in the most effectual manner, the North
German ports in the Baltic and North Sea.

One fine morning during the war, two coal-laden
brigs, one standing in and the other off (the wind
being from the north), sighted each other a little
to the south-east of Heligoland. The ships approached, and the skipper of the brig standing off
hailed the other vessel with—

" Where are ye bound ? "

" Hamburg," was the reply.

" Ye'll niver get there."

" What for, then ? "

" The blockade's on. We've been turned back biv
a Danish frigate. Aw'se gawn tiv New Deep, an'
then aw'll talegraph the owner."

" Aw'll hev a try ti get intiv the Elbe, onny way."

" Tisn't a bit use ; he's fired a shot through our
galley, an' our ceuk's cryin' his eyes out about his
fat."

" Eff aw cannot get in, aw let ti come back."

The ships separated, and the skipper of the vessel
standing eastward went below, and addressing himself to the lad in the cabin, he said—

" Boy, nip intiv the sail locker there, scrammel

ower the spare sails, an' ye'll find an awd trinnel auger lyin' o' the transom."

The boy did as he was ordered, and soon appeared with an old inch-and-quarter auger.

"Why, there's nee brace in't!" exclaimed the master. "Had away on deck an' get two bits o' fir out o' the galley, an' tell the ceuk for ti len' us his axe—an' luck here, divn't ye say nowt ti neebody about this auger, or else aw'll spanghue ye when aw come aft."

The boy returned with the cook's axe and two pieces of wood, when the master dismissed him with, "Gan away up intiv the fore-top, an' keep a good luck out, an' eff ye see a big ship wiv three masts, let me knaw thereckly."

As soon as the coast was clear, he proceeded to manufacture a brace for the auger, and having made the other piece of wood into a good-sized plug, he removed the cabin table and lifted the hatch, then taking a lighted candle, dropped quietly down on the cargo.

The vessel being laden with heavy unscreened coals, was by no means full at the ends, and the captain was able to remove one of the air ports in the lower hold, and after half-an-hour's hard work, during which time he anathematized the old auger on an average about twice a minute, he succeeded in boring a hole through the outside plank, thus permitting the water to come in with terrific force.

When this was done he replaced the hatch, and after a while went on deck, where the mate and crew were all mustered.

"Now then, my lads," he began, "what d'ye think on't now?"

"Why, aw hardly knaw what ti think," replied
one of the hands; "aw'se varry frightencd they
winnot let us gan in."

"Now, luck here," the skipper continued, "eff ye
leave all ti me, we'll be up above Cuxhaven ti neet;
an' eff we once get in, they'll let us out ageyn, cas'
aw knaw they niver stop onny ships iv ballast—on'y
ships wiv cargies."

"Varry weel, then," said the mate, "tell us what
we hev ti dee."

"Let all hands gan belaw, an' strip theirsels ti
their buff, all but their trousers, an' then come up
an' pump away till they come aboard on us."

"What daftness!" returned the mate, contemptuously; "what's the use o' the hands gannin' ti the
pumps when there's nee watter iv the ship?"

"How d'ye knaw there's nee watter i' the ship?"

"Why, nicely; she's as tight as a cup.   When we
jogged her out this moanin', we didn't get two buckets
out on her till she sucked."

"How much div ye think there's in her now?"

"Why, eight inches an' a-half, what she sucks at;
mevies she's drained half-an-inch mair."

"Put the rod down, an' see what there's in her,"
said the skipper.

The mate went to the companion, and returning
with the sounding rod, drew the box and let it
gently down the pump; on drawing it up, he
exclaimed, with horror—

"Why, bliss us all! the ship's sinkin'; it's ower
the rod an' two foot up the line."

"Aw thowt see," said the skipper, quite com-
posedly; and as the hands came on deck stripped

for their work, the boy from the fore-top sung
out—

"On deck there."

"Aye, aye," answered the captain.

"Here's a big ship."

"Where away?"

"Just o' the starboard bow," replied the boy.

"Had away, Bill," said the master to the mate,
"bring us me glass; an' here lads," he continued,
addressing the crew, "get to the pumps as fast as
iver ye can; they hev spyin' glasses aboard them
line o' battle ships lucks fifty miles an' mair."

The men went to the pumps, and the wind
freshening a little, she soon came up to the other
vessel, which was now flying the Danish flag, and
on attempting to pass her a shot was fired across
the collier's bows, most unpleasantly near. The
brig was hove-to, and the lieutenant, with about
half-a-dozen men, came on board, and walking aft,
he asked the captain in his sternest manner, and in
the Danish language, the following question:—

"Viste de ikke Elben var blokeret?"

"So it is, sir," replied the skipper, "a varry fine
day; 'specially for the time o' year."

The lieutenant waved his hand, and a young man
stepped forward.

"The lieutenant asks you," said he, "if you did
not come to know there was a blockade on the
Elbe."

"A blockade!" returned the master, scratching his
head in the most innocent manner—"what's a
blockade, mister?"

"You know," said the young man, who appeared

to rank as midshipman, " that we are at war with the Germans, and we are here to see that no ship shall come to the Elbe, or to the Weiser, or to the Eider."

" Aw see, sir," observed the skipper. " Aw knew there was war amang ye someway or other—nut that aw read the papers much meesell, but aw hear folks talk like; but there might hev been a snatch-block, or a cat-block, steed ov a block-ade, for owt aw knaw'd."

" Well, captain, you will have for to go back."

" Gan back ! " exclaimed the skipper, lifting up his hands—" that's just impossible."

" For what is it impossible ? " asked the mid-shipman.

" For what ? Luck at them men at the pumps, wiv the varry sharts on that they were born in ! The ship broke out wiv us, an' they've been pumping there two days an' two neets ; an' howiver they've stood it, Hiven above ony knaws, an' eff we put ti sea ageyn, she'll gan down under our feet."

The midshipman having interpreted the master's last speech to the lieutenant, he addressed some words to the men in the boat, which immediately returned to the Danish war vessel, and shortly afterwards she came back with more men, and after a few words from the man in charge of the boat, the young midshipman, addressing the skipper, said—

" Because that your ship will make so much water, our captain will let you go into the Elbe, and our men will help to pump till we are in as far as

Newerk, to rest your own crew ; then you must help yourself."

"Thenk ye, sir ; the captin's a gentleman, so is the lovetenant, and so will ye be eff ye live lang enuff."

The Danes worked the pumps till the vessel was abreast of Newerk, and after they had left her, the skipper turned to his own crew, saying : "Now, gan on me lads ; slash away at them pumps. She'll seun suck now—aw'se gawn down belaw for ti put the plug in ! "

OVER-DONE BLACK PUDDINGS.

GOOD many years ago, when wood ship-building was almost the staple trade of the Wear, a reaction took place, and three-fourths of the yards were for a time laid in, and consequently a large number of men were thrown out of employment. Some of them were fortunate enough to find work on the Tyne and at Hartlepool.

Three shipwrights, who had, with a number of others, secured employment at the building yard of Mr. Winspeare, at Old Hartlepool, lodged and boarded together ; and it was their invariable custom, after the day's labour was done, to form themselves into a committee for the purpose of settling the all-important question of the next day's dinner. On one particular occasion they had decided unanimously for a beefsteak pie, and the landlady was called in to take the necessary instructions, and she was at the same time particularly requested by one of the number to be sure and put "a canny bit black puddin' in't. Nowt iv the world," he observed, "bet a bit nice black puddin' iv a beefsteak pie; it meyd it as nice agyen."

The landlady promised faithfully to attend to the black puddings, and left the room.

On the next day, when the bell rung for dinner, the shipwright who had suggested the addition to the beefsteak pie was busy working a plank just taken from the boilers, and could not leave until it was set in its berth, a work of only a few minutes : the other two, who were working the other side of the vessel, consequently arrived first at the lodging.

The cloth was laid for dinner, and a pie in a dish of considerable size stood in the centre of the table. One of them evidently saw a favourable opportunity for a little fun, so he carefully removed the lid of the pie, and heaping a plate with the contents, he secreted it in the closet, then taking the two metal weights from a "wag o' the wall" clock which hung in the room, he placed them in the pie-dish, and just as he had succeeded in re-adjusting the crust, the other man entered the house.

" Holloa ! " he exclaimed, " hevn't ye gettin' started yit ?   Ye needn't ha' waited for me."

"Why," exclaimed one of the others, " we wannit iv a partickler hurry, so we thowt we wad wait for ye. Sit down, and cut intiv the pie."

Down they sat, and the late arrival plunged his knife into the crust, and had the lid speedily removed without noticing that the paste had been previously tampered with.   When the contents of the pie-dish met his ardent gaze, he exclaimed with unbounded delight—

"By gox! she knaws how ti mak' a pie, proper; here's lashins o' black puddin', lads. Had yer plates; this is a fust rate pie, an' nee mistake."

His fellow lodgers shoved their plates towards him, just as his knife and fork came down simultaneously on one of the clock weights. A puzzled expression stole across his hitherto beaming face, and he exclaimed, in a half-bewildered manner—

"Aw say, lads! eff them's black puddins, she's had them far ower lang i' the yuven!"

THE BIOGRAPHY OF CAPTAIN JAMES SOLLEY.

JAMES SOLLEY, master mariner without certificate of competency or servitude, stood five feet six and three-quarters in his stockings, and six feet four and a half in his own estimation. He was a good sailor sans doubt, but like the old well worn-out type of sea captain, was over boastful of his own accomplishments.

Captain James Solley was born in the parish of Bishopwearmouth, in the year 1797, and the insalubrious locality of Pudding-skin Lane.

The lifetime of Solley's paternal relative was devoted to agricultural pursuits and macadamization. In the last-named business or profession—*i.e.*, stone-breaking by the turnpike roadside—his last physical energies were exhausted. The father of James did

not marry until late in life, and his co-partner in the
holy estate was a middle-aged spinster, who since the
death of her parents had eked out a somewhat pre-
carious livelihood by the sale of spice horses, clag'em,
treacle balls, seed cakes, and other toothsome condi-
ments.

Somewhere about the average after marriage time
our friend James opened his eyes on the world in
general, and Pudding-skin Lane in particular.

When the embryo captain was about two years old
the family had a windfall, by which their position in
life was considerably altered for the better.   One
hard, dry, frosty day, the male parent Solley, having
finished his geological studies at the stone-heap, was
proceeding leisurely homeward along the Durham
turnpike, when something lying on the road before
him attracted his attention.   The sight of the object,
whatever it might be, had the effect of infusing
accelerated motion into the limbs of old Solley, and
arriving speedily on the spot, he picked up a leathern
bag, which had apparently, by the breaking of a
strap, become detached from the saddle of some
horseman.   From its weight Solley senior came at
once to the conclusion that it held money, and after
looking carefully around him, he shoved it into his
wallet, and continued his journey.   On his arrival
home, the bag was found to contain no less a sum than
fifty golden guineas.   Solley and his wife feasted their
eyes on the spade aces, and overpowered by the unusual spectacle, both maintained a lengthened silence.
At last Mrs. Solley swept the guineas back into the
bag, put it carefully away, and then the pair sat down
to hold a consultation.   Were they to proclaim their

good fortune to their neighbours ?—would this be wise ? would it be prudent ? would it not, on the contrary, be very foolish ?   They came to the latter conclusion, deciding to take no notice whatever, but if an inquiry was made they would produce the bag, and accept such reward as the owner might be disposed to give. Days, weeks, nay months, they kept the guineas sacred and inviolate ; but no reward was offered, no inquiries were made, and at length they finally resolved to use the money which a kind Providence had put into their hands.

They moved to premises of a more imposing character, near the Low Row; a veritable shop-window, and two half doors, stamped the building with such a thoroughly decisive business appearance, that customers were drawn towards it as small pieces of steel and iron are attracted by a magnet.

They laboured under one great disadvantage—neither Solley nor his wife could write. The former had by some means picked up a slight knowledge of reading, and could get along with plain print, when the words were not too long. It was consequently resolved that the male Solley should attend a night school, and become sufficiently acquainted with writing, and the simple rules of arithmetic, to enable him to keep something like an accurate account of the goods supplied to the various customers on credit. Solley soon found out a good schoolmaster, an old man whose educational certificate was a wooden leg; to him he went, and after some time he succeeded in gaining the required knowledge.

Time flew by ; young James had entered into his sixth year; the business, which might be characterised

18

as a multifarious grocery store, was prospering. The
finding of the guineas had become a thing of the past,
and the circumstance was seldom or never alluded to,
either by Solley or his wife.

One fine dry day, just about that period of the
year when winter begins to tread remarkably close
in the tracks of autumn, old Solley was pursuing
his usual occupation (which, by-the-way, he distinctly
refused to abandon, in spite of the entreaties of his
better-half), when a horseman halted at the stone-
heaps, and greeted the old man with the customary
salutation—" A fine day."

Solley assented, and said, " It is, very."

" Have you been long employed in this sort of
work?" asked the traveller.

" Yes, sir," replied Solley, " about forty years."

" Now, I suppose," pursued the horseman, in an
inquisitorial sort of tone, "you will occasionally
find things that have been lost on the road."

" No, sir; I never found anything in my life but
once."

" Aye," interposed the other quickly, " what was
that, now?"

" Why," answered the old man, whose prudence
and caution had evidently deserted him, " I once
found a leather bag with fifty gowlden guineas."

" Aye, a leather bag with fifty golden guineas;
how long is that since, eh, old man?"

" How long is it since?" repeated old Solley,
scratching the small patch of hair which still stuck
to him, " how long is it since? Why, let me see;
ah! yes, it was just before I went to school."

" To school!" exclaimed the other, in evident

disappointment, "then it couldn't have been mine. Good day, old man;" and before Solley could look up, the pattering of the horse's hoofs came faint and fainter from the distance.

Young Jim grew amazingly, was sent to school, and learnt a little, when his educational career was unfortunately stopped short. The Solley family met with a sad reverse, and it fell out thuswise: the old man was in a weak moment induced to put his name on some responsible part of a document known as a bill of exchange, merely to oblige a friend, who gave the customary assurance that it would be all right when it became due. It was "the old, old story"—the bill (like nine hundred and ninety-nine out of every thousand bills of the same character) came back on poor Solley, who had to provide funds for the original amount and sundry costs thereon.

This disastrous affair not only swept away the money made by Solley and his wife in so many years, but made also a savage attack on the turn-pike treasure trove.

The old man never blamed himself or his false friend, but persisted that the loss was solely attributable to the schoolmaster with the amputated limb and the timber substitute. "If that man had never learnt me to write, I wouldn't have put my name to that bill; how could I, tell me that?" and Mrs. Solley could only answer with a copious shower of tears.

The shop was still kept open, but the bright hopes entertained by the old couple of making a brilliant future for their only child had fled, and

young Solley, instead of been articled to the law
as his parents originally intended he should be,
found himself at the age of twelve years apprenticed
to the owner of a Sunderland collier. Jim went
through his sea apprenticeship (a remarkably hard
duty at this particular time) with credit to himself
and satisfaction to his owner and captain ; and after
making a few voyages before the mast, he became
mate, and ultimately master of the same craft in
which he had learnt the duties of seamanship.

As a shipmaster James Solley was quite up to
the mark, and his vessel was kept running between
Sunderland and Abbeville, a seaport on the Somme,
for some years. Jim's good humour and pleasing
eccentricities made him decidedly popular, and to
the close of his life his entry into the smoke-room
of any public-house in Sunderland, where a few
nautical men were gathered together, was hailed
with satisfaction and delight.

At the time of the occurrence of the one or two
important events we are about to relate, Jim's
parents were dead, he had taken to himself a wife,
and was the father of two or three children of both
sexes. His town residence was at this particular
period the upper part of a house in Littlegate, one
of a row which disappeared some years ago to
make room for the Almshouses at present standing
near Bishopwearmouth Church.

On one particular voyage, while discharging his
cargo of coals at Abbeville, Captain Solley (for by
this title we must for the future designate him)
went ashore early one morning with the cabin-boy
to make a few purchases, after which he called

at the office of his broker (whose name, by the way, was Jean Baptiste), still accompanied by the boy.

After the usual greeting, the broker said, "Capitaine Solley, I have the pleasure to make you this morning for your dinnaire one present of one ver fine what you call—*Levraut.*"

"A Lee-vro?" queried the skipper; "what's a Lee-vro, Mister John the Baptist?"

"*Un Levraut,*" said the puzzled Frenchman, "*un Levraut* is—is, *morbleu!* what you call this, capitaine?" and the broker put his hand to the side of his face.

"What div aw call that?" repeated the skipper; "aw call that yer whiskers."

"Vhiskare! no, zat is not what I shall make him. What you call this, sare?" and Monsieur Baptiste put his hand on his crown.

"That's yer heed," answered Solley.

"*Ah! oui, mon ami, mais sur la tete;* on ze top of ze head, what you call him, eh?"

"Oh, that's yer hair."

"*Certainement,*" exclaimed the broker, gleefully, "*un Levraut* is one hare."

"Oh," said the worthy captain, "aw see now; a Lee-vro's a hare, is he? Aw'se sure aw'se varry much obliged ti ye, Mister John the Baptist."

"Yes, sare, ze hare is here, and I have got some ver fine French beans for vat you call pickell; and *monsieur capitaine, votre garçon, le petit mousse,* he can take them to your ship *immediatement.*"

The hare and the French beans were accordingly confided to the cabin-boy, with special instructions from the captain to the cook, that as it was only nine o'clock, the latter was to proceed at once to prepare the hare for dinner, and that Solley himself would be on board by one P.M. to do full justice to the meal. With the usual "All reet, sir," the boy departed in the direction of the vessel.

Captain Solley went from the broker's office to a small *cabaret*, usually frequented by English shipmasters ; there he had his pipe and two sips of *café noir*, which, by-the-way, contained a powerful infusion of cognac. As the clock of the old church was pealing forth "the wee short hour ayont the twal," he proceeded to the vessel to dine, as per arrangement. The ship was lying in a quay berth, and as Solley approached her, he observed his mate sitting on the taffrail, and apparently jerking something over his right shoulder into the water at short intervals. On a nearer approach, he saw to his utter amazement that the man was coolly and deliberately throwing the French beans overboard. Having grave doubts as to the sanity of his chief officer, he vaulted over the rail, and rushing aft, exclaimed—

"Geodie! what are ye deein'?"

"What is aw deein'?" Geodie repeated, in accents of truly withering irony ; "what is aw deein'? Now, that's just what aw want ti knaw ; aw want ti knaw what aw's deein'. Somebody's been playin' a joke beyth o' ye an' o' me. Here hev aw been sittin' for the last quarter of an hour shillin' them beans, an' aw hevn't getten a single thing out o' them yit ; an' what's mair, aw dinnot think ye'll get a thimmelful o' them when they're all deun."

"Why, ye fond fuil," interrupted the skipper, "they

hevn't to be shill'd at all, ye eat them just as they are, when ye steep them intiv vinegar."

"Eat them just as they are!" said the mate, in slightly incredulous tones; "what! swads an' all?"

"Aye, ti be sure, ye ig'orant animal! there's nowt else but the swads."

"Why, aw hev seen folks, when they've been about two-thirds drunk, eat swads an' all at a pea-feast, but aw niver expected for ti liv ti see the day when onny-body wad eat them i' their sober senses iv a respect-able ship's cabin. Ye can hev all there's left," he continued, contemptuously, "but ye cannot get them that's geyn owerboard; some o' them's varry near as far down as Sent Valery bi this."

With a lowly-muttered inquiry as to the precise locality of "the nearest mad-house" the skipper went below. The boy had the table arranged for dinner— a not over-clean cloth, plates, knives, forks, a bread-basket, and the four seasons—pepper, mustard, salt, and vinegar.

"Is the dinner not ready yit, boy?" asked Captain Solley, after taking a by no means pleasant survey of the cabin.

"No, sir," was the reply.

"How's that?"

"Aw dinnot knaw, aw'se sure."

"Where's the ceuk?"

"He's i' the galley, sir; he's niver been seen since half-past nine o'clock this moanin'."

"An' ye've niver seen him since?"

"No sir, niver! He's had beyth the galley doors shut. Aw went on deck and spoke tiv him about twelve o'clock."

" What did he say ? "

" He said nowt, he on'y swore at us."

" Why, that's a queer thing!   Didn't ye tell him for ti hev the dinner riddy bi one o'clock ? "

"Yes sir, an' he tuk the hare fre' me an' went inti the galley, an' he said, ' All reet.' "

" Aw'll seun see what's the matter," the skipper indignantly exclaimed, and rushing up the cabin stairs, he was soon on deck : walking forward as far as the galley, he found the statement made by the boy to be quite correct, for the two doors were shut close, and not a sound could be heard from within.

The skipper knocked with a by no means gentle hand, and at the same time said, " Are ye there, Jack ? "

A half desponding, half surly " Yes " was the answer.

It was too late in the day for monosyllabism, and the captain, in an angry voice, asked if the dinner was ready.

The reply came, faint and sullen, " Nut yet."

Solley's patience was fairly exhausted, and he slid back the galley door on the starboard side, and immediately staggered back in amazement, for seated directly in front of a tremendous fire (the perspiration standing in big beads on his forehead, until, too large to sustain themselves, they trickled down his face) he beheld the cook with the large hare nipped closely between his knees, pulling away with both hands at the fawn-coloured fur.

" Why, Jack ! " exclaimed the captain, his astonishment growing upon him every moment, " whativer are ye deein' on ? "

"What's aw deein' on!" the poor cook repeated, looking up hopelessly into the face of the skipper, "aw's gettin' the hare riddy; aw niver had such a job i' me life, aw can tell ye! Aw started ti plote him at half-past nine o'clock, an' the stuff winnot come out, an' me fingar ends is that sair, aw can hardly bide them."

"The mate an' ye'll drive me past mesell!" shouted Solley. "Ye hevn't ti did that way, man; ye hev ti skinned like a ribbit."

"Skinned!" echoed Jack, "skinned! Why aw thowt aw had for ti plote it like a guse!"

"HE WADN'T TELL HIS NYEM FOR COFFEE."

YEARS ago, although still in the recollection of the writer, it was the invariable custom for our colliers to throw out the whole of their ballast in the roads off Sunderland harbour, excepting when the sea was unusually rough, and the weather too unfavourable to permit of this being done, and in such cases the ballast was carted away from the vessels while lying on the North Sands or Potato Garth, and other places, to ballast heaps (or hills as they were more generally called) located in different parts of the town—one of them being dangerously near the time-honoured church of Monkwearmouth.

Dean Stanley, by-the-way, had his attention drawn to this particular ballast heap, for in his lecture on

"The Early History of Northumbrian Christianity," he says, speaking of the venerable pile—"Through all these 1200 years it has witnessed many changes. It has been singed by the fire of the Danish pirates, battered by the Norman conquerors and Scottish marauders, and smothered by the ballast out of the ships from London."

Instead of one pilot to a vessel, as at present, it was customary in those days for three men to go on board from a pilot coble, their duties being not only the pilotage of the ship, but also to assist the crew to dispose of the ballast in the manner before alluded to.

One morning, just about the time when night and day were contending together for the mastery, a coble containing three hands rowed slowly out of the harbour's mouth, on the last quarter of the ebb, pulling away to the south-east. After about half-an-hour's easy rowing, they sighted a small vessel, which one of them pronounced "a Dutch or a Hannaveerin galley-hot." Hailing her, and ascertaining that she wanted a pilot, one man was put on board, thus only leaving two hands in the coble.

They then pulled away southward, and soon came in sight of a brig.

"That's the Hairyhadnee o' Poachmuth," exclaimed one of them ; "it's nee use gannin' tiv him, he winnot let us gan alangside eff we hevn't three hands iv the coble."

"Eff we can on'y get aboard on him, it'll be all reet ; let's mak' another hand."

"Mak' another hand!" demanded the other, "how are ye gawn ti dee that ? "

"Just hand me the map, an' that oilskin coat, an' aw'll seun let ye see how ti mak' another hand."

The mop and the oilskin coat were handed forward, the former was stuck over-end in a dignified and imposing position, and being covered by the oilskin coat and topped by the coble dish by way of a sou'-wester, all the outward semblance of a masculine piece of humanity was attained.

As soon as this matter was properly arranged, they rowed alongside the vessel, and in the uncertain morning light the skipper naturally concluded that there were not less than three hands in the coble.

Shinning up the side, the two nautical Frankensteins, by means of a long line, dropped their frail vessel a long way astern the brig, with the object of their own creation seated quietly on the foremost thoft.

"Holloa," exclaimed the master, "why hasn't the other man come on board?"

"Aw'll tell ye, sir," answered pilot No. 1, "he's not varry weel, poor fellow; an' besides, there's a nasty bit ov a lift on, an' we should hev somebody for ti tak' care o' the coble; an' aw'll sure ye it winnot mak' a mossel o' difference ti ye, maister, for without a word ov a lee, ye've gettin' two men aboard that can thraw mair ballas' than onny other three men out o' the pote o' Sunderlent."

The skipper being a reasonable and not unkind man, accepted the explanation, and the two pilots went to work to assist the crew in discharging the ballast, and after an hour they knocked off for the customary coffee. The captain coming on deck just at this time, and seeing the coble still astern, said to the pilots:

"Why don't you tell that man to haul alongside, and get his coffee with the rest?"

"Niver mind him, maister," one of the pilots replied, "niver mind him; he disn't care a pin about it. There he sits, luck ye," he continued, pointing his hand in the direction of the mop and oilskin, "there he sits; he wadn't tell his nyem for coffee!"

THE REGION OF THE SOUL.

MORE than thirty years ago, a regular company assembled almost nightly at the "Grace Darling Tavern" in Coronation Street, and over pipe and glass different subjects—political, social, and scientific—were debated in a friendly way. An old-fashioned sea-captain was a nightly visitor, and listened very earnestly to the debates, although he never took any part in them. One particular evening the region of the soul came by some accidental means to be the subject of discussion, and after strong arguments between the heart and the brain, one of the disputants, turning to the skipper, said — "What's your opinion, Captain S——?" "Why," replied the captain, "since ye've ax'd me, aw'll tell ye. Aw think it lies iv the nose." "In the nose!" they all exclaimed; "how d'ye make that appear?" "Why," replied the old salt seriously, "if iver a chap says 'Aw'll knock yer sowl out,' he allus hits strite out for yer nose end!"

PINCHARD AND THE SCRAPERS.

IN the month of April, some thirty-five years ago, the gay garlanded Quebec fleet sailed away from the Mark Quay. In one of the vessels was a truly eccentric sailor called Pinchard. After passing the Butt of the Lewis, some six days after leaving Sunderland, the skipper was rather astonished to see an addition to his crew in the person of a young man between fifteen and sixteen years of age. "Holloa!" exclaimed the skipper, "how did ye come here?" "Why," replied the youth, "aw stowed mysell away at Sunderland." "An' div ye think for a single moment," pursued the master, "that aw's gawn ti find ye wi' grub all the way tiv Quebec? What hae ye been?" "Aw've been a carpenter wi' Jacky * varry near three years." "Can ye caulk onney?" "Yis, aw can caulk a buth." "Then aw'll just tell ye what it is—aw've plenty oakum an' plenty o' pitch, an' a new set o' second-hand caulking irons aw bowt iv the Law Street, an' a good caulking mellet; so ye can gan ti wark an' caulk the decks frev the watter-way seam o' both sides right in tiv the hetch combins'; an' biv the time ye get that dune, ye'll hae wrought for yer passage." The difficulty was smoothed over; the lad set to work in fair earnest, and at the end of a fortnight his task was completed, the deck being caulked and properly paid from the water-ways into the hatch combings on port and starboard sides. The next morning one of the crew, after being relieved at

* The late John Hutchinson was generally called "Jacky."

the wheel, went forward, and addressing Pinchard, A.B., said, "What d' ye think we're gawn ti dee to-day, Jack?" "Aw divn't knaw," was the reply. "We're gawn to scrape the deck." "Nut likely." "But it's true, aw tell ye; the maister browt up fower scrapers an' laid them o' the top o' the capstan, an' aw heard him tell the mate." "Aw divn't care a d—n!" exclaimed Pinchard, indignantly, "aw'll neither scrape decks for him nor neebody else." "Aye, but how will ye get off?" asked his companion. "Aw'll seun let ye see how aw'll get off," replied Pinchard; "just ye watch me." Pinchard walked slowly aft, and after curiously eyeing the four scrapers lying on the head of the capstan, he accosted the skipper with—"Them's fower nice scrapers ye hev there, maister." "Aye," returned the captain, "they're good scrapers, Jack." "What might they cost apiece now, maister?" Pinchard asked in his smoothest manner. "They cost me one and ninepence." "One and nine apiece, maister," continued Jack; "how much is that for the fower?" "For the fower," replied the captain, "why it's—it's—let's see: fower shillings is fower shillings, an' fower nines is thirty-six, that's three shillings—siven shillings altogither, Jack." Pinchard took up the four scrapers in an apparently affectionate manner, and before the skipper could divine his object, he pitched them over the lee-rail into the deep waters of the North Atlantic, and turning to the captain with a self-satisfied smile on his good-humoured face, he said—"Put them down to me, maister, hinney; aw'll pay for them."

READING THE WILL.

[NOT EXACTLY AFTER WIL-KIE.]

"AW say, Geodie, Uncle Dick's deed at last."

"Aye, poor awd man, aw heered this moanin that he'd getten away."

"Aw suppose we'll get the bit property amang us?"

"Aye, there can be nee doubt about that; wee else hes he ti leav't tee?"

"Why, neebody sartain'y. Ye'll be at the funeral aw suppose?"

"Like a lowey."

The above conversation happened to fall out *en passant* between two men, a shipwright and a pilot, both nephews of the deceased gentleman yclept "Uncle Dick."

A day or two afterwards the old man was quietly and unostentatiously laid in the cold ground; the mourners returned from the church trying to look solemn under the circumstances. The funeral *cortege* comprised and numbered two nephews with their wives, two nieces with their husbands, and an intimate friend and companion of the deceased.

On their arrival at the house in which poor Uncle Dick had taken his final farewell of this world, they sat themselves down to listen with careful attention to the reading of the will.

The attorney read the document very slowly, and with good emphasis. In it the testator began by making certain statements, and preferring certain requests. In the first place he stated, that although weak in body, his intellectual department was still adequately furnished ; in the second place, he requested his body to be decently buried, and his just debts to be properly discharged. Then came the most important part of the document, that part relating to the disposition of his worldly goods, chattels, bricks and mortar. To the utter surprise of the nieces and nephews, their husbands and wives, all the real and personal estate of Uncle Dick was " given, bequeathed, and demised," with sundry " whatsoevers," " wheresoevers," and " notwithstandings," to his friend George Tate. A change of scene was instantly effected ; the facial expression changed as though by magic, and lively indignation superseded demure gravity. The shipwright nephew was the first to find his voice.

"Div ye mean ti tell me," he exclaimed, looking straight at the lawyer—" div ye mean ti tell me that he's left ivery thing ti Geodie Tate—nee relation, nut even a fifty-second cousin ? "

" You have heard the will read," replied the attorney, with cold dignity ; " it contains the last wishes and desires of your departed relative."

" Aw winnot believ't," shouted the pilot, excitedly ; " it's nowt but jokery-pawkery."

" He couldn't ha' been iv his reet mind," whimpered one of the nieces.

" Luk here !" said the shipwright, evidently making a strong effort to keep calm ; " div ye mean ti tell me that he wad iver ha' meyd a will like that, an' left all his awn relashons out i' the cawd, eff he'd been properly composite ? "

" I refuse to answer any more questions," the

lawyer returned. "If you think there is anything wrong with the will, you know where to look for your remedy."

"Aw hope he'll niver rest iv his grave," cried one of the nieces.

"To think how offens aw've cleaned up his house, and duen a fortnith's weshin' for the awd sinner," chimed in the other.

"We niver had broth since we've been married," said the shipwright, "but our wife allus tuk him a tin-canful, nice an' het."

"The roguish awd thief!" exclaimed the pilot, his indignation getting a complete mastery over him ; "aw hope he's gyen where he desarves ! Ti leave ivery blisséd ha'penny away frev his awn kith and kin ! He should allus ha' recollected that blood was thicker then watter."

"Now, luk here," said the fortunate legatee, rising to his feet, and speaking for the first time, "ye're all a pawsel o' fuils. How could the poor awd man think about blood bein' thicker then watter, when he was six times tapp'd, an' deed wi' the dropsy ?"

HOW CAPTAIN JOHNSON BROUGHT THE HORSE FROM TREPORT.

BILLY JOHNSON, the master of the collier brig *Betsey Jane*, more than half-a-century ago, was a stumpy little fellow—large head, shoulder-of-mutton hands, and legs slightly inclined to be bandy. Billy was chiefly engaged in the

19

French channel-port trade, running with his little vessel
to St. Valery, Etaples, Treport, and Ville d'Eu.

Billy had only made one voyage to London with
the *Betsey Jane*, and that was under exceptional circumstances.   A London coal merchant entertained
an idea of purchasing the vessel, and she was accordingly chartered for the Pool, in order that he might
have an opportunity of inspecting her previous to
consummating the purchase.

The *Betsey Jane* was, like the general class of old
colliers of her time, inclined to make a considerable
quantity of water in anything like bad weather, but
despite this failing, Billy was exceedingly reluctant
to give up his command, and to see the vessel he
had navigated safely for so many years pass into
the hands of strangers.

After the entire cargo had been discharged, the
intending purchaser came on board, and the vessel and
her outfit underwent a most rigid examination.   The
result of this inspection was apparently satisfactory,
and the coal merchant sheered up alongside Billy,
who was slowly walking the quarter deck in a
somewhat pensive mood, and asked the following
question—

" How many tons does she put out, captain ? "

" Three hundred and forty, sir," answered Billy,
with the utmost gravity.

" Nay," remonstrated the merchant, "you must
be wrong.   Your owner writes me two hundred and
forty."

" Aye, aye," answered Billy, " that's coals, mister :
but we allus pump out a hundred tons o' watter as
we come up."

The coal merchant looked thoughtful for a moment, bid Billy good day, went ashore, and the *Betsey Jane* was not sold. Johnson's excuse for this singular conduct was, that "he wasn't gawn for ti heave hissel out ov a buth eff he could help't."

On one occasion, while discharging his cargo at Treport, Billy received a letter from the Sunderland fitter, conveying the information that he—the fitter—had negotiated for the purchase of a horse from the merchant at Treport, and that the animal was to be brought to the Wear in the most careful manner, in the good ship *Betsey Jane.*

Billy, who had up to this time been totally unaccustomed to deal with live cargoes, was rather put out; and how to carry, and where to carry the horse, was a mystery he could not solve.

"Eff aw carry him on deck," said Johnson, "an' we hev ony bad weather, he'll get weshed owerboard; an' eff aw carry him i' the howld, an' we hev for ti batten all down, he'll mevies get scumfish'd. Aw'll ax the myate what he thinks about it."

Accordingly, a consultation was held between Billy and his mate, when the latter scouted the idea of the horse dying in the hold for want of air.

"Luk here, maister; all ye hev for ti dee is to put him down o' the ballas' amidships, tak' the awd flying jib, and pass'd under his belly, mak't fast tiv the bars o' the ballas' potes, guy him properly fore an' aft for ti keep him stiddy, an' there ye are, like a fiddle. Eff the ship rowls, an' he falls down, he'll be forced for ti stand up."

"Give us thy hand, Jack!" exclaimed the skipper delightedly, "give us thy hand! Thou niver should ha' been a myate ov a ship; thou should ha' been a hinganear, or a haircheteck, or else a cairt-reet. Why, the thing's as easy as winkin', when ye knawed. Put thy hand intiv the locker underneath my bedbuth, an' thou'll find the brandy bottle; we'll hev a drop apiece o' the heed o' that onnyway."

When the ship was discharged and ballasted, the horse was put on board, and secured in the manner suggested by the mate. The *Betsey Jane* then set sail from Treport with the wind from W.S.W., passed quickly through the Downs, and succeeded in getting the length of Yarmouth Roads, when the wind, in a fit of obstinacy, and out of pure perverseness, jumped round to the N.N.E., and poor Billy was, much against his will, compelled to come to an anchor. Shortly after bringing up, a Shoreham brig, also bound north, passed the *Betsey Jane* preparatory to bringing up, and in doing so carried away one of the bowsprit shrouds, and damaged the starboard cathead, still continuing on her way until a few hundred fathoms separated the vessels, when the hoarse rattle of her cable, as it ran rapidly out of the hawse-pipe, gave notice that she had also brought up.

"He's come tiv an anchor," said Captain Johnson. "Aw'll knaw we he is, an' aw'll mak' him pay for this damage, or else my nyem isn't what it is. Here, Jack," he continued, addressing the mate, "get the skiff out, an' pull away under his stawn, an' see what they call him; an' tak' one o' the men wi' ye."

The skiff was soon over the side, and the mate with one of the able seamen pulled away in the direction of the Shoreham vessel. They soon reached her, and pulling round the quarter, saw the name in well-defined white letters on the archboard.

"Now, Bill," said the mate to the seaman, "what d'ye they call her?"

"Aw'se sure aw dinnot knaw," replied the man.

"Ye dinnot knaw!" repeated the mate; "cannot ye read?"

"Nut me," was the answer.

"Why, here's a consawn!" exclaimed the mate, "Aw can read nyen; aw niver could. Whativer will we dee?"

"Ax them on deck; they'll mevies tell us," suggested the man.

They hailed the vessel, and the skipper, who had noticed the approach of the boat, looked over the taffrail.

"What's the nyem o' your ship, mister?" Jack asked, in his politest manner.

"It's on the stern," coolly replied the skipper.

"Aye, aw knaw that, but we cannot mak't out varry weel."

"Well, then, 'taint likely I'm agoin' to tell you," replied the skipper; and despite the most earnest and pitiful entreaties of the mate, the name of the Shoreham vessel could not be ascertained, and the pair rowed sorrowfully back to the *Betsey Jane*, with a short stroke, but elongated faces.

Captain Johnson was below when they came alongside, and that worthy emerged from the companion just as the skiff was hoisted in.

"Now, Jack," he said, addressing the mate, "ye've getten back."

"Aye," replied Jack, in a sulky tone of voice, "we've getten back."

"What di they call the ship?"

"Blist eff aw knaw."

"How's that then?"

"We couldn't read the nyem."

"Ye couldn't read the nyem!" echoed the skipper. "Why, didn't ye knaw ye couldn't read afore ye went."

"Wee says we couldn't read?" Jack demanded, somewhat indignantly.

"Why, didn't ye say ye couldn't read the nyem o' the starn?"

"Yis, aw did say see, an' what o' that? The nyem was printed o' the airchboard—iv—iv—Jawman text, an' there was nyen o' that sort o' printin' learnt at our skule."

A change of wind soon enabled Captain Johnson to weigh anchor, and the *Betsey Jane* arrived in Sunderland all well. She proceeded at once to Thornhill Wharf, and after the official visit of the Customs authorities, a boy was sent up to the fitter's to ask him to send down his groom. The horse was carefully slung, hove up out of the hold, and landed on the quay; the noble steed neighed in token of his delight at standing on *terra firma* once more. The groom had not arrived when the horse was brought ashore, and Captain Johnson proceeded in quest of him. An hour elapsed, but neither master nor groom appeared; the boy had returned to the vessel with the intelligence that "the fitter's man wad be down thereckly."

The mate showed signs of impatience, and at length resolved to take the horse to its proper destination himself, alleging as an all-sufficient reason that "the poor animal wad get its deeth o' cauld stannin' there."

"Dee ye knaw how ti manage him?" asked one of the men.

"Why, no," replied the mate, "aw cannot say aw dee; aw wish our Bill had a been here, he knaws all about it—he used for ti drive the milk barrels for Clegram o' Tunsull, or Pattison, aw forget which. But it seems ti me the maister's nut coming back wiv the fitter's hossler, as he said he wad, so aw'll et ti dee the best aw can. Slip down intiv the steerage, Tom, an' ye'll get about ten faddoms o' two-inch, an' aw'll bend that on ti the small kadge."

The rope and kedge were put ashore; and taking a turn round the animal's neck with the former, and making the other end fast to the small anchor, the mate mounted, placed the kedge in front of him, gathering up and arranging in the most careful manner the bite of the rope.

Having secured his novel deck-load, he proceeded on his way up the Pottery Bank into the High Street, and soon became the observed of all observers. Before reaching Church Street he was met by Captain Johnson and the fitter's groom, these two gentlemen having been busily engaged in celebrating the birth of their friendship in something hot and strong at "The Union Flag."

The skipper and groom were equally struck with amazement at the appearance of the mate seated on horseback, coolly smoking his pipe, with the kedge and rope before him.

"Why, whativer dee ye mean, Jack? an' where are

ye gannin ?" demanded Johnson, in an exceedingly angry tone.

"Gannin!" echoed the mate; "aw'se gawn to the fitter's house wi' the hoss. Aw couldn't keep the poor animal stannin' there for two or three hours parishin' like a thowl."

"But where are ye gawn ti tak' the kadge tee?"

"Where's aw gawn ti tak the kadge tee! Why, neeway; nee man should navigate a craft without takin' proper precautions. How div aw knaw what he'll dee? Eff he taks't intiv his heed ti run away, aw on'y hev ti thraw the kadge owerboard and bring him up."

An exquisitely-delightful smile illuminated Captain Johnson's features, and taking the groom by the button-hole, he said, in a triumphant tone—

"Aw dinnot think there's another man i' the world like our myate; he's a reg'lar geenus!"

THE KEELMAN PREACHER.

A SUNDERLAND keelman, who for many years had found pleasure and delight in making smart tracks on the broad and easy roadway that leads on to destruction, was suddenly awakened to the danger of his condition by hearing accidentally, or rather providentially, a robust and exceedingly powerful sermon preached by an itinerant evangelist of Primitive Methodist growth and culture, rich in the possession of the drive-it-homeism qualities of a Salvation Army captain. The keelman became a new man, was a member in class, a love-feast speaker, and ultimately a favourite local preacher. His sermons had unquestionably an individualised peculiarity, being wonderfully characteristic of the skipper and his employment ; and his quaint illustrations were so perspicuously given, that they became life-like pictures to the mind's eye of his not too highly refined congregations. For instance, while speaking of the great difficulty attending the rich man's entry into heaven, he once said—"Now, ye all knaw what a needle is, but still there's different needles ; the eye of a dawnin' needle's a lang way bigger then the eye ov a sewin' needle, an' the eye ov a sail needle's bigger nor beyth o' them. An' as for a camel, why, mevies there may be one or two on ye that's seen a camel iv a wild beast show, but the rest on ye knaws nowt about him. But just ti mak't plainer ti ye, aw'll put it this way— ye've all seen a keel, an' ye've all seen a lop o' the bed-claies, an' ye've felt him very offens when ye cudn't see him. Now, my frinds, it wad be far easier for a lop to drag a loaded hight-chawther keel up Bodawell Leyn, than for a rich man ti enter the kin'dom ov hiven."

On one occasion our keelman preacher had chosen for his subject the Prodigal Son, and gave to his hearers the following vivid, though homely, description of the career of the young spendthrift :—

"We are towld, my dear frinds, that when he'd wasted all his substance in riotous livin', there rose a mighty famine i' that land, an' he began for ti be in want. Now, that was a sure case, 'cas when the folks i' that far country could hardly get onny breed for theirsels, they wannit likely ti give him onny—it cudn't be expected. Eh, dear me! how misfortin' sifts frindships, an' shows us the difference between the pure and the sham. Talk about a refiner's fire!—a refiner's fire isn't in't. The fine chaps he stood wine, an' shampain, an' brandy, an' Havaner seegars for—where were they? Why, there wasn't one o' them wad treat him to a pennorth o' Dolly Reed's 'allsorts;' an' the fal-the-ral leet-o'-the-heel lasses he'd allus been makin' prisents tee, an' takin' ti balls an' plisure parties, where wa' they? Oh, they wer' there, but they went past him i' the streets, flirtin' their dandy parasowls, just as if he was muck an' rubbish. At last he hired his-sel tiv a citizen o' that country, an' he sent him away inti the fields ti feed the pigs; varry likely becas' the citizen fund he cudn't dee nowt else. Now, here, my dear frinds an' brethren, we're reminded o' the varry aw'd an' varry true sayin'— 'Hunger's a sharp thorn:' 'he wad fain ha' filled his belly wi' the husks the swine did eat.' Poor fellow! he must ha' been awful hungery. What's husks? Why, the outside o' seeds an' nuts. Ye've seen that thing like a canoe that comes off the outside o' the cocoa nut—that's a husk; there's just about as much nutriment i' them for a man as there is iv a piece ov awd shoe sole. Now, had they been proper pigs' weshins'—tatie peelin's an' greasy watter—he might ha' stayed his stomach a bit, poor lad. Now, let's luk upon the 'tother pictur —let's gan back ti the place ov his buth an' the home ov his childhood; let's see how the poor awd father's been getting on all this lang time. Eh, that was a sorrowful day for the awd man, when he saw the young spark gallop away down the lonnon wiv' his potion, all i' guineas, rattlin' iv his saddle bags! They say the Jews puts money iv a seck, and then tosses't about to get some o' the gowld off. That's called swettin', and he was swettin' his as he was gallopin' off; but it was nowt to the prespirashon he was gawn ti gi'd efter a bit.

"Did the awd man forget the son as the son had forgettin' him? Nut a bit on't! Neebody feels for a bairn like a father—except a mother. The awd man knew that lad wad come back agyen; something allus kept whisperin' tiv his hart that it wad be see, an' efter a sartain time had 'lapsed he began to luk for him every day. When he turned out o' bed iv a moanin', aye beyth winter an' summer, he wad allus walk ti the winder—bafore he put his stockins' and drawers on—an' pull the blind ti one side, an' luk varry anxious down the road leadin' ti the house, ti see if there was onny body comin'.

"One moanin' he went ti the winder as usual. It was summer time—about the end o' June or the beginnin' o' July—an' the roads was covered thick wi' dust, becas', dee ye see, it had been a varry dry season. Now, when the awd man pulled the blind ti one side on this pertickler moanin', accordin' tiv his custom, his two eyes beheld a chap toilin' away alang the dusty lonnon, an' just about a quarter ov a mile off. Poor fellow! Talk about a flae craw! Eff ye'd a puttin' him i' one o' Ralphy Lawson's fields, Ralphy's flae craw wad ha' been that much annoyed at the disgrace, that he wad ha' run away through Pennywell, an' niver stop'd 'til he gat tiv Offerton. His shoes—poor lad ! we'll call them shoes, but they were mair like Paddy's sedan ; eff it hadn't been for the nyem o' the thing, he might just as weel ha' been without them— there was nowt but the upper leathers. His trowsers an' coat was beyth fleein' away i' rags an' tatters ; as for a waiscut, he had nyen ; his hat was bash'd out ov all shape, the best hatter i' the countryside couldn't ha' tell'd the breed on't ; an' there was a short dirty pipe stickin' i' the hat-band. But spite ov all this, my frinds, though the family likeness was wesh'd out ov him like the colours out ov a bad cotton print, the awd man knew him thereckly. His eyes wasn't as good as they used to be, but he wasn't lukin' at the lad through his bodily vishon ; nut him. He was lukin' strite at him through the magynifyin' eye of FAITH ! His heart tell'd him wee he was, an' he lifted up his poor awd feyce, while the tears o' joy and thenkful- ness streamed down his cheeks, an' cried out aloud— 'It's my son ! it's my son ! Aw knaw him, aw knaw him, bi the cut ov his jib.' "

THEIR FIRST SIX MONTHS' BILL.

A STORY OF THE PALMY DAYS OF WOOD SHIPBUILDING.

LESS than half a century ago, it was quite an easy matter to commence wood shipbuild- ing. Timber merchants were obliging and gracious, iron merchants were pliant, and yellow-metal agents were accommodating. A few pounds for wages, a long jib crane, a boiler, and a saw-pit, comprehended the requisite capital stock neces-sary for embarkation in the then principal trade of the Wear. When the ship was built, launched, and sold, the accounts of the various tradesmen by whom goods had been supplied were settled, and the builder commenced another vessel on the same under-standing.

A number of small builders, especially in the neigh-bourhood of Hylton, were under the protecting wings of Messrs. Briggs, Hay, Greenwell and Sacker, and others. It is a notorious fact that during a short period of almost unexampled depression in the shipbuilding trade, Messrs. Greenwell and Sacker built a vessel at Pallion—under the superintendence of Mr. John Watson—on which every shipwright employed was in reality a master builder in tempor-arily reduced circumstances.

John S—— and William S—— were brothers, shipwrights and natives of South Hylton, in the parish of Ford, and county palatinate of Durham. One day the two brothers waited on Mr. Richard Greenwell, of the firm of "Greenwell & Sacker," large timber merchants, having their offices at this time in Villiers Street. After being shown into Mr. Greenwell's private apartment, William S—— (who had been delegated spokesman by the fall of a halfpenny, after its transitory spin in the air), stated his case as follows :—

"Mister Grinwill an' Sack-her, our awd man left us a bit money, an' me an' our Jack's seyved a bit mair since ; our Jack hes sixty-fower pund, an' aw hev fifty-six, an' we want ti' start shipbuildin'."

"Well, my good men," said Mr. Greenwell, who,

though an educated gentleman, invariably spoke with a strong Tyneside burr, "I don't see why you shouldn't start; sixty-four and fifty-six—that's one hundred and twenty pounds, and by working hard your two selves, this should pretty nearly pay all the other labour for a small vessel. I will supply you with English oak timber, Stettin and Dantzic, and all your Quebec stuff—you paying me when your ship is launched and sold ; and you can easily make the same arrangements for your iron and metal work."

"Varry weel, then, Mister Grinwill an' Sack-her," said William, "we've getten a yaird i' the Haugh o' the south side, and if we can get the keel-pieces we'll gan on thereckly."

" Good," was Mr. Greenwell's rejoinder ; " I will give you an order to the foreman of the timber yard to get whatever you may require."

The interview terminated, and in less than a fort-night the two brothers had a stem and a stern frame reared aloft, to the admiration and envy of their less fortunate neighbours.

The draughting and laying-down of the ship was to them a matter of great difficulty, being so entirely apart from their particular branch of work in the general constructive business of maritimal carriers. The brothers, however, secured the services of an old man who was considered, in those days of "rule o' thumb" building, eminently proficient in the theory, and also well grounded by experience in the practice, of all things appertaining to marine architecture.

John and William were too proud to acknowledge the fact of their being beholden to any one for assist-ance in the construction of their vessel, and she was laid down in a loft at Pallion, and the moulds for the frames were carried up on the shoulders of the two brothers by stealth and midnight. One day, when the vessel was timbered and ready for dressing and chocking, a friend was looking at her, and after expressing his admiration of the model, he put to John the pertinent question of "Wee drafted her, Jack?"

"We drafted her oursels," the elder brother answered with quiet dignity. "Aw drafted one side, an' our Bill drafted the tother."

One day, when the little vessel was planked, beams in, and ready for decks, Mr. Richard Greenwell drove up to the yard (or rather, to speak correctly, "so near thereunto as he could safely get," as they say in the charter-parties), and informed the two brothers that in consequence of large and extensive purchases of Baltic and Quebec wood goods having been made by the firm of Greenwell and Sacker, it had become incumbent on the part of those gentlemen to draw or value upon the said John and William S—— for the amount due for timber supplied, instead of allowing the account to remain open until the sale of the ship, as at first agreed. "It can make no difference to you, lads," said Mr. Greenwell; "we've drawn at six months, and before the bills comes to maturity your vessel will be launched and sold."

The brothers could not see it: they knew even less about drawing a bill than they knew about drawing a ship.

"Now, look here," the worthy merchant continued, "it's just this way, my lads; your account—here it is, look ye—comes to three hundred and eighty-five

pound, six-and-fourpence.' Very well then, we want
money unexpectedly, and you haven't any."

John and William understood and agreed with this,
and indulged simultaneously in an affirmative nod.

" Very well then, my lads—you see this ?   That's a
bill stamp, drawn for £385, 6s. 4d., for value received
in timber.   Now, if you write your names across this
bill stamp, I have nothing to do but go to my bankers
and get the money."

" What ! all the three hundred an' eighty-five ? "
asked Jack in astonishment.

" Yes, the whole amount," replied Mr. Greenwell.

" Why, that is wonderful—isn't it, Bill ? "

Bill thought it beat all he had ever heard or read
about.   The bill was duly accepted, and Mr. Greenwell went down the waterside to his conveyance, and
returned therein to Sunderland.

In due time their No. 1 vessel was built, launched,
and sold, and all accounts were honourably discharged
by the two brothers, save their acceptance to the
timber merchants, which was still running.   The bill
never troubled them in the least ; its existence dwelt
not in their memories, although they had been most
agreeably surprised at the large sum of money left
in their possession after paying, as they considered,
all their just and legitimate debts, and in counting
up the remainder they both expressed an opinion
that "ship-buildin' was a lang way better than iver
they thowt."

The time, however, was drawing nigh when their
pleasant vision would fade away.   One fine day,
when the two brothers, with two additional hands,
were busily engaged in timbering their second vessel,

Mr. Greenwell entered the yard—very warm, very red, decidedly angry, and in a palpable state of exasperation.

"My good men!" he exclaimed excitedly, holding out the bill, which was now decorated with two small bits of paper, "my good men, whatever in the world is the meaning of this?"

"Meanin' o' what, Mister Grinwill an' Sack-her?" asked Bill.

"Why, here's your acceptance to us, sir, for £385, 6s. 4d., sir, domiciled at the Union Bank of London, sir, and due the day before yesterday, sir, returned to us dishonoured, sir."

"Aw sure aw dinnot knaw what he means! Dis thou, Jack?"

"Nee mair then the man i' the moon," replied the elder brother.

"We dinnot understand a little bit what ye're talkin' about, Mister Grinwill an' Sack-her."

"Don't understand!" re-echoed the timber merchant, wrathfully, "don't understand! Why, men, you'll drive me insane. Didn't you accept a bill at six months for £385, 6s. 4d., for wood goods supplied by us for your vessel?"

"Oh! oh!" exclaimed Bill, a light dawning upon him—"oh! oh! that's it, is't; what about it then?"

"What about it, sir!" cried Mr. Greenwell, doing a short Indian war dance round the end of the sawpit, "what about it, sir! Why, it hasn't been paid, sir."

"Hesn't it?"

"No, sir, it hasn't, and you know it hasn't; you've never advised it, sir."

"Now luk here, Mister Grinwill an' Sack-her," said

20

Bill, very quietly, "we're on'y, two poor, simple men, but we're not exackly boan fuils, mind ye. Didn't ye say eff me an' our Jack put our nyems across that bit o' paper, ye could gan ti the bank an' get the money?"

"Of course I did, sir."

"Varry weel, then," exclaimed Bill, gradually warming up, "did ye gan ti the bank, an' did ye get the money?"

"Certainly, sir, certainly."

"Ye did," exclaimed Bill, after giving an exceedingly fair imitation of a savage war-whoop—"ye did, an' ye hev the feyce ti come here ti get it twice ower! Ye must be a roguish awd thief!"

JOANEY CARR'S FANCY.

Being a few pages culled from the Biography of a
Newfoundland Dog.

THAT man, almost without exception, has implanted within him a strong, and apparently irresistible, desire to fancy or to take what is generally termed "a liking" to certain specimens of the animal creation, ranged below his own peculiar indexed scale of humanity, is a fact that will be allowed to go undisputed. The feathered biped comes in for a large share of human regard. Some men go in persistently, and with an earnestness truly wonderful, for canaries, linnets, larks, and piping bullfinches; while others are severely stricken with the pigeon mania, and can talk of nothing but carriers, tumblers, jacobins, nuns, and the several other species in this particular ornithological class. Again, there are others who go in for poultry, and contrive to mix up a very little profit with a great deal of fancy.

Pets are selected from various other grades of animal life, but the real and almost universally acknowledged *amicus humani generis* is found in the class known as the canine ; and from that particular rank in creation came the subject of our present brief biographical sketch.

Joaney Carr was a keelman who occupied a house in Panns, many many years ago—long before the iron-horse became a thoroughly perfected invention— in the grand old times, when good money could be made by going in the unwieldly and unsightly river craft daily puoyed to and fro on the placid bosom of the Wear.

Joaney, at the period when our story commences, was a married man, and about thirty-five years of age. His wife, Phœbe Carr, was an industrious, hard-working little body, economical and tidy, frugal, but by no means parsimonious ; she always kept her house " as clean as print," and was never known to be froppish, peevish, or froward. In one particular branch of matrimonial industry Phœbe Carr had proved a decided failure : although ten years had passed away since her troth-plight was given to Joaney in his short jacket, blue stockings, and buckle shoes, she had up to this time neglected to present her liege lord with even one of those pledges of conjugal affection, invariably deemed by persons of both sexes to be the pure essentiality necessary to the true perfectionation of domestic happiness and connubial bliss. Joaney and Phœbe may have had leisure moments for regret at the loneliness of their household, but their grief was not of so intense a nature as to interfere with, or to unpleasantly disturb, the even quiet of their lowly domesticity.

One evening, after bringing his keel from Staith, Joaney was sitting before a well-scrubbed deal table, multifariously stored with provisions for the comfort of the inner man, and the general sustainment of the human structure. Phœbe was sitting knitting on a cracket by the side of a bright, cheerful fire, and looking in smiling approval on her good man's repeated, though invariably unrepulsed, attacks on the savoury viands before him.

Resting for a moment from his alimentary labours, Joaney turned himself towards the wife of his bosom, and in quick and decisive tones said, " Phœbe, aw've meyd up mee mine ti hev a dog."

" A dog!" Phœbe echoed, letting fall more than a half-a-dozen loops in her amazement; "a dog! What's put that intiv thee heed, Joaney, hinney?"

"Why, sis-thee, Phœbe, lass," Joaney answered, "aw've been thinkin' about it for mair nor a week. It'll be kind o' company i' the keel thou knaws, an' when ones gawn an' comin' ower land i' the dark neets; but mind thee, aw'se gawn ti hev' nyen o' them little messet things, that gans yelp, yelpin' about, they dinnot knaw what for; aw'se gawn for ti hev a Newfoun'lan', and aw' think aw' knaw where aw' can get one."

To Phœbe, Joaney's will was as imperative and steadfast as the laws of the Medes and Persians, so she carefully took up the fallen loops, rattled away with her knitting needles again, and looking over to the husband of her choice, said quietly, and in her most affectionate manner—

" Eff thou thinks see, Joaney, what for nut ? "

"Why, lucks thee," Joaney continued, after getting rid of a huge mouthful of beef-steak with some difficulty, and no little danger, " Billy Dawson, the offputher at Law Lam'ton, hes a grit big Newfoun'lan' —such a bonnie beast, as black as a sloe, wiv' a white breast. She's gawn to hev' pups, and eff aw ax him for one, he's sure to give us't."

"Vary weel, Joaney, hinney," said Phœbe, quiescently, " eff thou's tuen a fancy for one, ax him next tide, an' thou'll see what he ses."

Next day Joaney, after mooring his keel at Staith, stepped on to the quay where the offputter and his canine companion were standing together, and walking up to the pair, and patting the dog on the head, Joaney exclaimed, with rapture, " Eh, but she's a bonnie un' ! " and then turning to the offputter, he continued, " Aw'se gawn te ax ye for a favor, Mister Dawson, hinney."

" Is thee ? " the other inquired ; " what is't it to be, then ? "

"Why, it's just this, Mister Dawson, hinney," Joaney answered ; " aw want to see eff ye'll be as kind as to give us one of her pups ? "

"Why," said the offputter, " aw'se sure aw' wad like for ti 'blige thee, but our wife ses she winnot hev the trouble o' them agyen at nee price, so we're just gawn to keep one for the Newbottle under-viewer, an' the 'tothers is all gawn to be drowned."

"Now, Mister Dawson, hinney, dee let us hev one," Joaney pleaded. "Aw'll tell ye how ye can manage'd, an' aw'se sure the miss'us winnot object; syeve us one o' the drownded ones, an' aw'll tak't away as seun as iver it hoppens it's eyes, an' fetch'd up wi' new milk frev the cow."

"Varry weel, Joaney," said the good-natured staith official. "Mind aw'll not promise, but aw'll see what the wife ses, an' eff aw can syeve thee one, aw will."

With this they separated, and Joaney, after bestowing an affectionate parting pat on the head of the lineal descendant of the canine specimen,

> "Whalpit some place far abroad,
> Where sailors gang to fish for cod,"

marched down to Coxgreen for his customary pint of beer.

Time rolled on. The pup was saved for Joaney on the condition of its removal from the custody of the offputter as soon as its eyes had fairly opened on the world.

Joaney worked his tide, moored his keel at Staith, and went up for the dog at the appointed time. The night was wet and dreary, and when it was given to him he buttoned it up closely within his rough jacket and set off to walk "ower land." There was a strong east wind blowing, and the rain was falling like tramcar stock in a certain locality. But Joaney heeded not wind or rain; off he sped, through Coxgreen, by Grimestone banks, through Offerton and Penniwell, and so into Hylton Road proper.

When our brave keelman and his newly-acquired associate arrived at the unpretentious mansion at

Panns, Joaney plucked the little black object from the bosom of his jacket, and placing it on the table, rapturously exclaimed—

" There, Phœbe, lass, isn't he a fine 'un ! "

" Aw allus thowt," murmured Phœbe, putting the forefinger of her right hand in a somewhat nervous manner on the head of the pup, " aw allus thowt Newfound-lan' dogs was grit big uns."

" Wait till he gets tiv' his full size, woman," Joaney answered. " Then, luks thee, he'll be very near as high as the chimla-piece."

" But Joaney, hinney," Phœbe asked, apparently under a sudden economic influence, " winnot he eat a lot ? "

" No, lass," Joaney answered; " not half see much as thou thinks for."

The pup grew amazingly, and Phœbe had no longer a doubt but that the altitude of the chimney-piece would ultimately be reached.

In his infantile days " Coaley " (for by such name was the dog christened, probably on account of the duskiness of his coat) was a constant source of pain, trouble, and annoyance to poor Phœbe. On two occasions he had succeeded in climbing, after several presistent efforts, over the rim of the skellet pan, and had taken a header into the broth, set ready to warm up for Joaney's repast. One day the thrifty little woman, having laid a week's baking of bread in a large mug, found it necessary to leave the house in search of some article incidental to its domestic economy, and returning after a short absence, she found " Coaley " paddling in the dough, and gradually sinking deeper and deeper still, after the manner of poor Christian in the Slough of Despond. By the time Phœbe reached the mug, the puppy's head alone was visible, and that only partially so; "Coaley's" eyes, which at other times sparkled like diamonds of the first water, had now become veritable *paste.* The frantic housewife seized him firmly by the starboard auricular, and in the exuberance of her wrath she hurled him across the room, his woolly coat bearing away no inconsiderable portion of the kneaded flour. As "Coaley" landed on the floor, he gave utterance to a somewhat unmusical yelp, which, by the way, was almost strictly on the *Dough* Me Ri Sol Fa system. He rolled himself over and over and over, until the paste covered him like a white racing Mackintosh; then he sat up and looked at Phœbe in the most comical manner, while she, poor woman, sank down on a chair and burst into tears.

The greatest, the most flagrant, the most daring in its heinousness, of all the long list of "Coaley's" atrocities has yet to be recorded. When our hero was nearly six months old, a family affliction cast a transitory shade of gloom over the Carr household. An aunt of Phœbe's departed this life full of years, and, as a matter of course, the mortal remains of the poor old woman were to be consigned to the silent tomb in the long-established orthodox fashion, and Mrs. Carr, on the score of kinship, had to attend the funeral. Now, in all Phœbe's worldly possessions, if there was one thing more than another on which the little woman prided herself, that article was a black silk dress, which she had contrived to get made up for her years and years before. This sombre mantua was the joy of her heart and the

gem of her wardrobe. On the day of interment
Joaney's smaller but better half carefully brought
out the dress from a long box, something like a
sailor's chest, and after proudly surveying it for a
moment or two, she hung it on the horse, at a little
distance from the fire, so that the heat might take
out the creases; her bonnet was taken out and
placed on the top of the desk-bed, and then Phœbe
prepared to go to a Mrs. Smith's, the wife of a
sailor, a few doors off, who had kindly volunteered
the loan of a beautiful black lace shawl, brought by
her husband from foreign parts. The little woman
was neither vain nor proud, still she could not help
thinking, now and again, how she would excite
general admiration and even envy at the funeral.
Phœbe went off for the shawl, locking the door, and
leaving Coaley sole representative and family
occupant. Now Mrs. Smith was unfortunately a
bit of a gossip, and was in a more gossip-like
humour than usual on this particular day. She began
to relate to Phœbe certain family matters, and as
she discoursed glibly, she held in her hand the
coveted shawl, neatly folded, and used it occasionally
to point out, and, as it were, illustrate, the most
forcible parts of her conversation; and under those
circumstances poor Mrs. Carr was compelled to listen
patiently, although she began to have some slight
misgivings as to how Coaley might be conducting
himself. All things have an end, so had Mrs. Smith's
tale of family grievances; Phœbe at length got
possession of the shawl and departed, proceeding
at a rapid pace in the direction of her own house.
She opened the door, and on entering gave a piercing

scream, and rushed madly towards the fireplace. The scene almost beggars description, and only to the graphic pencil of the artist could we look for the true delineation. The clothes-horse had fallen on the fire, and the upper portion of it was blazing cheerfully, cracking and emitting sparks at short intervals; on the left-hand side of the fireplace Coaley and the black silk dress were holding a strong, although, as far as the dress itself was concerned, a by no means tough argument. Phœbe seized the poker, and the dog, ever alive to his own safety, began to make tracks for the door. He was too late; the now thoroughly roused little woman caught him a severe blow exactly on his philoprogenitiveness, and he ran yelping into the street, where he began to describe rapid circles, in the frantic though vain endeavour to lick the back of his head.

Coaley's exit from, and Joaney's entrance on, the scene, were simultaneous occurrences. Carr beheld with amazement his wife taking up the rent and torn dress, and sobbing meanwhile as though her heart would break.

"Why, what iv hivvan's good nyem's the matter now?" he asked, wildly.

"Oh deary, deary me!" groaned poor Phœbe, "aw'se a ruined woman; luk at mee beautiful black silk. There's a seet!" she continued, holding up the tattered garment for Joaney's inspection; "its for all the world like a herrin' net."

"A herrin' net, hinney," Joaney repeated, abstractedly. "A herrin' net. Its far warse, awd woman; it wadn't catch mackerell."

The poor aunt went to the grave unfollowed and unwept by Phœbe, whose full meed of sorrow was poured out on the shrine of the cruelly lacerated silk.

If time and space would permit we would be pleased to cull out and place before our readers a few more of the stirring incidents recorded in the complete history of Coaley—namely, how legs of mutton were stolen, how cocks and hens were literally bolted, and favourite tabbies wantonly destroyed.

Joaney and Phœbe were perpetually in hot water; day after day complaints were lodged, and sums of money demanded and paid, for Coaley's various acts of robbery and devastation.

One day, as the once happy couple were sitting together enjoying, or trying to enjoy, the mid-day repast, a dignified knock came to the door, and on Phœbe answering it, a pompous gentleman's gentleman, garbed in a magnificently gorgeous livery, entered the apartment. Phœbe looked at the brilliantly-adorned visitor in astonishment, while Joaney—who was just in the act of raising a pot of beer to his lips—gazed at the stranger more in alarm than surprise.

"Isn't your name John Carr?" asked the all-important flunkey.

"It is," assented Joaney, wondering what was to come next.

"Haven't you a dog called Coaley?" was the next interrogation.

Down went the pot with its contents, shivering itself on the flagged floor, while poor Carr exclaimed, in sorrowful tones—

"Oh dear me! what hes he been deein' on now?
He's varry near ruined us, an' now he's gawn to get us
transpo'ted, eff he disn't kill us outreet."

"You must come with me at once to Major C——."

"The Magistrate!" moaned poor Phœbe. "Oh,
lawks-a-daisy me! aw knaw'd it wad come to this.
Joaney, hinney, eff thou tes to gan to jail, aw'll gan wi'
thee."

The powdered functionary smiled.

"Come," he said; "my orders are to bring you to
the Major at once."

Phœbe wept, and Joaney put on his low crowned
hat, and went out with the flunkey—his mode of
exit exhibiting all that awful seriousness, and truly
impressive gravity, so frequently observed in William
All-in-the-Downs, when he leaves the court-martial
for the yard-arm.

Major C—— was seated at his ease in the library
when Joaney was ushered in.

"Ha! my good man," he said, in his usual stiff,
patronising way, "you, then, are the owner of the
Newfoundland dog."

"Aw cannot denied, sir," Joaney answered, "but
as aw'se a poor livin' sinner, aw nivver teached him
nee bad habits; nut even to sit up and smoke a'
hempty pipe."

"Ho! ho!" chuckled the Major; "then you don't
know what has really occurred?"

"No, sir," Joaney replied, meekly, "but aw wadn't
be astonished at nowt."

"My good man, your dog has done my wife and
me a service which can never be repaid. My little
daughter was in the Panns field with her nurse, and

while the girl was talking to some one, poor little
Florence, being unnoticed, strayed away and fell into
the river. But for your noble dog she would have been
drowned, and Mrs. C—— made inconsolable for
life. He sprang into the water, seized the child, and
brought her safely to the landing. My wife is determined to have that dog, and I am equally determined
she shall have her wish."

"Why, Mister Major C——," Joaney said, his
heart fairly bursting with joy to think he was going
to get rid of Coaley at last, "though aw wad be
varry sorry like to loss the dog, still, eff it wad mak
your good lady mair comfortable, why, then, aw say,
tak him."

"Mind you," the Major resumed, "I don't want
him for nothing. There's ten pounds ; now go and
bring the dog at once."

Joaney took the two notes, and saying, "Thenk
ye varry much, Mister Major C——," he left the
house, to return in about half-an-hour with Coaley in
safe custody. And so departed the only skeleton
from the Carr closet.

BALLADS.

THE LEGEND OF THE LAMBTON WORME.*

THE matin bell was ringing through
  The Sabbath morning air,
With beads and book, from Lambton Hall
  To chapel all repair—
Lords, ladies, vassals many, yet
  Young Lambton was not there.

He wander'd down the shady walk,
  With rod and line in hand,
Down where the river rushes o'er
  Its bed of silver sand,
And laves the basement of the bridge
  Where the gnarled oak trees stand.

He met a friar as he sped
  All on his sinful way,
With close-drawn hood and plaited cord
  Drawn round his cassock grey.
" Ho! why dost not thou yonder go,
  Thy morning vows to pay ? "

---

* This quaint ballad was first published by the author in the
Newcastle Weekly Chronicle.

" Now, foul thee fall, thou saucy friar,"
    Lord Lambton quicklie said ;
" I ne'er pay vows till eventide,
    And then to village-maid,
Beside the milk-white blossomed thorn,
    Or 'neath the oak tree's shade."

He turned him round a moment's space ;
    The friar was not there ;
But a gruesome, hellish, taunting laugh
    Came loud upon the air.
Lord Lambton's cheek it instant paled,
    And stirred his very hair.

But he laughed aloud defiantlie,
    And carolled forth a lay,
And down the river's grassy bank
    All heedless took his way,
And by a little well-spring side
    His angle he 'gan play.

An hour slowly passed away,
    And ne'er a fish he took ;
At length he drew a little worm,
    All writhing on the hook ;
E'en like a leech for size, but yet
    More ugly to the look.

With gruesome curses on his tongue,
    He plunged it in the well,
Then stood amazed and breathlessly,
    As bound by magic spell,
For once again that fiendish laugh
    On's ear loudly fell.

That night, all on his tap'stried bed,
  Lord Lambton could not sleep,
But restless tossed him to and fro,
  Till the sun 'gan upward peep ;
And when he thought on all his sins,
  Lord Lambton he 'gan to weep.

Early he sought the priest that wonned
  Within his father's hall,
And, kneeling to the good old man,
  Said, " At thy feet I fall,
To make confession of my sins ;
  Do thou for mercy call."

" Alas ! alas ! my erring son,"
  The aged priest then said,
" Saints laughed to scorn, Christ's love forgot ;
  And then, poor artless maid,
Confiding, trustful in thy love,
  So ruthlesslie betrayed.

" Now go to aid those Christian knights,
  With thy good trusty brand,
To win the city of Our Lord
  Out of the heathen's hand,
And fight for Christ, His sepulchre,
  All in the Holy Land."

Lord Lambton's boun' him and away,
  All in a monarch's train ;
And Saracens full many a score
  By his good sword were slain.
A better and a holier man
  He then came back again.

Meantime the worm it grew and grew
   So lithlie and so strong,
And stretched itself at morning prime
   An hundred yards along
The river-bank, and ofttimes wrought
   Sad devastating wrong.

Lord Lambton from his father heard,
   With horror and great dread,
How all that battled with the worm
   Had foul and fatal sped ;
Though cut in twain, the severed parts
   Were quick again re-wed.

He's boun' him to a wise woman,
   Ligged nigh to Chester town.
" Oh ! vengeance drear for all thy crimes,
   Lord Lambton, has come down !
List, and obey, and I will strive
   Thy happiness to crown.

" A coat of mail thou shalt prepare,
   Thigh clasps of steel also ;
Thy back and breast with good steel blades
   All studded in a row ;
And when the tide is ebbing fast,
   Into the river go,

" Near the worm-hill, where at mid-day
   He coils him three times round,
And when the water laves thy waist,
   Loud let thy bugle sound ;
Stand firm, and pray Our Lady's grace
   To spare thee thy death-wound."

21

Now when Lord Lambton blew his blast,
 As erst he had been told,
The worm awoke, and soon began
 T' uncoil him fold by fold ;
Then down towards the riverside
 The hideous monster rolled.

The water from its writhing sides
 Glanced off in flakes of spray,
As to the spot where Lambton stood
 It quicklie plied its way.
Oh ! gallant knight, now hold thine own,
 And to our Lady pray !

It coiled around the knight, but lo !
 As fold on fold it plied,
The good steel blades cut through and **through,**
 And, falling in the tide,
The severed portions by the stream
 Were swiftly downward hied,

And borne away upon the ebb
 Before they could unite,
Until the monster's head alone
 Glared fiercely on the knight.
Anon it fell into the stream,
 And vanished from his sight.

  . . . . . .

Now to this time the village swain,
 All in the grassy vale,

Hushes his vows of constant love,
  To tell the maid this tale,
What time the river ripples sheen
  Beneath the moonlight pale.

RALPH THE BOATMAN.

UPON the river's bank there stands
  A row of stately trees,
That, blushing, bend their leafy heads
  When kiss'd by summer's breeze ;
And 'neath those trees there stands alone
A cot with ivy overgrown.

The summer sun is sinking now
  Behind the western hill ;
The noise of toil in yonder town
  Has ceased, and all is still,
Save the glad birds, that flirt and sing,
And the tide's gentle murm'ring.

The boat is swinging idly now,
  The tide is turning slow ;
From the grassy bank you scarce may mark
  Its lazy, languid flow ;
And 'gainst an oak tree's rugged breast
The clumsy oars are laid to rest.

Ralph sits beside his cottage door,
  And puffs his " yard of clay,"

Anon he sends the faint blue smoke
   In eddying curls away ;
His face is tanned, and age and care
Have turned to iron grey his hair.

A little girl stands at his knee,
   Some ten years old or so ;
Her flaxen curls o'ercast a neck
   As white as driven snow ;
Her light blue eyes, you now can trace,
Are laughing in the old man's face.

" Dear grandpapa, do let me go."
   " Well, well, e'en as thou wilt ;
Thou hast thy mother's face and smile—
   Heav'n shield thee from her guilt ! "
A tear-drop glistens in his eye,
And he half checks a deep-drawn sigh.

Away with speed, like startled fawn,
   Along the grassy road,
The little fairy swiftly glides,
   And, where the path grows broad,
She turns and waves her hand amain,
And cries, " I'll soon come back again."

   .   .   .   .

A dozen years have passed away
   Since, in that little cot,
His daughter's smile like sunlight beam'd
   On all around the spot ;
Ten wintry seasons now have sped,
Since Ralph stood by her dying bed.

Squire Bracy proffered his false love,
   And she, poor artless maid,
Ne'er found the guile upon his tongue
   Till she had been betrayed ;
And only could his falsehood prove,
When virtue died with maiden love.

In grief for Bracy's want of truth,
   Sorrow for tainted name,
She slowly wasted, pined, and died,
   The victim of her shame,
And left Ralph's hope in future built
Naught but the offspring of her guilt.

One wild and drear November night,
   When, o'er the grassy shore,
The swollen waters hurried past
   With loud and angry roar ;
The boisterous wind howl'd out amain,
In torrents fell the wintry rain.

Ralph sat within his lowly cot,
   List'ning the wild winds cry,
And the hoarse murmur of the flood
   As it went rushing by ;
When, 'mid the roar the tempest made,
There came a piercing cry for aid.

He seized a line, he ope'd the door,
   And there a horseman stood.
" Oh boatman, boatman ! haste, and save
   My master from the flood ;
His steed has gained the northern side,
But he lies struggling in the tide ! "

Adown the river's bank he ran,
  And peering through the storm,
Soon spied amid the rushing stream
  A struggling human form ;
Ralph held his line prepared to throw,
And warned him with a loud " Holloa ! "

The man pray'd blessings on the voice
  That fill'd his heart with hope,
And trying hard to gain the bank,
  Cried, " Quick, throw out the rope."
Ralph stood prepared, but at that sound
He cast the coil upon the ground.

" Now, palsied be this arm of mine
  If it affords thee aid !
Squire Bracy, thou art he by whom
  My daughter was betrayed :
And she would haunt me from her grave,
Did I but stretch my hand to save ! "

Next morn they found the lifeless man
  Upon the river's shore,
And bore him up the grassy bank
  To Ralph's own cottage door ;
Ralph saw the face as there he lay,
And turned him from the sight away.

.   .   .   .

Now when the child stands by his knee,
  And upward turns her eye,
'Tis not alone his daughter's shame
  That makes him heave the sigh :
No ; in those features he can trace
Some likeness to the dead man's face.

THE LEGEND OF LOWTHER HALL.

"————————when the herté felté death
  Dusked his eyën two and fail'd his breath ;
  But on his lady yet cast he his eye."
                              —*Chaucer.*

" That terrible tempest's hideous wallis huge,
  Were maist grislie for to behold or judge."
                              —*Gawain Douglas.*

LOWTHER HALL stands high on the moor,
  And looks o'er the German sea ;
And Lowther's lord claims proud descent
  From the knights of Normandie.

And Lowther's child is fair to view
  As dawn of summer's day ;
And her heart's gone out to the fisher-lad
  That sails o'er Hendon Bay.

But fate has cast their lots apart,
  And though true love roams free,
'Tis hard to climb the barrier wall
  'Twixt high and low degree ;

'Tis hard to love through pride of birth—
  High lineage to disgrace,
Mixing vein-mud of Saxon churl
  With blood of Norman race.

But who can gauge affection's power ?
  " Love levels rank," 'tis said ;
And stronger grew the link between
  Low boy and high-born maid.

They met in secret, night by night,
   On the shingly beach below,
When the dark blue waters rippled bright,
   Beneath the moon's pale glow.

And tales were told, and pledges pledged,
   All else was little worth ;
They felt as they were all alone,
   With nought but love on earth.

     .   .   .   .   .   .

The fairy elf who ruled the storm
   On that sea-beaten shore,
She lov'd the fair-hair'd fisher-boy,
   Aye, long and long before.

No storm would sweep the ocean's face,
   No gale disturb its rest,
While his frail bark with tawny sail
   Rode slowly o'er its breast.

The sprite would follow his coble's track,
   And low soft music make—
Her elf-locks flashing in the tide,
   Like foam, all in his wake.

But all unconscious was the youth
   Of the love the sea-nymph bore,
And the high-born maid of Lowther's blood
   Was ever his mind before.

     .   .   .   .   .   .

When autumn days were short'ning fast,
   And wheaten ears were seen,
Glowing in rays of noonday sun,
   In bright and golden sheen,

One moonlight night, on the lone moor edge,
 The lovers twain had strayed,
List'ning the splashing sound on shore,
 By dancing wavelet made ;

While whisper'd words of tend'rest love
 Blend on the maiden's ear ;—
'Twas but the oft-repeated tale,
 She knew before perquier.

A shadow dark now intervenes
 Before the moon's pale light,
And the wrathful face of Lowther's lord
 Gleams on the lovers' sight.

The maiden's shriek is borne afar
 Across the deep blue wave !
For in her father's hand there shone
 The steel of a naked glave.

No time to sue, no time to pray,
 No power to fight or flee ;
The fisher's blood dyes red the blade—
 His form cast in the sea !

 .   .   .   .   .   .

The lifeless corse of the fisher-lad
 Was now the storm-elf's care,
And deep down in her own sea-home
 His grave was fashion'd there—

His grave, where ocean's scentless flowers
 Bloom far from human sight,
Springing from coral beds bedeck'd
 With shells of pearly white.

She kiss'd the cold lips of the boy,
  Toy'd with his flaxen hair ;
Never a requiem sung or said—
  Never a word of prayer ;

But to the surface of the sea
  With light'ning speed she rose ;—
Its breast like gentle dreamer's heav'd
  In calm and soft repose.

She waved her wand o'er ocean wide,
  And invocation made :
" Come, destroying wild wind, come—
  My call must be obeyed.

" From Berga and from Jutia's coast,
  Come swift, thou east wind, on :
Gather, each league, in strength and force,
  Storm-breath ! euroclydon !

" Madden the waves, and hurl them forth
  Foam-lash'd to western land ;
And break them white with angry roar
  On proud Dunelmia's strand.

" Ocean ! expand and burst thy bonds,
  Level the hill to plain ;
Glut well thyself with death and spoil—
  Avenge me for the slain ! "

The moon was veil'd, the sea-mew shriek'd,
  Each boat sped swift to shore,
For far away in the darken'd east
  Was heard the storm-wind's roar.

The ocean vast, which erstwhile lay
  In calm and gentle sleep,
Woke up, and leagues of feather'd spray
  Ruffled its bosom deep;

Glancing in purest silvery sheen,
  In the dim, uncertain light,
Like plumage of the wild sea-bird,
  Winging its rapid flight:

And huge green waves came on eftsoons,
  Marshall'd with east wind's roar;
Curling with hate, they broke in foam,
  Lapping the sandy shore.

'Till crazed amain by wild storm blast,
  They rose a liquid wall,
And dash'd with angry force upon
  The banks 'neath Lowther's Hall.

The clayey barriers crumbled down,
  High dashed the wild, white spray;
And the firm-built walls of Lowther's Hall
  Lay buried in the bay!

Loud shrieks for help were heard above
  The wind and mad sea-roar,
As the Lowther name and Lowther race
  Perish'd for evermore!

THE WRECK OF THE OLD *CECROPS.*

(A TRUE STORY OF THE SEA.)

" ' 'BOUT Cap'en Webb no doubt it's true, an' he's all
    that you say ;
But there's bin swimmers good as he—I've known
    'em in my day."
Jim Veitch spoke thus—a smart old tar—as he quaffed
    his pint of beer,   [leer.
And looked upon the lot around with a self-assertive
" Yes, what I say, my lads, is true, believe it as you
    may ;
I knew a man, aye, just as good—poor Andrew
    Thompson Kay.
We was shipmates in the *Mary Jane*, and in the
    Rainbow too,
An' divin' tricks 'ud make you stare I've hoff seen
    Andrew do.
Some on ye knew the old *Sea-crops*—a rum old craft
    was she,
All *clatter-wedged* in every butt, that's what she used
    to be ;
And then her *huttin's*, fore an' aft—my eye ! they
    warn't no joke,
A three-inch lanyard warn't enough them blessed
    seams to choke.
' Hardweather Hoskins ' had that brig the time I'm
    telling you,
And Andrew sail'd afore the mast—the life of all the
    crew.
She left the Wear for *Poachmuth* bound, and a
    hard October gale

Caught them midway o'er Boston Deeps, an' stripp'd
  off every sail ;
She held her way with scarce a rag much bigger than
  your hand,
An' that same night she went ashore, outside the
  Scroby Sand.
The angry waves ran roarin' high when the *Sea-*
  crops struck the ground,   [around.
An', lash'd an' beat to yeasty foam, kept hissin' all
The crew war' in the tops—for why, the sea a clean
  breach made,
An' bulwarks, stanchions, boats, war' gone as decks
  to sea she laid—
The seethin' waters all below, and aloft the murky
  skies ;
An' there they cluster'd in them tops, with death afore
  their eyes,
For well they knew the old *Sea-crops* must soon to
  pieces go,
And each prepared to meet his fate—as only sailors
  know.
Old Hoskins he was in the main, with Andrew by
  his side,
Watchin' the sea now making fast, as stronger grew
  the tide ;
When Andrew said—'My lads, it's plain she cannot
  stand much more ;
To stay with you will do no good : I'll have a try for
  shore.
The risk is great, but there's a chance that I the land
  may reach ;
The strong flood-tide is setting fast towards the
  Yarmouth Beach."

''Tis but to try,' old Hoskins said; 'but from the
    Scroby Sand
No livin' man in such a sea can ever swim to land—
Except through Him who holds each wave within
    His mighty hand.
But should you reach the shore alive, tell my old
    wife from me,
I've only gone a bit before—an' say, it had to be.
Tell her to keep her spirits up, and not to grieve
    an' cry ;
Her days are lengthenin' out full fast, she'll join me
    bye an' bye.
Tell her, my lad, we'll meet above, in that bright and
    happy home,
Where rough nor'-easters never blow, where shipwrecks
    never come !'
He grasp'd in farewell grip the hand of Andrew
    Thompson Kay,   [hissin' spray.
His thin locks flutterin' in the breeze, white as the
'Good bye, my lads !' then Andrew said. ' If I can
    gain the land,
The Yarmouth boatmen won't be slack to lend a
    helpin' hand ;
I'll do the best to reach the shore that mortal man
    can do,
And if the *Crops* but holds this tide, there may be
    help for you !'
From the main shrouds, with desp'rate leap, he
    plunged, devoid of fear,
And rose, to hear beyond the roar his comrades'
    ringin' cheer—
A ringin' cheer, while open-jaw'd grim Death went
    prowlin' round ;

A cheer!—aye, lads, 'tis on the sea true British pluck
    is found!
Breasting the sea with sturdy stroke, brave Andrew
    cleft his way,
Borne shorewards on the turgid waves, crested with
    snowy spray;
Now in the hollow trough he strove, now on the
    billow's crown,
Hove skyward in a shower of foam, then sinkin'
    faddoms down;
Offen's, 'twixt hope an' grim despair, some sign of
    land to mark,   [waters dark.
Peerin' with anxious surge-blash'd eye across the
At length both strength and hope were gone, an' he
    could do no more,
He ceas'd to swim, his feet dropped down; when, lo!
    they touched the shore.
Vigour an' faith were born anew; but oft the greedy
    wave,
In wild back-sweep would suck him down, to share
    its watery grave.
At last he reach'd the glad dry land, when strength
    an' senses fled,
And Andrew fell, a lifeless lump, upon the shingly bed.

    .   .   .   .

The Yarmouth boatmen found him there, above the
    tidal flow.
In using means to bring him round, you bet they
    were not slow;
They chafed his limbs, they rubb'd his hands,
    pour'd brandy down his throat,
Till Andrew found his voice an' cried, 'Be quick an'
    man your boat!

The old *Sea-crops* is lying now upon the Scroby
  sands,
And, in an hour or two at most, she's gone with all
  her hands !'

    .   .   .   .

The boat was manned, the darin' crew went plunging
  on their way ;
The dawn was near, for in the east shot glim'rin'
  streaks of grey ;
They reach'd the Scroby, white with foam, an' though
  they pull'd all round,
No vestige of the old *Sea-crops* to this day has been
  found."

CLICK'EM AND CATCH'EM.

MARK FORTIN' at steeith had just moor'd his keel,
An' the neet was that dark it wad freeten the deil ;
Ye could not see yer thumb eff ye held up yer hand,
When Mark started off for ti come ower land.
      Singing Fal the lal, etc.

He call'd at the Reed Dog, but he didn't stay lang,
Smok'd his pipe, had some talk, an' sung a bit sang ;
He'd had nowt ti drink for ti mak' him feel queer—
On'y two pots o' rum and three quairts o' beer.
      Singing Fal the lal, etc.

As he cam' on past Painshaw it cam' on ti blaw,
An' his shoe sole cam' lowse, but poor Mark didn't knaw,
An' as he kept walkin' it flopp'd, div ye see,
Sayin' " Click'em and catch'em " as plain as could be.
      Singing Fal the lal, etc.

His hair it stood up wiv the fright an' the fear,
An' he dursn't luck round for ti see wee was near ;
But he set of ti run at a bonny round pace,
As if life an' death did depend on the race.
        Singing Fal the lal, etc.

But the faster he ran, tiv his horror and pain,
The quicker the shoe gav' the dridful refrain ;
For " Click'em and catch'em " was dinn'd in his ear,
Till he felt he was likely ti drop down wi' fear.
        Singing Fal the lal, etc.

Tiv Offerton he ran, his heart pitty-pat,
Reet intiv the Inn, like a weel-scadded cat,
His breath was maist gyen, but he just mey'd a mint,
Cryin' " Shut tee the door, there's the auld man behint !"
        Singing Fal the lal, etc.

THE KEELMAN'S MESSAGE.

AIR—"*'Twas between Hebburn an' Jarrow.*"

" Now, Jack, tak' a message for me,
    Ti-day, when thou gans ower land ;
An' as thou gans up ti the steeith,
    Give a luck ti my keel wi' thy *hand*.
Thou cannot for sartin get wrang,
    Eff wiv her thou isn't acquent—
Her ruther-staff's nicely *black'd* ower
    Wiv a brushful o' bonnie *reed* pent.
        Then, Jack, tak' a message, etc.

22

" Just luk inti Mall o' the Wood's,
    An' give her this tenpence as weel ;
It's pay for them to quairts o' yall
    Aw gat when aw moord the keel.
An eff thou sees Skinny Dick Todd,
    Just thou tell the roguish awd thing,
The canary's turn'd intiv a hen,
    An' never a note it'll sing.
            Then, Jack, tak' a message, etc.

" Tell the offputher aw've been varry bad,
    Or to send word wi' thou aw'd nee call ;
Eff aw dinnot load big roundy coal,
    He can just fill the keel up wi' small.
Aw was gannin across Boylin' Hill,
    For the burd a bit grunsel ti seek,
When aw fell *belly*-flap o' my back,
    An' aw hevn't been weel for a week."
            Then, Jack, tak' a message, etc.

Printed by WALTER SCOTT, *Felling, Newcastle-on-Tyne.*

Lightning Source UK Ltd.
Milton Keynes UK
UKHW031531220621
385967UK00006B/1057

9 781146 547062